Learning Through Touch

Supporting children with visual impairment and additional difficulties

MIKE McLINDEN AND STEVE McCALL

David Fulton Publishers

LONDON

David Fulton Publishers Ltd
The Chiswick Centre, 414 Chiswick High Road, London W4 5TF
www.fultonpublishers.co.uk

British Library Cataloguing in Publication Data
A catalogue record for this book is available from the British Library.

ISBN 1 85346 841 X

Typeset by BookEns Ltd, Royston, Herts.
Printed and bound in Great Britain by the Cromwell Press

LGDgm

Learning Through Touch

Contents

Acknowledgements

We wish to acknowledge the support and guidance offered to us by a large number of people who, either directly or indirectly, have helped us bring this text to fruition.

First, we would like to thank the teachers, too numerous to mention individually, who granted us access to children in their classrooms, and who provided the invaluable feedback and insights which have helped shape our ideas over the last ten years. We would also like to express our gratitude to the children and their parents, and especially to the parents who permitted us to refer to their children in our case studies.

Our thanks to our colleagues at the School of Education, University of Birmingham, who have been so supportive of our efforts to complete this text, unselfishly providing us with time and resources at a time of ever increasing professional commitments. In particular, our thanks go to Chris Arter for providing study leave cover, and to Jenny Whittaker for her cheerful assistance in helping us to proofread and prepare the final draft of this text, as well as helping us prepare the diagrams for publication. A big thank you also to Roberta Roberts for her helpful comments on earlier drafts of Chapter 2.

A special mention to Jane Whitaker (illustrations in Part 1) and Ed Sellman (illustrations in Part 2) for their inspired line drawings and for helping to bring the text to life. Our thanks must also go to the children and staff in the MSI unit at Victoria School in Birmingham for providing us with the opportunity to photograph them at work and play.

Finally, we would like to acknowledge the support of our families, and particularly our long-suffering wives, Neek and Jan, for their encouragement and support throughout the planning and writing of this book. It is no exaggeration to state that without their support this text would never have been completed.

Mike McLinden and Steve McCall
School of Education
University of Birmingham
Spring 2002

Preface

There is no agreement in the literature about how to describe children who have severe visual impairment in combination with additional educational needs. In the United Kingdom, the term 'multihandicapped and visually impaired' (MHVI) has given way in recent years to descriptions of children who have 'multiple disabilities and visual impairment' (MDVI). We acknowledge that no single definition can capture satisfactorily the wide range of conditions which combine with visual impairment to produce multiple disabilities, and so we have adopted the abbreviation 'MDVI' for this text on the pragmatic basis that it is the one that is currently in general usage in the field.

We use MDVI as a broad term to refer to children who, in combination with a visual impairment, have a range of additional impairments which might be physical, emotional, behavioural and/or sensory in nature. Much of the text is concerned with children who have been assessed as functioning at 'early' stages of development. In terms of educational attainment many of these children will have been assessed as working 'within' Level 1 of the core subjects of the National Curriculum (NC) and may continue to work at this level throughout their educational career.

Of particular relevance when planning the curriculum for these children will be the recently published QCA/DfEE guidelines which offer support for the planning, development and implementation of the curriculum for pupils with learning difficulties (QCA 2001a). These guidelines relate to all pupils aged between 5 and 16 who have learning difficulties 'regardless of factors such as ethnicity, culture, religion, home language, family background or gender, or the extent of their other difficulties' and includes pupils who are unlikely to achieve above Level 2 of the NC at Key Stage 4 (QCA 2001b: 4). Within this population there are children who show an uneven profile of development, and in some areas of function will be working at a relatively higher level than others. Children who have MDVI require significant adaptations to be made in order to have access to the curriculum and in the majority of cases will attend specialist schools where children with a range of severe and complex needs are educated.

Throughout this text we use the generic term 'visual impairment' to describe the broad continuum of sight loss in children and young people aged 0–16 years. When a distinction is necessary, the term 'blind' or 'educationally blind' is used to refer to children who rely predominantly on methods which incorporate a tactile component, while the term 'low vision' is used with reference to children who are taught through methods which utilise vision.

In line with common practice we have adopted a 'child first, disability second' approach throughout the text, i.e. 'child who has MDVI'. Although this usage can at times appear rather cumbersome, it acknowledges the fact that the child rather than the impairment/disability should be the main emphasis in any description.

There is no common agreement in the literature on how the term 'touch' should be defined. Indeed, Hull (1993) reported that the 'vocabulary used in the psychology of touch is more confused than the area itself; there is seldom misunderstanding as to the type of perception or processing that is being discussed, but writers are often unsure as to the correct term to describe it' (p. 4). Hull illustrated this point by reference to the terms *tactile*, *tactual* and *haptic*, which he noted were used almost interchangeably 'reflecting the author's background rather than the type of perception that is being described' (p. 4). This lack of consistency suggests that we need to offer some clarification about how each of these terms is used throughout this text.

In line with the work of Schiff and Foulke (1982) we use 'touch' as a general term to describe the sense through which information is received by specialist receptor systems in the skin and body. This includes both 'passive' and 'active' touch, the latter term referring to 'the active exploratory and manipulative use of the skin, and hence stimulation of receptors systems in the muscles, tendons and joints – the kinaesthetic system' (Schiff and Foulke 1982: xi). 'Passive' touch is generally used in the literature to refer either to the actions involved in 'being touched' either by an object or by another person (as in the act of massage), or to contact with an object that does not involve independent exploratory and manipulative action. As we shall see in the text, the distinction between active and passive touch is a particularly pertinent one when considering children who have severe physical impairments.

The term 'tactile' has been adopted to refer to the physical features or properties of an object which can be detected through the sense of touch, for example its contours, surface temperature, texture and/or weight. 'Tactual' and 'haptic' are used interchangeably in the literature to refer to active exploratory and manipulative touch (Schiff and Foulke 1982). For the purpose of this text our preferred term is 'haptic' rather than 'tactual'. The recently introduced National SEN Specialist Standards (TTA 1999) state that teachers working with children who have visual impairment should be able to demonstrate knowledge and understanding of 'the principles of haptic perception'. This suggests that in time haptic will be the pre-ferred designation in the field. As Schiff and Foulke (1982) note, however, whether the terms 'haptic' or 'tactual' 'differ only superficially or in some more palpable way is an issue . . . not resolved' (xi).

Overview

It has been well documented in recent years that a significant proportion of the population of children with visual impairment have 'additional' or 'multiple' disabilities which include intellectual, physical, sensory or emotional difficulties (e.g. Best 1992; Clunies-Ross and Franklin 1997). The proportion of children with multiple disabilities within this population is likely to increase and this change inevitably has significant implications for the knowledge, understanding and skills required by practitioners working in the field of sensory impairment.

In essence the concept of 'multiple' disabilities concerns the combined influence of disabilities on development (McLinden 1997). The prefix 'multiple' or 'multi' serves to highlight the synergetic effect of the combination of the disabilities and emphasises the interactive or multiplying effect which exceeds the sum of each individual disability (Best and Brown 1994).

Goold and Hummell (1993) report that multiple disabilities restrict the individual's exploration and understanding of the world, and when defining 'multisensory impairment' Best and Brown (1994) refer to a 'situation' rather than a 'condition', the situation being characterised by an individual being unable to:

- gather sufficient information from the environment to learn independently;
- make sufficient use of the environment to function independently.

Given the wide range of educational needs created by multiple disabilities, the role of touch in a child's learning can easily be neglected. The ways in which children and young people who have visual impairment make use of touch for exploration and learning has been relatively well researched, particularly in relation to reading through touch (e.g. Millar 1997; Tobin 1994; Warren 1994), the perception of tactile shape (e.g. Millar 1997) and tactile diagrams (e.g. Unger *et al*. 1997). However, much of this research has been undertaken with children and young people who have no additional difficulties. We know relatively little about the ways children who have multiple disabilities use touch when engaging in their environment, although this is an area of increasing interest to researchers (e.g. Davidson 1985; McLinden 1999; McLinden and Douglas 2000; Nielsen 1988; Rogow 1988).

A common feature of children who have multiple disabilities is their increased dependency on other individuals to structure their learning experiences. In examining how a child who has MDVI uses touch in his or her learning, we need to explore therefore the wider context within which these interactions take place, and to acknowledge that effective learning through touch rarely takes place within a 'social vacuum'.

The theme of *independent* activity is one which runs throughout the research literature in relation to the early haptic development of children who follow normal patterns of development. However, research into children with multiple disabilities needs to account for the fact that a significant proportion of this population require, to a greater or lesser extent, continuing support from an adult partner throughout their education. Therefore, in line with the work of Bozic and Murdoch (1996) this book has a wider focus than that of the child; it also considers how the child's use of touch is mediated through their interactions with adult partners.

This text is an attempt to synthesise different elements of practice and research that relate to the role of touch in the development of children who have multiple disabilities which include visual impairment. A central focus of the text is to explore ways in which effective learning opportunities can be provided to encourage these children to become 'active constructors of their own understanding' (Daniels 1996: vii), rather than merely passive recipients of sensory information supplied by others. We start from the premise that adult partners supporting children who have MDVI require appropriate knowledge and understanding of basic principles underpinning the role of touch in learning in order to promote effective learning opportunities. Given the wide range of needs of these children it is not possible to explore in depth all the aspects relating to touch in their education. Instead we have identified four related themes which serve as a focus for the text (see boxes opposite). We will return to these themes again in Chapter 10.

This book is divided into three parts. Part 1, 'Finding out about Touch', consists of four chapters which provide a background to the sense of touch. Chapter 1 is written in an interactive style based around a series of guided 'reflective' activities adapted from professional development sessions we have run. Touch is an intimate sense and we feel that focusing on your own use of touch as an initial point of reference helps you to understand not only the nature of this complex sense, but also the importance of careful observation and reflection, skills which are so valuable when working with children who have multiple disabilities.

Chapter 2 provides a summary of the anatomy and physiology of the sense of touch and introduces a number of key terms which are useful when discussing the role of touch in a child's learning experiences. Chapter 3 explores in further detail how touch is used to acquire different types of sensory information and considers

- The learning experiences of a child who has MDVI will incorporate a range of sensory information, some of which will be distorted in quality and/or quantity. In order to work effectively with the child, the adult partner requires knowledge and understanding of the child's level of sensory function, namely how the child receives, interprets and consequently acts upon different types of sensory information during a given task.

- In considering how a child processes and acts upon sensory information, a distinction can be made between information received from within the body and information which is external to the body. This external information can be broadly divided into information which informs us about the world which is relatively distant to our bodies (for example through the 'distant' senses of vision and hearing), and information which is close to the body (for example through the 'close' senses of touch and taste). In the absence of consistent information through the distant senses, the information received through the close senses increases in significance in a child's learning experiences.

- For a child who is more reliant on information received through the close senses, his or her learning experiences can provide imprecise information about the world if they are not mediated at a level appropriate to the child's needs. This can have an important bearing on the child's knowledge and understanding of the world at critical stages in early development.

- The child's adult partner will need to have knowledge and understanding of his or her role in mediating the child's learning experiences through each of the senses to ensure that these are appropriate to the child's individual needs.

Four related themes guiding the development of effective learning experiences through touch.

the different functions of 'interactive' and 'non-interactive' types of touch. Chapter 4 explores the early development of sensory and cognitive abilities in children following 'normal' patterns of development, and the links between touch and the other senses during early development are outlined.

Part 2, 'Identifying Barriers to Learning', consists of five chapters. In Chapter 5 we consider the implications of a visual impairment for learning through touch and offer an overview of the research literature in this area. The impact of additional disabilities on learning through touch are explored in Chapter 6, and we

discuss how appropriate opportunities can be provided to reduce potential barriers to learning. Chapter 7 explores principles underpinning assessment of touch,
and provides a summary of a number of commonly used assessment procedures.
Chapter 8 has as its main focus the role of touch in communication for children
who have MDVI and considers the crucial role of the child's communication partner. This chapter also includes a discussion of 'transitory' symbols which have a
tactile component, such as hand-over-hand signs, and which are used to support
and develop the communication of children who have MDVI. Chapter 9 considers
the design and use of more 'permanent' tactile symbols such as objects of reference
and Moon, and considers their applications for supporting the learning of children who have a visual impairment. This chapter includes a discussion of emergent literacy through touch and the role of the adult partner in supporting a
child's early literacy development.

Part 3, 'Finishing Touches', consists of two chapters. Chapter 10 expands upon
the themes we presented in the boxes on page xv and considers in further detail
how they can be of value in developing and structuring appropriate learning
experiences through touch. In the final chapter we offer our thoughts on a number of issues which have relevance to the role of touch in the learning experiences
of children who have MDVI. We begin by revisiting the broad spectrum of need
within the population and then consider briefly the implication of this heterogeneity for future research. This is followed by a short discussion of developments in
Information and Communication Technology (ICT) as well as issues relating to the
continuing professional development (CPD) of those supporting children with
MDVI.

A series of 'portfolio' activities are included at the end of the text. These have
been designed to draw out the key issues from the book and to explore implications for your practice. A number of these activities are designed to cross reference with relevant extension standards included in the National SEN Specialist
Standards (TTA 1999). Completion of these activities can be used as evidence of
knowledge and understanding and incorporated into a portfolio of continuing
professional development.

PART 1

FINDING OUT ABOUT TOUCH

CHAPTER 1

Reflecting on Touch

Introduction

Which sense would you most hate to 'lose'? It's a question that is usually only ever asked by, and of, people who have all their senses 'intact'. It typically gives rise to a conversation about the relative merits of sight and hearing, for example, 'I couldn't stand to lose my sight because I wouldn't be able to see the beauty of the world around me' or, 'It would be awful to lose your hearing because you'd be cut off from what other people are saying'. Consider for a moment however a world without your sense of touch. It would be a strange world. Imagine eating without being able to feel the texture of food, embracing your partner without feeling his or her caresses, carrying a suitcase without feeling what you are holding. Imagine a world where tennis players have no 'touch', doctors cannot feel for lumps, and it's not just your mouth that's numb when you leave the dentist. A world where you can't feel the wind on your face, the sun on your back or the good earth under your feet. In short, a world where you would experience your life as if you were watching a film with smell and taste supplements – a very strange world indeed.

As we can easily appreciate, touch has a unique role in providing us with the experience of 'being present' in the world. However, unlike vision or hearing, touch generally requires direct contact with a source before we can receive and process information about it, but even the very word 'touch' is somewhat misleading. Clearly we can also use our sense of touch to acquire information about a source without making physical contact with it, for example when we 'warm' our hands over an open fire.

In this introductory chapter we are going to explore some of the key functions of the sense of touch and consider its particular role in providing us with sensory information about the world. As we have hinted, we consider touch to be a very immediate and intimate sense, a sense all of us employ constantly but few of us reflect upon in any depth. To help us in our exploration we have incorporated five 'reflective' activities into this chapter. These activities are designed to supplement the content of the chapters that follow and you might find it helpful to revisit them during the course of your later reading in this book. Each reflective activity comprises two or three tasks which can be completed using readily available resources including parts of your body, items of clothing, or indeed, this book itself! At the end of each activity you will find a short commentary which addresses the question *'What does this activity tell us about the sense of touch?'*. There are no 'right' or 'wrong' answers to these activities, and this commentary is only intended to help you compare your ideas with our own.

Reflective Activity 1: Acquiring sensory information about your body through touch

The first activity considers how we acquire particular types of information through touch in the absence of visual information and focuses on different areas of your face, i.e. your lips, your chin and your cheeks.

---

a. For the first part of this activity gently place the pad of your index finger onto a part of your lip for about five seconds. Without moving your finger, and without pressing, what sensory features of your lip are immediately apparent through touch? For example, does your lip feel 'cold' or 'warm' to touch? Now gently touch at least three other areas of your lips using the same finger pad. What additional sensory information about the features of your lips do you acquire? What sensory information do you acquire about your finger pad through your lips?

---

b. Repeat the activity, but this time place the pad of your finger onto a part of your cheek. Remember to keep your finger still.

---

c. Repeat the activity but this time place your finger pad onto a part of your chin.

What does this activity tell us about the sense of touch?

This first activity provides us with information about an important aspect of touch, namely that gentle, static touch can provide some information about characteristics such as temperature and general surface quality, i.e. surface texture. This type of information is fundamentally different from that provided by our other senses. For example, by *looking* at your lips in a mirror you become aware of important defining features such as their shape and colour. However, when *touching* your lips without the use of visual information, you may have become aware of other properties of your lips, for example, the distinctive feel of the skin which covers the lip when compared with the skin of the cheek. You'll notice that in the first component of this activity it's quite difficult to separate out the sensation of 'touching' from the sensation of 'being touched'. The touch receptors in our finger pads and our lips are closely grouped, making them relatively 'sensitive' areas of our bodies.

As we shall see, there are a number of types of touch receptors within the skin which provide us with different types of sensory information depending on the type of touch that is employed. Within this activity you were requested not to move your finger over the surface of the skin but to consider what type of information you received through a static or 'passive' type of touch. Before moving on to the next activity, you may wish to repeat this activity on one or more parts of your face. This time however, gently rub your finger pad across the surface of the skin being felt. How does the surface of the skin feel when a more 'active' touch is employed compared with the more 'passive' type of touch used earlier?

Reflective Activity 2: Acquiring information about external sensory features

The focus of Activity 1 was very much on your own body and, in particular, areas of your body which you are unable to see without the aid of a mirror. The second activity is designed to explore how we can use touch to acquire information about objects or 'sensory stimuli' which are external to our bodies, for example our clothes.

a. Lightly rest the finger pads of one hand on the surface of an item of clothing you are wearing and leave them stationary for approximately ten seconds. What particular sensations do you experience when your hand is passive on the clothing?

b. Now lightly rub your finger pads gently across the surface of the clothing. What additional information do you receive once you begin moving your finger pads across the clothing?

What does this activity tell us about the sense of touch?

Activity 2 demonstrates how important movement can be in acquiring information through touch. Although a 'passive' hand or finger on an object provides some important information about its particular features, it is not until we move our fingers across a surface (or indeed, the surface of the object is moved under our fingers) that fine details such as the subtleties of the texture or particular features such as seams, folds and creases become apparent.

We can immediately begin to make a broad distinction between two types of touch which we use to find out about the world, namely 'active' and 'passive' touch. 'Active touch' can be described as a process of exploring an object in order to acquire information about it. In comparison 'passive touch' may be described as touch which involves your skin coming into contact with objects but which does not involve 'active' manipulation on your part. The information you receive when you place the palm of your hand onto a table top without moving it, or the feeling you experience when somebody massages your shoulders are examples of different types of this more passive type of touch. In general, research findings support the view that active touch is a 'superior' mode of exploration to passive touch (e.g. Appelle 1991) although, as we shall see later, this is very dependent on a range of factors including our familiarity with the object, or the feature of the object, which is under investigation. Further, the distinction between active and passive touch is somewhat blurred by the fact that the touching we employ during our everyday activities can rarely be described as either purely 'active' or 'passive'.

Consider for example the information you receive through touch when bending down to stroke a purring cat which is rubbing its side against your bare ankles. The stroking action performed by your hand is a good example of a more active type of touch in that it involves independent activity on your part. Indeed, by varying the type of stroking action you perform on the cat's fur you can find out different types of information about its particular sensory features, for example how 'smooth' it feels when stroked one way but not the other. In some respects the cat's movements in brushing its body firmly against your ankles can be described as 'passive' touch in that it does not involve active manipulation on your part. However, it is unlikely that your ankles will remain 'passive' as the cat brushes against them, and indeed, you may find yourself attempting to move your feet away from the cat's body. This example shows that although the distinction between active and passive types of touch is a useful one, the way we normally make use of touch during our daily lives is actually rather more complex than such a broad distinction might suggest.

Although you weren't asked to perform Activity 2 in the dark, consider how useful independent activity in touch can be in providing us with information when we are deprived of vision. Imagine you are in a cinema and the lights are down. What specific movements might your fingers make to work out whether the surface of the chair you are sitting on is made from cloth or nylon? Typically you would run your finger tips from side to side across the surface. If it's a very old cinema seat you might experience that slightly spikey sensation as the short fibres of the plush seat covering rub against your fingers. The hand movements we make to find out about the features of an object are often described as 'exploratory strategies'. These strategies have been widely investigated by researchers and provide valuable insights into the way we seek out and process information using our hands. In our next activity we are going to look briefly at the role that exploratory strategies can play in helping us acquire particular types of sensory information.

Reflective Activity 3: Role of exploratory strategies

In this third activity you are going to explore a number of different parts of your own body, namely your face, ears and hands. Compared with the first activity however your fingers will be performing slower, more deliberate movements. You may find that you prefer to carry out this activity in a place where you are not being watched!

a. Lightly trace your forefinger along the profile of your face, starting at your forehead and working down to your chin. As your finger moves down the contours consider carefully the type of sensory information you are receiving about the shape of the various parts of the face, for example your nose, your lips and your chin.

b. Lightly trace the forefinger of one hand across the external contours of one of your ears, starting with your finger close to your inner ear and working down towards the ear lobe. As your finger moves across the contour of the ear consider carefully the different type of sensory information you are receiving. Now use both your forefingers to simultaneously trace around the external contours of both ears. Are you able to feel any differences between the tactile features of each ear?

c. Place the palm of either your right or left hand onto the back of your other hand. The hand on top is referred to as the 'manipulating' hand; the hand underneath is the hand that is being 'manipulated'. With the 'manipulating' hand spend approximately 30 seconds carefully investigating the features of the other hand. You should pay particular attention to any features which you can feel underneath the surface of the skin, for example the structure of the bones in your hand. In addition, pay careful attention to the type of hand movements that are made to investigate the various components of the 'manipulated' hand.

What does this activity tell us about the sense of touch?

This activity provides further insights into the role of hand movements in finding out information through touch. The movements in the earlier activities were relatively fast and simple to execute and provided information about particular properties, including surface temperature and texture. In order to accurately determine other features of an object or part of the body, such as its surface outline (or contour), we need to use more subtle and refined types of hand movements. In this case we employ 'contour following' movements – a slower procedure that involves precise and distinctive hand movements.

In the third component of this activity by pushing, prodding and manipulating the more 'passive' hand, you are able to find out something about the salient features of its internal structure which are not directly accessible through vision. You can use your fingers to 'feel' structures under the skin such as the bones in your hand even though you are not able to make direct physical contact with them. We make use of this important function of touch to discover information which may not be apparent through our other senses, for example, if we are not well we might feel our throat with our fingers to determine whether our glands are enlarged.

Reflective Activity 4: Manipulation of objects

The fourth activity provides an opportunity to investigate different types of portable and 'freely manipulable' objects (i.e. objects that are not attached to other objects) in order to gain information about their features. As you do so pay careful attention to the type of movements your hands make when you explore each object, for example for shape, weight and/or surface temperature. You should also consider precisely how your two hands work with one another as they manipulate various features of each object.

a. Select a portable and freely manipulable object which you can hold in either one or both hands, for example this book or a pen. Without looking at the object spend about 20 seconds exploring its features using just one hand. You should then use both hands to investigate it for another 20 seconds, again, without looking at it if possible. What additional movements were you able to make when you manipulated the object with both hands which you were not able to make with one hand?

b. Select another portable and freely manipulable object and, without looking at it, explore its main features for approximately 20 seconds using both hands. What comparisons can you make with the first object in terms of relative size, shape, texture, etc? What types of exploratory movements did you use to find information about the properties of this object?

What does this activity tell us about the sense of touch?

This activity is different from the earlier ones in that it provides an opportunity to manipulate unattached objects using either one or two hands. This activity helps us find out about the ways in which our hands complement each other when investigating the properties of an object. You will have noticed that each hand assumes quite distinct roles at different points in the investigation process. For example, while the left hand grasps the object, the right hand may exert pressure by 'squeezing' it in an attempt to determine its hardness. The right hand may then grasp the object while the left hand exerts pressure.

This activity shows how the hands can assume quite distinct roles during the manipulation of an object. Indeed, a differentiation is made in the literature between the 'executive' role of the hand, i.e. when it is used for grasping and holding, and the 'perceptual' role of the hand, i.e. when it is used for seeking out sensory information. Further, this activity demonstrated the importance of 'complementary bimanual activity' (i.e. using one hand to complement the action performed by the other hand), which represents an important developmental milestone in young infants, something we will explore further in Chapter 4.

Reflective Activity 5: Oral exploration

The fifth and final activity in this chapter is of a different nature to the others in that the main focus is on the role of the tongue rather than the hands in acquiring sensory information. It is an unusual activity as it explores areas of the mouth and teeth which are not easy to observe through vision.

---

a. Using the tip of your tongue, lightly trace along the inside contours of your upper and your lower lip. Do you notice any differences in the features of your upper lip in comparison with those in your lower lip?

---

b. Using the tip of your tongue lightly trace along the upper row of your teeth. What particular features do you notice about the cutting edges of different teeth? What does this suggest about the sensitivity of the tongue? Is it possible to count the number of teeth you have in your upper row using your tongue alone?

What does this activity tell us about the sense of touch?

This activity highlights the role that parts of the body other than the hands can play in acquiring information through touch. The first component demonstrates the dexterity of the tongue and how effective it can be in acquiring particular types of sensory information. By tracing along the contours of your lips your tongue can acquire some information about surface texture, shape, relative size and possibly the surface temperature of each lip.

The second component shows how the tongue can make very subtle distinctions between surface textures. You might have felt slight ridges on the edge of your two front teeth. If you have ever lost a filling you will have noticed how 'large' even very small cavities can feel when you explore them with your tongue. This activity also serves to highlight the length of time and the degree of concentration required to process certain types of sensory information effectively. You may have noticed for example how easy it was to lose track of where you got up to when counting your teeth, requiring you perhaps to start again at a known reference point.

Assumptions underpinning reflective activities

The activities in this chapter were selected not only to provide you with opportunities to reflect upon your own sense of touch, but also as a platform to begin to consider the implications of touch for children with a visual impairment, and in particular those who have additional needs which may serve as barriers to *independent* learning. In designing these activities and asking you to carry them out, we have made a number of assumptions about you. For example we have assumed that you have:

- sufficient free movement in your arms, hands and fingers to be able to explore and manipulate objects *independently*;
- the ability to understand and employ a range of different types of exploratory strategies in order to acquire sensory information about objects and object features;
- fully functioning senses of vision and touch, allowing you to compare information you receive from touch with information you receive from your sense of vision;
- an appropriate level of understanding of the purpose of the activities and how they are designed to serve as a foundation for your later reading.

As you read through the subsequent chapters in this book you may wish to reflect on the extent to which each of these assumptions applies to a particular child you know who has a visual impairment and additional needs. If you are not familiar with children in this population, you may wish to relate your thoughts to a young infant who is still developing his or her abilities to utilise information through touch. Is the infant able, for example, to independently manipulate different types of objects? Is he or she able to select from a range of strategies to acquire information about different objects? Further, to what extent is the infant able to utilise information from other senses in order to acquire different types of information about an object, for example, bringing the object to his or her visual field to find out what it is?

Summary

In Chapter 1 we have provided opportunities for you to explore different aspects of the sense of touch through a number of reflective activities. The activities incorporated in this chapter were designed to offer insights into how the sense of touch can be used to acquire sensory information about the world. We highlighted an important distinction between 'active' and 'passive' types of touch, a distinction which is expanded upon later in the text. Further, we made a number of assumptions about the abilities which could be utilised by the reader in performing each of the tasks and considered possible implications for those with less developed independent abilities. This information will be useful in your reading of Chapter

2, in which we explore in further depth the processes by which information is received through touch and then transmitted to the brain for processing through a complex series of pathways.

Recommended reading

Connolly, K. (ed.) (1997) *The Psychobiology of the Hand*. Cambridge: MacKeith Press.

Heller, M.A. and Schiff, W. (eds) (1991) *The Psychology of Touch*. Hillsdale, NJ: Lawrence Erlbaum Associates.

Schiff, W. and Foulke, E. (eds) (1982) *Tactual Perception: A sourcebook*. Cambridge: Cambridge University Press.

CHAPTER 2

The Anatomy and Physiology of Touch

Introduction

In Chapter 1 we explored how the sense of touch serves as an interface between our body and the external environment and how it allows us to acquire information about the physical world. Before we can recognise, or 'sense' the properties of an object through touch, the sensory information we receive through the skin (for example temperature or texture) has to be transmitted to the brain for processing through a complex sequence of pathways. In order to understand the way this information is received, transmitted and processed we will need to consider both human anatomy (i.e. the *structure*, form and relationships of different parts of the body) and human physiology (i.e. the *function* of the parts of the body and how each of these parts works). In this chapter we provide you with a broad summary of these complex issues, and introduce a number of technical terms that will serve as a useful foundation for later chapters.

Receiving sensory information

A sense organ has been defined as 'a tissue system sensitive to energies generally applied from the environment but also sensitive to those applied within the body' (Bartley 1980: 13–14). Touch is one of the five sensations (touch, vision, taste, smell and hearing) which can be directly related to specific sensory organs (skin, eyes, mouth, nose and ears). The body receives and processes additional kinds of information through receptors, not all of which are linked to discrete sense organs. This includes vestibular (balance), proprioceptive (body space and position), as well as homeostatic (body temperature) information (Bartley 1980; Rosen 1997). These receptors can broadly be divided into those which provide us with information about what is happening *within* our bodies, and are therefore helpful in knowing, for example, about body space and movement (i.e. proprioception), and those which provide us with information about the world *outside* of our bodies, for example receptors located in the skin, eyes, ears, nose, etc. (i.e. extero-ception) (Pagliano 2001).

Each of the sensory organs contains nerve cells or sensory *receptors* that are designed to turn sensory information into 'electrical' activity. This electrical activity travels through the nervous system and is transmitted to the appropriate areas in the brain. For the purposes of this text, we use the term 'perception' to describe how input to the sensory receptors is transformed into what we actually see, hear, feel, taste, smell, etc. However, before we think about perception in relation to the sense of touch, first we will consider the anatomy and physiology of the sense organ through which we initially receive tactile information from outside of our bodies, namely the skin.

Skin

Although we do not usually think of it as such, the skin is, in fact, the body's largest organ. In addition to its sensory role, the skin has a number of other functions. For example, it protects our internal organs from infection and radiation and provides our bodies with a waterproof membrane. You will be aware from your own body that most of our skin is covered in hair (with some areas having more hair than others), which helps maintain our body temperature. However, a number of areas of the skin do not have hair, for example the palms of our hands and the soles of our feet. The technical term used to describe the non-hairy parts of the skin is 'glabrous'. Although the hairs themselves are not sensitive to touch, nerve fibres wrapped around the base of each hair provide us with a sense of 'touch' if the hairs are moved, or indeed 'pain' if a hair is plucked from the skin.

The skin is made up of two main layers:

- **Epidermis** or outer layer. This consists of flattened cells that are constantly being worn away and replaced from the inside. Certain parts of the body, for example the sole of the foot, will usually have a thickened epidermis.
- **Dermis** or inner layer. This contains hair follicles, sebaceous glands, sweat glands, blood vessels as well as the nerve endings which can transmit pain or detect stimuli such as temperature or pressure.

There are two main types of nerve endings found in the skin:

- free nerve endings;
- nerve endings incorporated within another structure, e.g. Pacinian corpuscles, Merkel's discs.

A cross-section of a sample of human skin which includes the various nerve endings is shown in Figure 2.1. However, depending on the location of the skin,

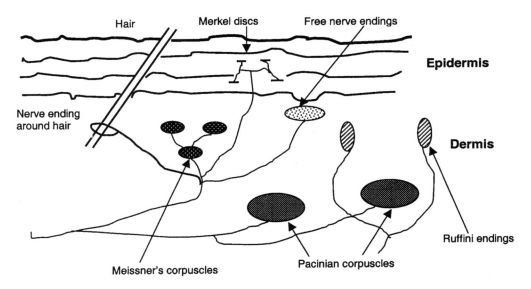

Figure 2.1 Diagram of a cross-section of human skin showing nerve endings

the number and types of structures found there will vary greatly. For example, there are no hair follicles in glabrous skin, nor are Pacinian corpuscles found in the skin of the cheek (Cholewiak and Collins 1991). Further, the nature of our skin surface changes depending on its location on the body; compare the texture of the skin found on the palm and back of your hand.

The nerve endings (also referred to as 'tactile' or 'skin' receptors) located within the skin are commonly classified according to how they react to particular stimuli (Goldstein 1989):

Mechanoreceptors receptors that respond to indentations of the skin, for example when a finger touches the back of the hand. Two types of mechano-receptors have been identified – rapidly adapting (RA) and slowly adapting (SA).

Thermoreceptors receptors that respond to temperatures or changes in temperature, for example when picking up a hot saucepan handle, or when eating a cold ice lolly.

Noiceptors receptors that respond to stimuli which damage the skin, for example intense heat which results in a burn to the skin, or a painful prick from a thorn.

Many of the different types of tactile receptors shown in Figure 2.1 were named by anatomists in the nineteenth century, which accounts for their rather obscure names. (e.g. Merkel's disc, Meissner's corpuscle, etc). Although experimental studies by these anatomists suggested a direct relationship between different sensations and particular skin receptors, more recent studies have not always supported these early findings, and some of the suggested relationships have proved tenuous. A summary of the location and possible modalities of sensation associated with the skin receptors is shown in Figure 2.2. However, as Cholewiak and Collins (1991) note, the *exact* correspondence between the structures in the skin and their function is not yet known. Further, these descriptions are greatly simplified, and to some extent, as Royeen and Lane (1991) note, 'all receptors respond to all inputs' (p. 115). However, for the purposes of this discussion we will just concentrate on the stimuli to which recent research suggests each type of receptor responds 'best'.

We have already noted that touch receptors are not just located in the skin. There are also receptors that form part of the *proprioceptive* system and provide information about stimuli from within the body such as the movement of the limbs. The proprioception receptors are found in the joints, tendons and muscles, and information we receive through these receptors informs us not only about the stationary position of our limbs (i.e. limb position) but also provides us with information about their movements (*kinaesthesia*) (Eliasoon 1995). In short, proprioception informs us where each of our limbs is in relation to the rest of our body, information that is essential to help us coordinate any action involving our limbs.

There appears to be a clear distinction between the proprioceptive sensations which arise from *within* the body and are linked to the movement and/or position of the limbs, and the touch sensations that come to us from our *external* body surface. However, these sensations are also linked because when we move our joints, we also inevitably stretch and compress our skin. Royeen and Lane (1991) suggest therefore that 'because there is frequently a close interaction between touch, and joint and body movement, it sometimes is difficult to separate the influence of these two sensory systems' (p. 109).

We rely on our proprioceptive systems all the time. Hold a small object, such as a pen, behind your back. Using just a thumb and two fingers on each hand transfer the pen from hand to hand. Now manoeuvre the pen as follows but try not to let your hands touch each other: twirl the pen around in one hand and alternately grip the tip and then the bottom of the pen with the other hand. You'll notice that you have a very good idea where your hands are in relation to each other even though they don't come into direct contact. All day we perform complex and sophisticated manoeuvres of this kind using touch, frequently without the need to look.

Without proprioceptive information we wouldn't be able to position our hands to perform these sophisticated actions. This particular type of perception has been described as 'conscious proprioception' as it involves the conscious awareness of the position of the body parts and their movements and, as noted above, contributes to the maintenance of balance and limb movement control as well as the evaluation of the shape of an object when held in the hand (Martin and Jessell 1991).

Type and Description	Location	Sensation
Free nerve endings – nerve endings in the skin which have been linked with the sensation of 'pain' and 'temperature'.	Dermis, joint capsules, tendons, ligaments, deep dermis	Pain, temperature
Hair follicle	Dermis	Hair displacement, pain
Meissner's corpuscles – small/well-defined field. Respond mostly only at the beginning and at the end of the stimulus. Classified as rapidly adapting (RA) *mechanoreceptors* which respond best to slower movements.	Particularly dense in sensitive areas of skin, e.g. finger pads and tip of tongue, glabrous (i.e. non-hairy) skin	Edges, location and timing of stimuli
Pacinian corpuscles – large, indistinct field. Activated only at the beginning or end of a *pressure* stimulus, for example when an object touches the skin and when it is removed from the skin. Classified as rapidly adapting (RA) *mechanoreceptors*.	Subcutaneous tissue, glabrous (i.e. non-hairy) skin	Pressure, vibration, cold
Merkel's discs – small, well defined field. Respond continuously to stimulation but is relatively 'slow' to adapt response. Classified as slowly adapting (SA) *mechanoreceptors*.	Epidermis of skin, glabrous and hairy skin	Pressure/direct impact
Ruffini endings – large, indistinct field. Classified as slowly adapting (SA) *mechanoreceptors*.	Joint capsules, connective tissue, glabrous and hairy skin	Skin stretch, also linked with sensitivity to heat

Figure 2.2 Locations and modalities of sensation associated with skin receptors (adapted from Goold and Hummell 1993; Royeen and Lane 1991; Goldstein 1989)

Transmission and processing of tactile stimuli

Sensory information we receive through our touch receptors is transmitted to our brain through pathways within the body. In this chapter we are only going to explore two pathways which we consider to have particular relevance to this book, although before we look at these two pathways we need to explore the central nervous system (CNS). You might find this section difficult to follow but we will attempt to summarise it at the end. Much of our explanation is based on two sources which we can recommend: Goold and Hummell (1993) and Royeen and Lane (1991). If you would like to explore this subject further you should refer to the recommended reading section at the end of the chapter.

Central nervous system

To understand how the various types of information we receive through touch are processed you will need a basic knowledge of the main structures involved in processing information within the CNS. Look at the greatly simplified diagram of the brain and the spinal cord in Figure 2.3.

The brain is made up of two hemispheres (also referred to as *cerebral hemispheres*) which consist of nerve cells and nerve fibres. Each hemisphere is divided into four broad *lobes* which correspond in position to the bones of the skull beneath which they are located, i.e. the *frontal, temporal, parietal* and *occipital* lobes. Of particular interest to our description is the *parietal lobe,* located at the top of the brain towards the back of the head, similar in position to where one might wear a skullcap.

The outer layer of each hemisphere is referred to as the *cortex,* and you will probably be familiar with the term *visual cortex* which is commonly used to describe the area of the brain where visual information is processed. We are particularly concerned in this discussion with the *somatosensory cortex,* a term which derives from the Greek word 'soma' meaning 'body'. The main role of the somatosensory cortex is to provide us with perception of sensations (Tortora and Anagnostakos 1987). As you can see from Figure 2.3 the somatosensory cortex is located in the *parietal lobe,* it is responsible for processing the information which has been transmitted through the somatosensory pathways from the somatosensory modalities (i.e. the tactile receptors we looked at in Figure 2.2). You will probably already be aware that input from the right side of the body is processed by the left hemisphere of the brain and vice versa. For example, damage (lesions) to the somatosensory cortex on one side of the brain may lead to loss of touch sensation in the opposite half of the body (e.g. hemiplegia).

The brain has a role which extends beyond simply interpreting the messages it receives from our skin and joints. The way we interpret sensation is affected by

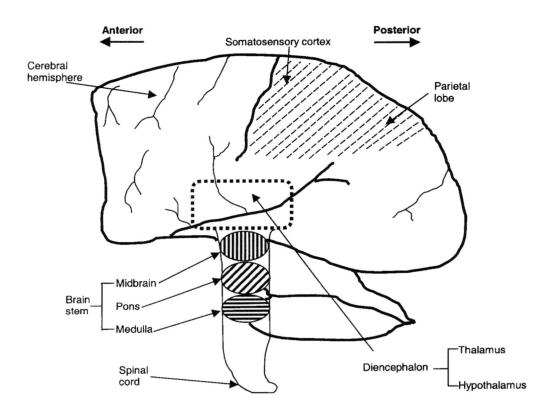

Figure 2.3   Diagram of main structures involved in processing somatosensory information within the central nervous system (CNS) (adapted from Goold and Hummell 1993)

'cognitive' factors such as memory, the amount of attention we are paying at the time to information received through our sense of touch, our motivation, the demands of the task in hand, etc. In fact we often ignore and occasionally misinterpret the sensory information we receive through the skin. For example, a colleague of ours describes an incident from his adolescence when he was sitting with his girlfriend in a dark cinema. He misinterpreted the swell of her shoulder for the swell of her breast. The more he fondled her shoulder the more aroused he became at what he imagined was his first sexual encounter. It was only after the final curtain when the lights were turned on that he was enlightened, if rather disappointed!

In order to reach the somatosensory cortex, the information we receive through the tactile receptors in the skin has to pass through one of our two processing systems along the spinal cord to the *reticular formation* in our brain. The reticular formation has an important role in both the arousal and inhibition of our sense of touch and can filter out sensory information. After passing through the reticular formation, the information from our touch sensors is then transmitted to the *thalamus*. The thalamus serves as an important integrating centre for input from all our sensory systems with the exception of the olfactory system (Goold and Hummell 1993; Martin and Jessell 1991). In very basic terms, the thalamus 'sorts out', or filters, various types of sensations and then transmits information to the somatosensory cortex.

Processing pathways

Figure 2.4 provides a schematic representation of the two main pathways which transmit information from the skin to the brain:

- dorsal column medial lemniscal system (DCMLS)
- anterolateral system (ALS)

We need a basic knowledge of these systems to understand how different types of sensory information are transmitted and processed. Further, as we will see later, these systems may have a direct bearing on the barriers to independent learning through touch that some children experience and may help to explain aversion to touch or 'tactile defensiveness'.

Dorsal column medial lemniscal system

The dorsal column medial lemniscal system (DCMLS) is the more sophisticated of our two transmission systems for touch. Primarily it has a discriminatory and exploratory function. It transmits tactile (i.e. 'vibratory' and 'touch–pressure') information as well as proprioceptive information and is associated with 'the functions inherent in tactile discrimination or perception: detection of size, form, texture, and movement across the skin' (Royeen and Lane 1991: 115).

The areas of the brain responsible for processing the information received through the DCMLS include the somatosensory cortex, as well as particular areas of the posterior (or the back) of the parietal lobe which are associated with the manipulation of objects and as such 'are important in discerning their tactile qualities (haptic perception)' (Royeen and Lane 1991: 115). Within the parietal lobe components of both *tactile* and *proprioceptive* input converge prior to transmission to the anterior (i.e. front) motor planning areas of the brain, and so the DCMLS has a role in object manipulation as well as 'motor planning' (Royeen and Lane 1991).

To make more sense of this you may find it useful to think back to manipulating the pen (p. 16). Although you could not see the pen you could use particular types of sensory information to continue your exploration. Central to this

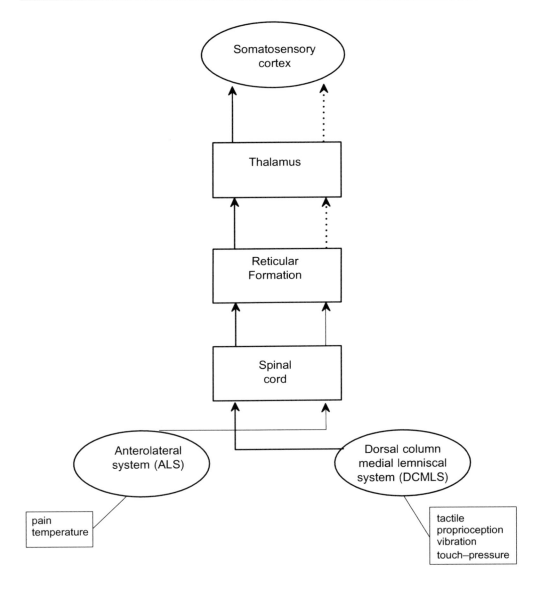

Figure 2.4 Simplified diagram of somatosensory system showing anterolateral system (ALS) and dorsal column medial lemniscal system (DCMLS) (adapted from Goold and Hummell 1993)

process was the proprioceptive information which informed you where your hands were in relation to each other. This information was transmitted mainly through your DCMLS. In addition to information about the location of the pen, you received information about its external features such as its hardness, temperature and shape, again information which was transmitted mainly through your

DCMLS and which converged in the parietal lobe. You were able to use this information in planning your next action with the pen.

Anterolateral system (ALS)

Goold and Hummell (1993) report that the ALS is mainly 'survival oriented' and as such serves a protective function. It appears to be a more primitive system than the DCMLS and is made up of three smaller pathways which serve primarily to mediate pain and to provide gross information about touch and about temperature. As Royeen and Lane (1991) note, 'most fibres within the anterolateral system terminate within the reticular formation' (p. 116), and do not continue to the somatosensory cortex (this is illustrated in Figure 2.4 with a broken line). Although the ALS can detect the *position* of objects it is reported that it cannot provide information on their *movement* across the skin.

Ayres (1972) has proposed that many aspects of touch which are associated with aversion to touch, or 'tactile defensiveness', are theoretically linked with transmission through the ALS pathways and with the interpretation of this input by the brain. Further, Goold and Hummell (1993) state that the ALS has links with the *limbic system* (a region of the brain which is associated with emotional responses) as well as with the *hypothalamus* (a region of the brain which is associated with autonomic regulation): 'Such links may assist in explaining why certain forms of touch make us feel happy and content, or cause us to shrink from the person touching us, increase our respiration rate, and perspire' (p. 36).

This is important information for those people who work with children who are resistant to touching or being touched. It raises a possibility that this 'tactile defensiveness' may have a physiological explanation, although as we consider later in the text, for children who have a visual impairment, there may be other reasons which account for their resistance to certain tactile experiences.

Overlapping functions of DCMLS and ALS

A useful way of distinguishing between the two systems is to consider the ALS as a 'protective' system which is oriented towards protecting the individual from pain or injury. In comparison, the DCMLS can be described as a 'discriminatory' system which allows the individual to find out about the world through the exploration of objects and sensory features. However, it is important to note that although it was originally thought that the roles of the two systems were quite distinct, there is evidence of functional overlap between them. For example, Royeen and Lane (1991) report that the DCMLS has been found to play an important role in the localisation of pain (more traditionally linked with the function of the ALS), and there is evidence that individuals with damage to the DCMLS retain some basic tactile discrimination abilities through the ALS even though these abilities have traditionally been considered the preserve of the DCMLS: 'Thus, some aspects of pain are transmitted through the dorsal column medial lemniscal system, and some aspects of tactile discrimination must be carried in the anterolateral system' (p. 117).

As we suggested earlier, a basic understanding of the two processing pathways provides a means of explaining why some children demonstrate avoidance to touching or being touched, in that damage to one of the systems may result in increased dominance of the other system. The more primitive 'protective' system (the ALS) is thought to be less vulnerable to damage than the 'discriminatory' systems (DCMLS). Goold and Hummell (1993) propose that damage to the DCMLS may result in 'domination' by the ALS, which triggers protective responses regarding touch: 'Such withdrawal from touch potentially limits exploration of people and objects in the environment, inhibits development of discriminatory touch and reduces the opportunities for social and information touch' (p. 36). This avoidance of particular types of touch may be one manifestation of 'tactile defensiveness', an area which we explore in Part 2.

Summary

The main purpose of this chapter has been to provide a basic overview of the anatomy and physiology of the sense of touch, and in particular to highlight the various components involved in the reception, transmission and processing of tactile information. This is a complex and technical area where knowledge and understanding is still at an emerging stage. We have seen that we receive information about touch through sensors or receptors in our skin, our joints, muscles and tendons. There are various types of receptors with each responding to a particular sort of stimulation. For example, the skin contains some receptors that respond to pressure or vibration and others that detect edges. Our joints contain proprioceptive receptors that are activated when we move and help us to coordinate our movement by informing us about the relative position of our body parts.

Information from the 'tactile' receptors is transmitted to the brain through two main pathways. One carries information we obtain through active exploratory touch and includes information about pressure, vibration and proprioception, while the other system is designed to carry basic information that helps 'defend' the body by relaying information about pain and temperature. It has been proposed that imbalances between these systems may explain the phenomenon of 'tactile defensiveness' observed in some people although, as we will see later, this is a complex issue, and for some children who have a visual impairment we can also consider other possible explanations.

Recommended reading

Cholewiak, R.W. and Collins, A. A. (1991) 'Sensory and physiological bases of touch', in Heller, M. A. and Schiff, W. (eds) *The Psychology of Touch*. Hillsdale, NJ: Lawrence Erlbaum Associates.

Goldstein, E.B. (1989) *Sensation and Perception* (3rd edn). Belmont, CA: Wadsworth Publishing Company.

Goold, L. and Hummell, J. (1993) *Supporting the Receptive Communication of Individuals with Significant Multiple Disabilities: Selective use of touch to enhance comprehension.* North Rocks, Australia: North Rocks Press.

Heller, M. A. and Schiff, W. (eds) (1991) *The Psychology of Touch*. Hillsdale, NJ: Lawrence Erlbaum Associates.

Roberts, R. and Wing, A. M. (2001) 'Making sense of active touch', *British Journal of Visual Impairment*, **19** (2), 48–56.

Royeen, C. and Lane, S. (1991) 'Tactile processing and sensory defensiveness', in Fisher, A., Murray, E. and Bundy, A. (eds) *Sensory Integration: Theory and practice*. Philadelphia, PA: F. A. Davis.

CHAPTER 3

Functions of Touch

Introduction

Although our knowledge and understanding of the role and functions of touch has increased enormously over the past hundred years, we still don't have a straightforward answer to the question 'What is touch?' During the first quarter of the twentieth century David Katz, a German scientist, reported his detailed observations on touch and noted:

> On the one hand, we find touch a slow, impoverished modality compared with vision; on the other, it is an expert system by which we can identify small objects with great accuracy ... It is a conglomeration of partly overlapping sensations rather than a single sense modality. At the same time, the hand has been considered a unitary sense organ like the eye. (Katz 1925/1989)

This description of touch hints at the frustrations felt at the time by researchers who were trying to define the parameters of touch. Over 70 years later Suzanna Millar, an experimental psychologist working at Oxford University, was continuing the challenge to capture touch's multifaceted nature:

> Touch conveys information about a number of different, although often overlapping, skin sensations. Inputs can arise from vibration or temporally spaced pulses, from pressure which gives impressions of hardness or softness, from shear patterns that convey impressions of rough and smooth surfaces, dry or wet textures. Hot and cold temperatures are also sensed. The impressions can all be used to identify objects. (1994: 16)

Katz and Millar demonstrate neatly the complex and contradictory elements of a sense which provides us with so many different forms of information that Millar concluded that it may actually be misleading to speak of a distinct 'sense of touch'. Given that touch is so difficult to define in the abstract our aim in this chapter is to try to identify the various functions of touch as they appear within our own daily experiences.

Exploring the functions of touch

The activities in Chapter 1 provided us with some insights into an important function of touch, namely its 'information seeking' role. By performing these activities we were able to acquire information about features of objects and about parts of our body. This active use of touch to seek out and acquire information has been termed 'haptic' touch, with the term haptic deriving from the Greek word *haptikos* meaning 'able to touch'. The 'haptic system' has been defined as a distinctive perceptual system, oriented towards discriminating and recognising objects by handling them as opposed to looking at them (Bushnell and Boudreau 1993). 'Haptic perception' has been described therefore as perception which has 'an inherent bias towards the way objects feel, and not towards how they might look' (Klatzky *et al.* 1987: 367). In Figure 3.1 we provide examples of the different kinds of information about the properties of objects that can be received through haptic perception, together with comparative terms that can be used to describe them.

Object property/ Sensory feature	Examples of comparative terms used to describe object properties		
Vibrations	'RAPID'	←——————→	'SLOW'
Surface texture	'ROUGH'	←——————→	'SMOOTH'
Wetness/dryness	'WET'	←——————→	'DRY'
Surface temperature	'HOT'	←——————→	'COLD'
Shape	'COMPLEX'	←——————→	'SIMPLE'
Slope	'STEEP'	←——————→	'FLAT'
Curved	'CURVED'	←——————→	'STRAIGHT'
Hardness/softness	'HARD'	←——————→	'SOFT'
Weight	'HEAVY'	←——————→	'LIGHT'
Elasticity	'STRETCHY'	←——————→	'FIRM'
Pliability	'PLIABLE'	←——————→	'RIGID'

Figure 3.1   Examples of sensory information acquired through haptic perception (adapted from Heller and Schiff 1991 and Pagliano 1999)

However touch is not always concerned with an active search for information; we can also acquire information through touch incidentally. We have already noted how it is possible to obtain information about objects and sensory experiences through our tactile receptors without our bodies contacting the objects directly. Examples include the 'whole-body' vibrations that we might experience sitting in a chair when a heavy lorry passes by outside; the 'warmth' we feel when sitting close to an open fire or the impression we 'feel' through our hands when we run a stick along railings.

We also use touch in other ways that are not *primarily* designed to obtain information. Touch serves an important and elaborate role in our daily interactions with people, for example, when we kiss, hug or shake hands. This kind of touch has been described as 'interactive' (Goold and Hummell 1993) and various examples of interactive touch are provided in Figure 3.2.

These interactive functions are distinguished from 'non-interactive' functions of touch that we perform on ourselves (such as rubbing a leg which has cramp or feeling the temperature of our forehead). See Figure 3.3 for more examples of non-interactive touch.

The 'information seeking' functions of touch we explored in Chapter 1 were 'non-interactive' in that they did not involve anyone else. However, we could have easily made them interactive by performing them with a partner. People working with children who are blind often employ particular types of interactive touch. For example, an adult wishing to draw the attention of a child to a particular feature of an object might explore it 'coactively' with the child using a 'hand-over-hand' technique in which the adult places his or her hands on top of the child's. We discuss the use of such techniques in Part 2.

In the next section we consider the different ways we use our sense of touch to seek out and acquire information with a particular focus on the distinction between 'active' and 'passive' types of touch.

Active and passive touch

Much of current research on processing sensory information through touch has been shaped by the theories of Katz (1925/1989), Revesz (1950) and Gibson (1962, 1966). Each of these authors has been influential in the development of the concept of 'haptic touch' as a distinct perceptual system. A common theme running through their research is their focus on hand movements (Heller 1991).

The work of Revesz was highly influential in defining the vocabulary of touch and drew heavily upon comparisons between touch and visual perception. Revesz made a distinction between 'visual form' recognition and 'tactual structure' recognition. He suggested that the eye takes in the 'form' of an object as an immediate

Type of touch	Function of touch	Example
Autocratic	Primary purpose of touch is to control	Holding another person's arm to prevent them moving away
Casual touch	Accidental touch as a result of casual contact	Brushing your body against another body when in a crowd of people
Extraneous touch	No interactive purpose or reason for the touch	Resting hand on another person's shoulder as a resting place
Habilitative touch	Primary purpose of touch is to achieve a specific therapy goal	Massage to relax a child's feet
Informative touch	Primary purpose of touch is to convey information	Finger spelling onto another person's hand
Intimate touch	Primary purpose of touch is private and expresses intimacy	Hugging another person
Malicious touch	Primary purpose of touch is to harm or injure	Pinching another person's shoulder
Nurturing touch	Primary purpose of touch is to foster a close emotional bond	Holding a baby in your arms
Protective touch	Primary purpose of touch is to protect another person from danger	Stopping a child falling down a stair
Recreational touch	Primary purpose of touch is to amuse	Tickling a child's tummy
Requisite touch	Primary purpose of touch is to carry out caregiving requirements	Bathing and dressing a child
Social touch	Primary purpose of touch is to express a social message	Shaking hands to say hello or goodbye

Figure 3.2 Examples of 'interactive' types of touch (adapted from Goold and Hummell 1993)

Type of touch	Function of touch	Example
Casual touch	Accidental touch as a result of casual contact	Brushing your arm against another part of your body
Extraneous touch	No specific purpose or reason for the touch	Resting hand on another part of your body as a resting place
Habilitative touch	Primary purpose of touch is to achieve a specific therapy goal	Massaging your leg to relieve cramp
Intimate touch	Primary purpose of touch is pleasurable contact	Stroking parts of your own body
Malicious touch	Primary purpose of touch is to harm or injure	Pinching your own arm
Perceptual touch	Primary purpose is to find out sensory information about part of the body	Feeling temperature on forehead with hand
Requisite touch	Primary purpose of touch is to fulfil functional health care requirements	Washing your own body

Figure 3.3 Examples of 'non-interactive' or 'personal' types of touch: focus of touch is own body (adapted from Goold and Hummell 1993)

impression, through spatial examination, whereas the hand is predominantly concerned with the 'structure' of an object, through serial or linear examination. He concluded that in comparison with vision, recognition of an object through haptic touch is a different, and relatively slow process involving a manual analysis of the relationship between an object's parts. Figure 3.4 illustrates, in very basic terms, these differences in relation to the visual and haptic exploration of the outline of a raised symbol of a face.

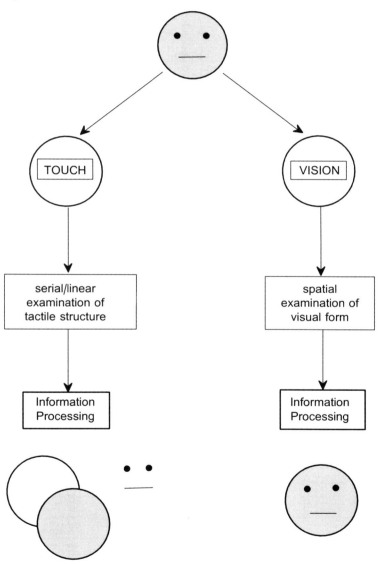

Figure 3.4   Exploration of raised symbol through touch and vision

Whereas we get an immediate impression of the whole face through vision, touch is sequential and requires a series of separate explorations, in order to:

i.   establish the outline shape (a raised circle);
ii. examine the texture within this shape (raised hatching);
iii. distinguish the features (raised 'eyes' and 'mouth').

Revesz (1950) emphasised the importance of independent activity in haptic exploration and proposed that 'active' haptic exploration, or the 'dynamic tactile process', is therefore superior to 'passive touch', or the 'static tactile process'. He argued that passive touch enables us to gain a very limited appreciation of the form of an object although he did note that it could be useful for detection of some broad properties of an object such as its surface temperature. Revesz (1950) insisted that clear impressions could only be gained tactually when touching involved movement, and that for 'successively progressing impressions and their connections, movement is indispensable' (p. 97).

The influential experimental psychologist J. J. Gibson backed up this notion of the 'superiority' of active touch. Gibson defined 'active touch' as touch which provides us with information about objects and surfaces in the environment, and viewed 'passive' touch as only bringing to our attention events at the surface level of our bodies. The experimental work of Gibson (1962, 1966) confirmed the importance of movement in haptic perception and demonstrated that activity or 'active' touch (and especially activity that was self-directed), resulted in better object perception than 'passive' touch. Gibson (1962) investigated different forms of passive touch and although he found that moving an object over a 'passive' hand (Figure 3.5b) provides better discrimination than just placing an object on the hand (Figure 3.5a), he concluded that neither of these conditions were as accurate as the 'active' touch conditions where subjects were able to freely manipulate objects (Figure 3.5c, 3.5d).

However, this view that active touch is superior to passive touch doesn't hold true in every situation, and indeed some scientists (e.g. Heller 1986; Magee and Kennedy 1980; Schwartz et al. 1975), have argued that it may be unhelpful to establish a rigid distinction between the notions of active and passive touch. Their findings suggest that we need to be careful about separating out activity from passivity in our attempts to classify touch. For example, some electronic braille writing devices contain a small tactile display which allows the writer to feel what they have written. Instead of moving the finger along a row of braille letters in the normal braille reading style, the reader's finger remains still (i.e. passive) while the letters are raised sequentially under the finger in a single 'refreshable' braille cell.

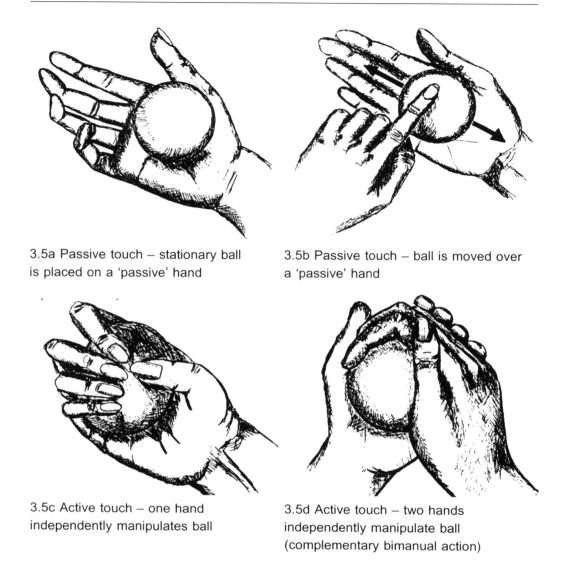

3.5a Passive touch – stationary ball is placed on a 'passive' hand

3.5b Passive touch – ball is moved over a 'passive' hand

3.5c Active touch – one hand independently manipulates ball

3.5d Active touch – two hands independently manipulate ball (complementary bimanual action)

Figure 3.5a–d   Examples of 'active' and 'passive' forms of touch

Appelle (1991) suggested that the distinction between active and passive forms of touch may not even be valid when related to real life exploratory activities. He argued that the manipulation of objects is neither exclusively active nor passive because of the 'numerous starts and stops during object inspection' (p. 169). You can demonstrate this to yourself by picking up any light object you have near you. As you explore the properties of the object pay particular attention to the relative roles of each hand at different stages in the process. You will probably observe a highly complex sequence within which each hand performs both active as well as passive manipulatory actions on the object. Such observations led Millar to conclude that a division between 'active' and 'passive' touch may not in itself be sufficient to explain these complex processes (1997). She proposed that under some conditions active touch could not be considered as superior in that 'It may convey little in the absence of prominent features or prior information that can provide anchor cues for systematic exploration. By contrast, prior information can produce efficient recognition also by passive touch' (Millar 1997: 21).

We will continue to concentrate on hand movements and in the next section we consider the different ways we are able to use our hands to gain information through touch.

Exploratory procedures

The reflective activities in Chapter 1 revealed a range of strategies that we employ to acquire information about the properties of objects. For example, if we place a finger pad on the surface of an object we receive information about its surface temperature, but only limited information about its shape and size. To acquire information about the shape and size of an object we need to use more sophisticated strategies such as exploring its contours.

Two American psychologists, Susan Lederman and Roberta Klatzky, investigated in some detail the strategies used by individuals with mature haptic abilities when manipulating a range of objects. They described the strategies they observed as 'exploratory procedures' (EPs), and defined an EP as 'a stereotyped movement pattern having certain characteristics that are invariant and others that are highly typical' (Lederman and Klatzky 1987: 344). An example of an EP is the 'rubbing' motion that we make with our finger pad on the surface of an object to determine its texture. This EP was termed 'Lateral motion' to describe the lateral movements made with the finger pads.

Klatzky and Lederman proposed that the careful observation of hand movements could help reveal something about 'the underlying haptic representation of objects in memory and the processes by which these are created and utilised' (1987: 344). They established links between particular EPs and the perception of specific object properties and found that information about the most obvious or 'salient' properties of an object such as texture, temperature and hardness was extracted using hand movements that were 'spontaneous' i.e. fast and simple to execute. These properties required only brief repetitive hand movements which could be applied over a small part of the object.

We can demonstrate this if we close our eyes and rest the finger pads of one hand on the surface of an object for a couple of seconds. Although we do not have time to explore the object, this brief 'haptic glance' provides us with important information about a number of its sensory features, for example hardness, temperature and/or texture. You may wish to refer to back to Figure 3.1 to see whether there were any other properties you recognised. You may, for example, have gathered some information about the shape of the object's surface but it will almost certainly have been limited. As we found in Chapter 1, in order to accurately determine the shape of an object we need to use a different type of EP called 'contour following', a much slower procedure. A summary of the six EPs identified by Lederman and Klatzky, with examples of the sensory information acquired about an object using each EP, is shown in Figure 3.6. An illustration of each of these EPs being used to explore a sponge ball is shown in Figure 3.7.

EPs can be very useful in helping us to make sense of hand movements and, as Klatzky and Lederman argue, they can 'serve as "windows" through which the haptic system can be viewed' (Lederman and Klatzky 1987: 344). However, this work by Klatzky and Lederman relates exclusively to the use of touch by individuals who have 'mature' haptic abilities, and assumes that these individuals have the means to execute a wide range of relatively sophisticated exploratory strategies in order to seek out sensory information about an object.

Infants (or older children with relatively immature or restricted abilities) will use touch in different ways to adults. If we observe young infants we won't see

Exploratory procedure (EP)	Example of sensory information acquired about object through EP
Lateral motion EP (rubbing finger across surface of object)	Texture
Pressure EP (squeezing, poking object)	Hardness
Static contact EP (fingers resting on object surface)	Temperature
Enclosure EP (holding/grasping object)	Shape/size/volume
Unsupported holding EP (holding object in hand)	Weight
Contour following EP (tracing along contours of object)	Global shape, exact shape

Figure 3.6 Range of exploratory procedures (EP) and examples of sensory information acquired about object through EP (adapted from Lederman and Klatzky 1987)

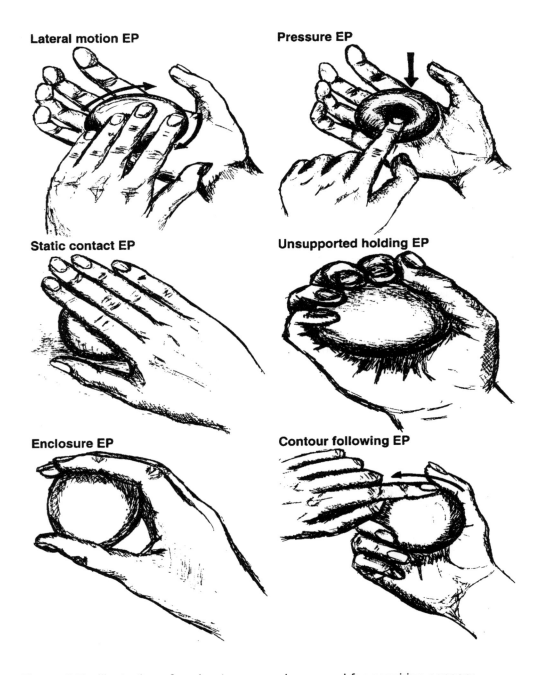

Lateral motion EP

Pressure EP

Static contact EP

Unsupported holding EP

Enclosure EP

Contour following EP

Figure 3.7 Illustration of exploratory procedures used for acquiring sensory information about a sponge tennis ball (adapted from Lederman and Klatzky 1987)

all of the exploratory strategies described by Klatzky and Lederman. For example, during the first few months of a baby's development the mouth plays a key role in exploring the properties of objects. As the infant's visual and haptic abilities emerge the tendency to 'mouth' rattles or toys diminishes and their manual abilities mature. We will explore the pattern of this early developmental process in Chapter 4.

Summary

The sense of touch has a number of functions which can be broadly divided into interactive and non-interactive types of touch. Within these functions, touch can be used to acquire sensory information about people, objects and sensory features through the process of haptic perception. Although research findings support the view that 'active' touch is generally a superior mode of exploration to 'passive' touch, the role of 'passive' touch should not be underestimated and, as we shall see, for children who have multiple disabilities, passive forms of touch may constitute an important source of sensory information. We considered the haptic exploratory procedures used by mature explorers and noted important differences in the strategies used by children with less developed haptic abilities.

Recommended reading

Bushnell, E. W. and Boudreau, J. P. (1991) 'The development of haptic perception during infancy', in Heller, M. A. and Schiff, W. (eds) *The Psychology of Touch,* 139–61. Hillsdale, NJ: Lawrence Erlbaum Associates.

Goold, L. and Hummell, J. (1993) *Supporting the Receptive Communication of Individuals with Significant Multiple Disabilities: Selective use of touch to enhance comprehension.* North Rocks, Australia: North Rocks Press.

Millar, S. (1997) *Reading by Touch.* London and New York: Routledge.

CHAPTER 4

Early Development of Sensory and Cognitive Abilities

Introduction

In this chapter we consider the development of sensory and cognitive abilities and examine how they are linked. It is extremely difficult to provide a simple overview of this topic. The processes are subtle and, for people without a grounding in psychology, even the basic language used to capture the processes is technical and perhaps, sometimes, impenetrable. Nevertheless we need to address the issue in order to understand touch in relation to children who function at 'early developmental' levels.

As we have already seen, the workings of touch are complex. They involve the triggering of the touch receptors that send signals along the pathways to the brain (sensation). The processing of this incoming information takes place in the 'perceptual system', which along with the 'memory system' and the 'attention system' has a role in *cognition* – the use and handling of knowledge.

It is difficult to know how very young babies use their senses and how they think. In fact some scientists have argued that newly born children make little or no differentiation between the senses at birth and that the senses exist in a 'primitive unity' (Bower 1977) in which newborns may not be aware whether they are seeing, hearing or touching something (Barraga 1986).

In our very early life we seem to respond primarily to touch, taste and smell – the senses that very young babies draw upon when breastfeeding. These senses (sometimes referred to as the 'close' senses) seem to be relatively well developed at this early stage, although you will probably have witnessed a newborn infant displaying a 'startle' reflex to loud sounds, demonstrating that hearing can also provide very young infants with some information about the world at a distance. Sensory and cognitive abilities become progressively more sophisticated and increasingly differentiated during the early months of development although, as we will now discover, there are differing views as to how these abilities develop.

Development of early haptic abilities

Within the first year early haptic activities typically progress from simple reflexive behaviours present at birth to well-integrated coordination of vision, reaching and grasping. In the first 16 weeks it is generally believed that early grasping (or prehension) activities are based on reflex actions which provide young infants with both 'survival capabilities', e.g. sucking and rooting, as well as 'protective responses' (Case-Smith 1995). Most of us will have experienced the 'instinctive' or 'automatic' grasping response of the infant when placing a finger or a small object into the palm of a young baby's hand (see Figures 4.1a and 4.1b).

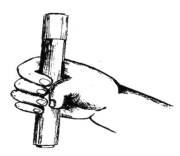

Figure 4.1a   1-month old infant – reflexive grasp of finger placed in hand

Figure 4.1b   1-month old infant – reflexive grasp of pen placed in hand

Voluntary grasping emerges alongside instinctive grasping, and at approximately 4 months babies demonstrate a more refined grasping activity incorporating visually directed reaching (Connolly and Elliot 1972). At about this age babies can use visual information to prepare the hand for grasp, and are able to open and shape the hand according to the size and shape of the object *before* they grasp it (Corbetta and Mounoud 1990) (see Figure 4.2).

Figure 4.2   5-month old infant adjusting grasp prior to picking up toy

Between 9 and 10 months infants become able to isolate the movements of the index finger and thumb from the other movements of their hand and fingers (Pehoski 1995). This is the precursor of the 'radial digital grasp' (Erhardt 1994) that dramatically opens up the ways infants can interact with objects. Radial digital grasp enables infants to adjust an object while holding it; to poke it with the index finger; to pick up small objects using a precision grip between the radial fingers and the thumb (Bayley 1969; Folio and Fewell 1983) and to let go of objects held in the hand using a controlled grasp release (Pehoski 1995) (see Figure 4.3).

Figure 4.3 9-month old infant picking up a toy using a radial digital grasp

The roles of the emerging visual and haptic systems

The intricate relationship between visual and haptic systems has been the focus of a number of experimental studies (e.g. Hatwell 1987, 1990; Rochat 1989; Ruff 1982). Rochat, for example, proposed that vision serves as an 'organiser' of different types of sensory information, allowing the infant to view the object from different perspectives and to learn about its properties. This supplementary information helps babies to organise the tactile and kinaesthetic information they receive through touch.

Based on these findings Pehoski (1995) proposed that in young babies vision has been shown to be 'an integral part of the process of grasp and manipulation and in fact may be the early motivator for object exploration and drive some of the more refined manipulative actions such as fingering an object' (p. 141).

Further, Stilwel and Cermak (1995) reported that young babies use their sight to monitor early exploration through the haptic system. They do not so much use sight as a substitute for touch but rather to *guide* their haptic manipulation, in order to make the sensory input more meaningful.

The role of the mouth

As we saw earlier, the mouth is an important source of information for the developing child, and the relationship between the hand and the mouth has been studied extensively. At 2–4 months haptic activity seems to be primarily geared to transporting objects to the mouth (Pehoski 1995). This observation is supported by the research of Ruff (1984) who highlighted the importance of the mouth during the first four months in developing the use of two hands to explore objects. Ruff claimed that the development of bi-manual coordination is initially linked to the oral system. Object exploration using both mouth *and* hand continues to be a major component in the infant's interaction with objects up until 7 months of age and it is not until after 12 months that manual manipulation of objects replaces the mouthing of objects.

There is also evidence in the research literature to show that the mouthing of objects takes a number of different forms. For example, mouthing can be 'active' or 'passive' and it appears to follow a developmental progression. Thus Ruff (1989) reported that 'mouthing' for a 12-month-old had a different function from 'mouthing' for a baby at 4 months. She proposed that for the older infant the mouth is used essentially as a location to rest objects in a 'place-holding' action, and no longer serves such an 'important exploratory' function (see Figures 4.4a and 4.4b).

Figure 4.4a 'Active mouthing': 4-month-old infant 'explores' toy using hand and mouth

Figure 4.4b 'Passive mouthing': 12-month-old infant rests object in mouth

Early development of cognitive abilities

The haptic and visual development we have outlined above occur as both the body and the mind mature. The development of babies' purposeful exploration of their environment is inextricably linked with the growth of their understanding and knowledge about the world. Inevitably this development of the mind is much more difficult for scientists to investigate and explain than the development of physical processes. A number of different models have been put forward to explain the cognitive development of children. The one that has arguably had most influence on our understanding of early child development is that proposed by the Swiss scientist Jean Piaget.

Jean Piaget

The work of Piaget (e.g. 1926, 1953, 1954) has laid the foundations for research into children's exploratory activity through touch and the role of touch in cognitive development. Exner and Henderson (1995) put forward two components they consider to be fundamental to the 'Piagetian view' of this area:

- object manipulation is critical in order for the child to learn about the individual properties of an object;
- mental activity is considered to be more likely to occur when the child is actively involved in manipulation of objects than when the child is passive.

As a biologist, Piaget was strongly influenced by the work of Charles Darwin, and he viewed learning essentially as a process of adjustment to the environment. Piaget developed a complex model in which the active behaviours of the child were referred to as 'schemes', which were adapted through mechanisms he called 'accommodation' and 'assimilation' balanced by a process of 'equilibration' (Piaget 1926).

Piaget (1953) outlined three broad periods of development: the sensorimotor, pre-operational and operational (concrete and formal) periods. Of particular relevance to this chapter is the early cognitive development that takes place in the 'sensorimotor' period which covers the first two years of a child's life and comprises six stages. In Figure 4.5 we provide a summary of the stages within the sensorimotor period, with a brief description of behaviours that might be observed within each stage.

You will notice from Figure 4.5 that the concept of 'circular reactions' features in Piaget's explanation of children's early actions with respect to 'self' and the environment, and he proposed that these were related to early forms of 'intelligent' activity. Piaget drew upon the work by Baldwin (1925), who had described 'circular' actions as involving the repetition of an action by a baby in order to produce 'pleasant stimulation'. The distinction between 'primary' and 'secondary' circular reactions within the sensorimotor period provides a means of analysing a child's interactions with a range of objects. It allows us to determine whether the child's behaviours are differentiated according to the properties of the object, or whether they are undifferentiated. For example, a child displaying 'differentiated' behaviours might *shake* a rattle, *wave* a flag, or *drop* a wooden cube onto the floor to listen to the sound it makes, whereas a child displaying 'undifferentiated' behaviours may mouth each of these objects or bang them repeatedly on the table.

Stage I (0–1 month) is termed a 'Reflexive Stage' and is based upon early physiological reflexes to external stimuli, e.g. the baby grips an adult's finger.

Stage II (1–4 months) is characterised by use of a range of undifferentiated schemes or 'Primary Circular Reactions' on objects, e.g. the baby repetitively bangs or taps an object primarily to obtain pleasure.

Stage III (4–8 months) is characterised by 'Secondary Circular Reactions', behaviours which are repeated to produce effects in the external environment. Although goals are not set before starting action patterns, there is heightened interest in the outcome of the activity, e.g. the effect on the environment of dropping an object onto the floor.

Stage IV (8–12 months) is termed 'Coordination of Secondary Circular Reactions'. Within this stage the infant is viewed as having a greater experience in interacting with objects, and a range of familiar objects are used appropriately. There is evidence of the child being able to establish a goal prior to the start of an activity in certain contexts, e.g. the child sees a cup, picks it up and drinks from it.

Stage V (12–18 months) is termed 'Tertiary Circular Reactions'. This stage is considered to be the beginning of mental representation and includes the achievement of object permanence, i.e. the child realises the cup exists even if it is out of sight.

Stage VI (18–24 months) is viewed as a transition stage, between sensorimotor and 'preconceptual' thought.

Figure 4.5   Summary of stages within the sensorimotor period (Piaget 1953)

Although Piaget's work has had a strong influence on views about early childhood development, some of the assumptions underlying his theory of early child development have been brought into question. Sutherland (1992) suggested that although Piaget's ideas were a significant influence at the time, 'research on babies has since undergone a revolution' (p. 8), and concluded that their relevance, particularly to the first months of development, is dubious. Further, Sutherland (1992) claimed that the first stage within the sensorimotor period (i.e. Reflexive Stage), 'more than any of his other stages, has been shown to be wrong' (p. 8). He proposed that recent work on early child development shows that 'the onset of intelligent behaviour has been successively moved back to perhaps a few hours after birth', suggesting that a case could be made 'for combining at least the first two stages (reflexes and primary circular reactions)' (p. 12).

Despite these criticisms, the work of Piaget remains a significant influence in research in early child development and provides us with useful reference points for assessing and interpreting the haptic behaviours of children who have special educational needs. As we shall see in Chapter 7, a number of assessment tools developed for use with children with severe learning difficulties are explicitly based upon the progression outlined within Piaget's sensorimotor period of development.

We now consider briefly an alternative model of how children's thinking develops. This is a model which was proposed by the psychologists J. J. and E. J. Gibson and it is worthy of consideration because of the links made between haptic perception and cognitive development. Further, some of the key vocabulary developed in this model is often used in describing a child's early haptic interactions with objects.

J. J. and E. J. Gibson

J. J. Gibson proposed that infants were far more capable at birth than Piaget's model implied, and introduced the complex notion of 'perceptual systems' (Gibson 1966: 47), proposing that even newly born infants had a capacity to learn and differentiate about the perceived world 'through coordinated systems of action, some of which are already functioning in this capacity at birth' (Lochman 1986: 25).

Gibson proposed that through active exploration an infant learned about the 'affordances' or particular properties of objects, e.g. texture, shape, weight and substance.

This model was further developed by Gibson's partner E. J. Gibson, who made a clear distinction between actions that were 'executive', e.g. reaching, grasping, locomotion, etc., and actions that were 'information-gathering', i.e. linked to the perceptual systems, although she acknowledged that the distinction was not rigid given that executive functions such as lifting could also be 'informative', i.e. exploratory. In contrast to Piaget's definition of the first stage of the sensorimotor period, E. J. Gibson proposed that although the possibilities for executive actions (that is reaching, holding and grasping) were 'minimal' in very young infants, opportunities for exploratory activities *were* available and could be 'used in functional ways even in the newborn' (E. J. Gibson 1988: 6). The role of executive actions in early cognitive development was highlighted with particular emphasis on the way they changed the affordances of things and places, providing new occasions for information-gathering and for acquiring knowledge about the environment. Further, as 'new actions become possible, new affordances are brought about; both the information available and the mechanisms for detecting it increase' (E. J. Gibson 1988: 7).

In summarising the development of the infant's physical and sensory abilities, E. J. Gibson highlighted the reciprocal links between the infant and the environment, arguing that the action systems and sensory systems equipped the infant to discover the world and, in addition, motivated the child to use these systems 'first by exploring the accessible surround, then acting on it, and (as spontaneous locomotion becomes possible) extending his explorations further. The exploratory systems emerge in an orderly way that permits an ever-spiralling path of discovery' (E. J. Gibson 1988: 37).

Within this model Gibson proposed that as new 'exploratory systems' developed, new 'action systems' emerged which then made 'new tasks' with objects possible. Three phases of exploratory development in the first year of life were outlined to illustrate how the infant develops 'the capability to discover what the world affords and what to do about it' (E. J. Gibson 1988: 34). A summary of these phases is presented in Figure 4.6.

What relevance does this model of development have to our understanding of how children with multiple disabilities develop their haptic abilities? The notion of 'affordance' provides a useful means of analysing a child's interactions with different objects to determine what the properties of each object 'affords' the child, for example, whether they bang it, tap it or shake it. Gibson proposes that learning about affordances of objects entails 'exploratory' activities and through such exploration a child learns about the particular properties of objects, e.g. texture, shape, weight and substance. This model suggests also that we need to consider

---

Phase 1: 0–5 months

- The hand and mouth have different functions. The hand only achieves 'exploratory' skill at around 5 months, when it is used for transferring objects to the mouth for examination;
- in contrast to the work of Piaget, who considered young infants 'egocentric', perceptual systems are externally directed and the child perceives events as external 'distal happenings in the world';
- early exploratory activities are relatively 'immature and unskilled' but they are 'spontaneous and directed' – infants therefore display 'neonatal control of exploratory activity'.

Phase 2: 5–9 months

- Increasing capabilities of the visual system and development of muscular components involved in reaching, grasping and fingering;
- as the hands become active and controllable, a new set of 'affordances' is opened up for the baby's discovery. Objects can be displaced, banged, shaken, squeezed and thrown – actions that are considered to have 'informative consequences' about an object's properties.

Phase 3: 9 months +

- Characterised by 'ambulatory exploration' (i.e. independent locomotion);
- termed a 'cognitive revolution' as infant's horizons are expanded by the acquisition of self-initiated, self-controlled locomotion;
- new kinds of exploratory activity become available for learning about the wider world.

Figure 4.6 Summary of early exploratory development: 0–12 months (adapted from E. J. Gibson 1988)

carefully how the term 'exploratory' is used to describe a child's actions with objects. For example, a distinction can be made between the 'manipulation' of an object, for example holding a spoon to eat, and active exploration of the object which is designed to gather information or 'knowledge' about it. As E. J. Gibson notes, 'a sequence of acts termed exploratory will have some outcome and will not be random. It will have a perceptual aspect, a motor aspect, and a knowledge-gathering aspect' (1988: 5).

However, as we noted earlier, many children with MDVI will have limited motor abilities, or demonstrate an aversion to touch, and will therefore be reliant on others to assist them in 'gathering knowledge' about their environment. We consider the role of the adult partner in supporting the learning experiences of these children in Part 2.

The distinction made by Gibson between the 'executive' and 'perceptual' functions of the hand also has direct relevance to children who have physical impairments as it suggests that even though a child may have limited *executive* abilities, for example not being able to grasp and hold a string of beads in two hands as the result of cerebral palsy, the child may still be able to use these abilities to gather *perceptual* information about an object, for example tapping the string of beads against a table top with one hand as a way of gathering information about it. This distinction is explored further in Vignette 4.1 at the end of this chapter.

A more recent developmental model for the emergence of the haptic abilities of the young infant has been outlined by two developmental psychologists, Emily Bushnell and J. Paul Boudreau (1991), within which explicit links are made with the exploratory procedures we discussed in Chapter 3. We provide a brief summary of this model below and show how it too can have relevance to our understanding of the emerging haptic abilities of children who have multiple disabilities and visual impairment.

Early development of exploratory procedures

The role of exploratory procedures (EPs) was introduced in Chapter 3 and it was noted that much of the research in this area has only limited relevance to the developing child with relatively immature manual abilities. Bushnell and Boudreau argued therefore that 'connections established between particular hand movements and certain object properties are important to the development of haptic perception because during the first year of life, infants do not motorically execute the full range of movements encompassed by Klatzky and Lederman's EPs' (1997: 4).

They proposed that finding out which qualities an infant can perceive by touch is a matter of finding answers to the following two questions:

- How can infants move their hands?
- What do infants want or need to know about objects?

Although a full account of their model is not possible within the scope of this text, Bushnell and Boudreau provide a helpful overview of the literature which relates to the development of manual behaviours during infancy. They identify a developmental sequence with three broad phases within which they relate the very early manual behaviours of young infants to the exploratory procedures outlined by Lederman and Klatzky (1987) (see Figures 3.6 and 3.7, pp. 34–5). A summary of this overview is presented in Figure 4.7.

Bushnell and Boudreau proposed that in order to perceive a particular property of an object an infant must be able to perform the requisite hand movements. For example, to determine the texture of an object a child would need to be capable of rubbing a finger across its surface.

An infant between 0 and 3 months may be able to obtain some haptic information about an object by 'clutching' it (for example, surface temperature and possibly size), but she or he could not yet obtain precise haptic information about its shape. It is only when the infant has developed more sophisticated exploratory strategies, such as using one hand to hold the object and one to explore it (described as 'complementary bimanual activity') that he or she may be able to determine the shape of an object. This skill doesn't usually develop until children are about 12 months. Such milestones in motor development are considered by Bushnell and Boudreau to set the 'lower limits' for when certain haptic sensitivities might be present. The infant's level of 'cognitive' development then determines whether he or she is able to perceive a particular attribute as soon as 'motor development' permits or whether it takes a period of time for the infant to become aware of that attribute, even if he or she has use of the appropriate motor activity.

Although it was developed for children following a normal pattern of development, the sequence outlined above can provide useful reference points for investigating the range of exploratory strategies used by children who have multiple disabilities (McLinden 2000; McLinden and Douglas 2000). For example, although a child may have restricted physical abilities which serve as a barrier to wholly independent manipulation of an object, he or she may still be able to perform a range of actions which provide the child with information about the haptic properties of the object. A vignette of Lana, a 7-year-old girl who attends a school for children who have severe learning difficulties, is presented below to illustrate this point (Vignette 4.1).

Phase 1 (0–4 months)

- Infants clutch an object tightly in one or both hands and possibly bring it to the mouth. This behaviour is considered to be largely controlled by the palmar grasp reflex which is present even before birth;
- there is limited movement of the fingers, which are restricted to opening and closing synergistically, in a 'kneading' pattern;
- the 'clutching' behaviour is considered to be similar to the 'enclosure' EP identified by Lederman and Klatzky (1987). The 'kneading' behaviour is considered as a rudimentary form of the 'pressure' EP;
- oral exploration can be considered as a *separate* modality to manual exploration, as the movement young infants make with their mouths are more 'intricate' than the clutching they are able to engage in with their hands. Particular tongue movements (i.e. pressing the tongue against the roof of the mouth and drawing it backwards over the surface of the mouthed object in a cyclical fashion) can be considered to be analogous to the 'pressure' and 'lateral motion' EPs described for the hand;
- infants in this phase might be able to haptically perceive temperature, size and perhaps compliance, but would not be expected to perceive texture, weight or exact shape with any precision as they are unable to perform the hand movements related to the EPs necessary to perceive these properties, e.g. lateral motion, contour following. However, active tongue movements could permit young infants to perceive hardness and texture *orally*.

Phase 2 (4–9 months)

- Manual behaviour with objects is characterised by repetitive finger and hand movements and includes scratching object, rubbing, waving, banging, squeezing and poking, passing from hand to hand;
- these manual behaviours are carried out with just one hand – the other hand serves to stabilise the object against a surface or helps to maintain the infant's sitting posture;
- manual behaviours are considered to be similar to a number of EPs and are more intricate than the clutching and kneading described in Phase 1, i.e. poking objects is considered to be similar to the 'pressure' EP; kneading, scratching and rubbing similar to the 'lateral motion' EP; waving, banging and passing objects hand to hand is considered similar to the 'unsupported holding' EP;
- infants may be expected to haptically perceive texture, hardness and weight with some precision, as well as temperature and size. However, these hand movements are not yet sufficient for accurate haptic perception of exact shape.

Phase 3 (9/10 months)

- By 9–10 months infants have developed torso strength and postural control which is necessary for independent sitting, allowing the second hand to be used in object manipulation;
- this phase is characterised by 'complementary bimanual' activities where one hand supports or positions the object while the other hand either manipulates it or acts on it with a second object;
- bimanual activity is considered to relate to the 'contour tracing' EP, enabling infants in this phase to haptically explore and perceive shape.

Figure 4.7 Summary of development of manual behaviour during infancy (adapted from Bushnell and Boudreau 1991)

Vignette 4.1   Lana

According to her records, Lana was born with 'severe spastic quadriplegia' and was diagnosed as having 'epilepsy with convulsions' for which she receives regular medication. She has had limited independent movement in her legs since birth and is unable to sit up unsupported. She spends much of her time in class positioned in a standing frame and moves within the school in a wheelchair. Lana has been diagnosed as having optic nerve hypoplasia and she has shown no clear visual response to light or objects in her environment, although there has been some evidence of visual response to bright objects under ultra violet light. Lana has restrictions in her ability to independently grasp and hold objects, and although there has been some 'co-active' exploration of objects and their properties with her teacher and her Learning Support Assistant (LSA), Lana is generally reluctant to work co-actively with others.

In an attempt to maximise Lana's learning experiences through touch her class teacher, in collaboration with a qualified teacher of children with a visual impairment (QTVI) and Lana's LSA, carefully observed her interactions with a range of hand manipulable objects, each selected to provide Lana with opportunities to perform different types of actions (e.g. strings of beads, plastic tubes, sponge balls, etc.). Based on these observations it was noted that Lana used a limited range of actions in her interactions with different types of objects. For example, an object was usually taken towards her mouth where it was either inserted *into* her mouth (plastic tube), or tapped lightly against her lips or teeth (string of beads). In addition Lana was observed on a number of occasions lightly rubbing a soft object (sponge ball) against the surface of her cheek.

These observations of her haptic activity were then analysed with respect to the descriptions of exploratory procedures in an attempt to determine whether the observed behaviours could be linked to information gathering about particular object properties. For example, it was noted that the end of the plastic tube was inserted into her mouth. This observation suggested that through this action Lana may be able to perceive at least the object properties of *temperature* and *size* as well as limited information about *shape*. Further, Lana was observed holding the tube so that it resisted gravity (unsupported holding EP), a behaviour which may be used to perceive the object property *weight*.

Lana was also observed performing a range of more 'complex' actions on objects. Two frequently observed behaviours were noted during the observation of her haptic behaviour (i.e. tapping the object against her teeth and against her lips) which could not be compared directly using the descriptors of haptic behaviours. These behaviours may have been used to gather additional sensory input about certain properties of the object. Thus, by tapping the beads against her teeth, Lana may have been able to find out something about their particular sensory features, for example how hard they are. This particular action may serve a similar role to (or have 'functional equivalence' with) the pressure EP which consists of squeezing an object with the fingers or palm of the hand.

Based on these observations it was speculated that Lana may be able to haptically perceive the object properties of *texture* and *hardness* with some precision. However, Lana was not observed using 'complementary bimanual actions' i.e. one hand holding object, the other hand squeezing it, which suggested that she might not be expected to perceive object *shape* with any precision. Examples of the range of haptic behaviours observed when Lana was presented with the selection of objects is presented in Figure 4.8 showing possible links between the EP and the information that may be acquired about the properties of the selected objects.

Exploratory procedure	Description of haptic behaviours	Example of information that may be acquired about properties of object
Static contact	Touches ball with hand Touches beads with hand Touches cheek with ball	Temperature (texture?)
Pressure	Squeezes ball in hand Clutches beads in hand Taps beads against teeth	hardness (size?)
Lateral motion	Rubs ball against cheek Rubs tube against cheek	texture (temperature?)
Enclosure	Inserts tube into mouth Inserts beads into mouth	size/volume (temperature? texture? hardness?)
Unsupported holding	Beads held in hand and brought to mouth	weight
Contour following	No evidence	—
Complementary bimanual activity	No evidence	—

Figure 4.8 Summary of Lana's haptic behaviours with selection of objects showing possible links between EPs, observed haptic behaviours and information acquired about an object.

Lana's class teacher found this exercise to be useful in developing a programme with the aim of providing Lana with structured experiences to develop her knowledge and understanding of different types of objects and their sensory features. The objectives of this programme included:

- to establish a regular and predictable routine within which Lana gains experience of selecting and manipulating different types of objects;
- to extend the repertoire of objects to provide different types of sensory experiences, e.g. *hard* objects (e.g. plastic balls) and *soft* objects (e.g. sponge balls); objects which could be safely inserted into the mouth for oral

manipulation (e.g. plastic tubes) and objects which incorporated a range of additional sensory features (i.e. objects which produced sounds);

• to provide Lana with opportunities for greater independence in her exploration of objects through the use of regular periods within an enclosed learning environment such as a Little Room (considered in further detail in Chapter 6) within which she can select and manipulate different types of objects.

Summary

There is general agreement that haptic perception in the sighted infant improves significantly during early development and that vision plays a key role within this progression. Findings to date suggest that vision does not act as a substitute for haptic perception, but rather serves as a guide or 'mediator' of haptic perceptual activities. By the middle of the first year vision has a crucial role in relation to early haptic activity, a finding which has significant implications for development in infants who are deprived of accurate visual information.

In this chapter we presented a summary of two influential models of early cognitive development, each of which offers potentially useful points of reference for analysing the haptic activities of children who have multiple disabilities. A model of the early haptic development of exploratory procedures was also outlined. Finally we provided a vignette of a child who has MDVI to illustrate how careful observation of the child's interactions with objects can be useful in planning an appropriate intervention programme.

Recommended reading

Bushnell, E. W. and Boudreau, J. P. (1991) 'The development of haptic perception during infancy', in Heller, M.A. and Schiff, W. (eds) *The Psychology of Touch,* 139–61. Hillsdale, NJ: Lawrence Erlbaum Associates.

Bushnell, E. W. and Boudreau, J. P. (1997) 'Exploring and exploiting objects with the hands during infancy', in Connolly, K. (ed.) *The Psychobiology of the Hand.* Cambridge: MacKeith Press.

Exner, C. E. and Henderson, A. (1995) 'Cognition and motor skills', in Henderson, A. and Pehoski, C. (eds) *Hand Function in the Child: Foundations for Remediation.* St. Louis, MO: Mosby-Year Book.

Warren, D. H. (1982) 'The development of haptic perception', in Schiff, W. and Foulke, E. (eds) *Tactual Perception: A sourcebook,* 82–129. Cambridge: Cambridge University Press.

Warren, D. H. (1994) *Blindness and Children: An individual differences approach.* Cambridge: Cambridge University Press.

PART 2

IDENTIFYING BARRIERS TO LEARNING

CHAPTER 5

The Impact of Visual Impairment on Early Haptic Development

Introduction

As we have seen in previous chapters, vision has an important role in coordinating haptic activities in infants and it provides a powerful incentive for them to reach out, grasp and manipulate objects. Research findings generally support the view that although the haptic and visual modalities have distinct encoding pathways, by the middle of the first year vision exerts control over early haptic interactions with objects.

In this chapter we begin to apply some of the information we have provided so far about touch to the particular circumstances of children who have reduced vision. In particular, we consider the significance of vision and touch in a child's early learning experiences, and focus on the potential impact of a visual impairment upon early development in this area.

Visual impairment

Children described as having a 'visual impairment' are not a homogeneous group. Children who have no vision make up a small part of this group, probably less than 20 per cent (Best 1992). Most children with a visual impairment have sufficient sight to use it as their main medium for learning, in spite of a reduction in the quality and/or the quantity of visual information which they can draw on.

Visual impairment is caused by a wide range of conditions, some of which affect the eye itself (e.g. cataracts), and others which result from damage to the optic pathways to the brain (e.g. optic atrophy) or to the visual cortex itself. The extent of the impact that a visual impairment has on early development will depend on a range of factors including:

- the personality of the child;
- the age of the child at the onset of the visual impairment;
- the promptness of the diagnosis;
- the degree and nature of the visual impairment;
- the degree and nature of any associated disabilities which limit the child's ability to compensate for the reduction in visual information;
- the effectiveness of intervention.

Vision plays an important role in linking different types of sensory information. When we hear a loud noise, if we are fully sighted we can turn to where the sound came from and see what made it. If we smell food burning in the kitchen, we can use our vision to decide whether we need to act promptly to remove the pan from the heat source. If we feel an unfamiliar object at the bottom of a bag we can lift it out and look at it. Vision is therefore often described as a sense which *integrates* and thereby helps us to 'make sense' of the information we receive through our other senses.

As we saw earlier, we can make a distinction between the senses which provide us with information about the world which is close to us (e.g. touch and taste), and senses which provide us with information about the world at a distance (e.g. vision and hearing). When the distance sense of vision is impaired, young children may be able to compensate to some extent by making greater use of their other distance sense – hearing.

However, it is important to recognise that vision and hearing operate in different ways and have different functions. Geenens (1999) describes these differences very clearly:

> Sight is continuous, but it can be turned off at will by closing the eyes or averting the gaze. Sight is the principal medium used to construct knowledge of the environment and differentiate oneself from it. It directs behaviour by providing feedback about the consequences of acts on the environment and, in particular, on others, for example, empathy.

> Hearing cannot be turned off even during sleep, but is discontinuous, since the listener has little or no control over the production of sound by persons and objects in his environment. Hearing does not require active scanning, although its resolution can be enhanced by selective attention to one set of acoustic signals over others occurring simultaneously. Hearing is the main channel for processing oral language, for conveying complex information about events remote in time or space, and for many aspects of thinking. (p. 156)

The assumption, therefore, that hearing can compensate for a visual loss is not well founded. Indeed, it can be argued that no one sense can fully 'compensate' for another.

Warren (1994) identifies three major challenges which face children in their efforts to construct their knowledge of the environment when they have little or no sight:

- a restriction in the extent of the environment that the infant can engage;
- lower stimulus value on the part of the environment that the infant encounters;
- a lack of appreciation of the infant's impact on the objects manipulated.

Thus a young child with a visual impairment may not only have access to a relatively limited environment, but the objects that are in their limited environment may not be stimulating enough to motivate the child to explore them. Further, the child may not appreciate the effects of his or her actions on any objects that have been manipulated. Consider as you look around you the wide range of objects in your immediate environment which attract your visual attention through their bright colours or interesting shapes. Now close your eyes and consider the number of objects that attract your attention through the interesting noise they make. Even this simple exercise shows clearly that if you have no vision the environment may afford little motivation to you to reach out and explore.

Toy manufacturers exploit the powerful effects that colour and shape have in motivating young children to reach out and manipulate objects. Once children make contact with objects, vision also encourages the child to sustain their exploration of the object by feeding back information about the effects their actions are having on the object, for example, being able to *see* that a sponge ball changes shape when squashed.

The child who has little or no vision can obviously draw some information through the distant sense of hearing but will be heavily reliant on information received through his or her close senses. Rogow (1988) argued that exploration through touch is essential in order for children who have visual impairment to 'achieve intimate and direct contact with the physical world' (p. 71). However, in the absence of the integrating function that vision performs, the information that young children receive through touch may be fragmentary and difficult to assimilate. Griffen and Gerber (1982) suggested therefore that information through touch needs to be 'systematically acquired and developmentally paced in order for environmental stimuli to be meaningful' (p. 116), in other words careful structuring will be required before touch becomes an effective way for children to learn about their environment.

Review of research findings

Warren (1994) suggests that it is reasonable to assume that restricted vision has implications for the early development of children who have severe visual impairment. However he concluded that it is difficult to make comparisons between the development of touch skills in children who are blind and children who are fully sighted 'because of the contradictions that exist in the research literature' (p. 39). Warren reports that although there is evidence of possible 'developmental' lag in some areas it is inconclusive. Part of the difficulty stems from the low incidence of severe visual impairment in early infancy, and the wide range of additional impairments reported within this population. In addition, the role of the environment is rarely taken into account in research studies, and as Warren has pointed out 'we have to wonder what the norms would be if more ideal environmental circumstances were provided for all blind infants' (1994: 39).

One relatively recent research study investigated the role of vision during early development in relation to the independent use of a spoon when feeding (Ross *et al*. 1997). The findings underlined the importance of visual feedback in controlling complex action patterns among infants who were fully sighted: 'Visual feedback not only informs the child when his spoon has food in it but seems to direct how the spoon should be used and where in the bowl to direct it' (p. 13).

Detailed video analysis revealed that the role of vision in monitoring actions gradually changes. For example, in the initial stages the child needs constant visual feedback but 'As the child's control over the trajectory of the spoon becomes more integrated, requiring fewer steps, his attention and visual system can be freed to perform other tasks' (Ross *et al*. 1997: 6).

Through detailed observations of the infants who performed this movement without the use of vision, Ross *et al*. proposed that the two potential challenges facing these infants as they develop this basic skill are:

- **Lack of incentive** – the child who is blind can't see other people performing the task and so is not motivated to develop the skill.
- **Lack of visual models** – the child who is blind has no 'model' on which to base his or her physical actions, e.g. gripping the spoon in order to fill it. Lack of feedback contributes to this situation as the child may not know whether the technique has been successful until the spoon enters the mouth.

Although short studies such as this provide useful insights into the early development of touch in children who are blind, the most informative findings come from longitudinal case studies. Longitudinal studies enable researchers to monitor particular areas of development in individual children over a period of time. However, due partly to the cost and time required, few longitudinal studies of this type have been undertaken with young infants who are blind or have severe visual impairment. A notable exception is a longitudinal study that was carried out by Selma Fraiberg, a therapist working in the USA.

Selma Fraiberg's longitudinal study

Fraiberg studied ten infants who were born blind and tracked their development between the ages of 1 and 11 months. Prior to commencing the study Fraiberg had noticed that the hands of the young infants who were blind did not reach out to attain objects or to get information about them and 'remained in a kind of morbid alliance with the mouth. They could bring objects to the mouth to be sucked. But, when the hands were not serving the mouth in some way, they were typically held at shoulder height with stereotyped inutile movements of the fingers' (Fraiberg 1977: 10).

Fraiberg compared this behaviour with that found in sighted infants and concluded that the fingering games and organisation of the hands at midline were largely facilitated by vision, and that the tactile engagement of the fingers required simultaneous visual experience to ensure its repetition. Of particular interest are Fraiberg's observations in relation to one of the children that she called 'Peter'. Fraiberg described Peter as using his hands in similar ways to the mouth in that they 'clawed', 'bit' and 'pinched', often in an 'aggressive' manner, rather than engaging in manual exploration of objects for 'pleasure'. Further, she noted that Peter seemed to need to go through a longer stage of throwing things than is typically found in a sighted child, which she speculated was part of a 'process of separating the skeletal muscles from the mouth' (Fraiberg 1977: 47).

Fraiberg observed that children at a similar age to Peter who were sighted were beginning to learn to move around the environment independently and so had ways of channelling their physical energy which were denied to Peter. She noted that when Peter was provided with opportunities to channel his physical energy in focused ways, the aggressive acts of pinching and clawing people and objects diminished quickly.

Fraiberg noticed that blind children's hands frequently made particular movements in response to pleasure or interest before they became able to reach out intentionally towards objects or people. She worked closely therefore with the mothers of the infants teaching them to identify their child's expressions of interests or affection by looking for clues in their hands rather than their faces, viewing this as an important way of encouraging early bonding experiences between mother and child. Significantly, Fraiberg also encouraged the development of 'mutual touch' techniques, a touch equivalent of pointing at an object. This ensured that the child was aware that the object they were feeling was the same one that the mother was talking about.

Another child in the case study, 'Robbie', provided some useful insights into the development of 'object permanence', a significant milestone in early development where children realise that an object 'exists' separately from their immediate experience of it (see Figure 4.5, p. 42). Fraiberg noted that at 10 months and 10 days, Robbie was observed for the first time 'fingering' an object in what appeared to be a truly 'exploratory' manner. In Fraiberg's words, Robbie realised 'it is a thing which has qualities of its own, independent of his own activity' (p. 192). Prior to this observation Robbie's actions with all objects had been largely based on banging, grasping, dropping and throwing, and he showed little discrimination in the range of actions performed on different objects. Three weeks after this observation Fraiberg reports that Robbie reached towards an object in response to a sound cue alone for the first time, and three days later he began to crawl for the first time. This significant move followed months of intensive input during which time his environment was structured in such a way that Robbie could learn that the information from his hands and from his ears could be coordinated and 'could provide him with reliable information about the world' (p. 3).

Fraiberg's study suggested that the infants who were blind did not reach for objects on the cue of sound until the age of about 10 months, whereas infants who were sighted reached for objects at 4 or 5 months of age. In addition, whereas infants who were sighted brought their hands to midline for mutual fingering at 4 months, Fraiberg reported that the infants who were blind demonstrated only 'chance' midline hand encounters at this age and showed no coordination of the activities of two hands until a number of months later.

However, Warren (1994) concluded that evidence indicating a delay in this area of early haptic development is contradictory, and states that 'with respect to midline bimanual activity, there is a discrepancy between Fraiberg's conclusions and those from other work' (p. 31).

Warren cites work by Norris *et al.* (1957) and Ferrell *et al.* (1990) to demonstrate that other research has not found the same discrepancies in the use of two hands. Norris *et al.*, for example, found that on the Cattell Scale of Infant development, babies with a visual impairment demonstrated grasping behaviours at equivalent ages to fully sighted children following normal patterns of development. Children who were blind did show a delay in reaching for objects and less than a quarter of the sample passed the 'unilateral reach' item at the normative age of 6 months, however by 9 months they found that more than three quarters of the children who were blind could pass this item. Warren adds that most of the sample in the Norris study were reported as being blind from retinopathy of prematurity and had been born up to three months prematurely, suggesting that if 'a three-month correction factor is applied, then even the unilateral reaching item shows age appropriate achievement according to the Cattell norms' (p. 31).

These contradictory results indicate the difficulty facing researchers when attempting to account for the full impact of visual impairment on early haptic development and show how much further research in this area is required. We consider the issue of designing appropriate research methods for investigating this kind of question in Chapter 11.

Summary

In the absence of consistent visual information children who have visual impairment will be more reliant on information received through their other senses, including touch, for their learning. Although there is evidence to support a delay in the development of early haptic abilities in children who have visual impairment, the small number of subjects used in the studies and the individual variance noted within the subject groups makes it difficult to reach any definite conclusions. In this chapter we have considered the potential impact of a visual impairment on early haptic development. In Chapter 6 we explore the possible impact of a visual impairment in combination with additional disabilities.

Recommended reading

Fraiberg, S. (1977) *Insights from the Blind*. London: Souvenir Press.
Lewis, V. and Collis, G. M. (1997) *Blindness and Psychological Development in Young Children*. Leicester: British Psychological Society.
Mason, H., McCall, S., Arter, A., McLinden, M. and Stone, J. (eds) (1997) *Visual Impairment Access to Education for Children and Young People*. London: David Fulton.
Warren, D. H. (1994) *Blindness and Children: An individual differences approach*. Cambridge: Cambridge University Press.

CHAPTER 6

The Impact of Additional Disabilities on Learning Through Touch

Introduction

Estimates of the number of children with a visual impairment who have additional disabilities vary. For example, a survey by the Royal National Institute for the Blind (Walker *et al.* 1992) highlighted that 56 per cent of children with a visual impairment have another permanent illness or disability, and 27 per cent have three or more additional impairments. One conclusion of the survey was that the poorer a child's sight was, the more likely it became that additional impairments 'in the areas of communication (hearing and speech), physical integrity and mental functioning' would be found present (p. 8). A more recent national survey (Clunies-Ross and Franklin 1997) found that approximately one third of the estimated 20,000 children with a visual impairment in the UK were described as having 'multiple disabilities'.

Within the population of children who have been identified as having multiple disabilities and visual impairment (MDVI) there is a wide continuum of sight loss. Although relatively few of these children may be diagnosed as 'educationally blind', it is often very difficult to measure with any certainty the degree of functional or useful vision available. In Chapter 5 we looked at the impact a severe visual impairment can have on children's early learning through touch, and we saw how sensory information acquired through the other senses becomes more important in the absence of consistent visual information. This chapter provides an overview of potential barriers to independent learning through touch for children who have multiple disabilities which include a visual impairment, and explores how appropriate learning opportunities can be provided in order to remove these barriers.

Barriers to independent learning

The term 'multiple disabilities' covers a wide range of sensory, intellectual and physical impairments which can occur in a range of combinations. The combinations occurring among children described as having MDVI include:

- visual impairment in combination with delay in 'cognitive' abilities (i.e. severe/profound learning difficulties);
- visual impairment in combination with additional sensory impairment (i.e. hearing impairment; impaired haptic system);
- visual impairment in combination with restrictions in manual abilities which serve to limit independent manipulation of an object (e.g. cerebral palsy);
- visual impairment in combination with restrictions in gross motor abilities which serve to limit independent mobility (e.g. spastic quadriplegia);
- visual impairment in combination with severe medical needs which limit the child's ability to independently manipulate objects (e.g. dependence on medical equipment such as an intravenous drip may restrict independent interactions with objects).

As we saw in Chapter 5, in much of the learning of children who are fully sighted, vision links up and gives meaning to information they receive from their other senses. If the quantity or quality of visual information is reduced it follows that children's ability to integrate information will be affected and this is even more likely to happen if one or more of the other sensory channels are also impaired. Impairments to the other senses and how they impact on learning might include:

- impairment of tactile sensation, for example hypersensitive skin, which may serve as a barrier to the child's participation in, and enjoyment of, different tactile experiences;
- limited proprioceptive feedback may serve as a barrier to children's ability to monitor where their limbs are in relation to the rest of their body;
- impaired hearing may serve as a barrier to the location of sounds in the environment.

Factors which might compound these effects include:

- medication which can affect the child's moods and general arousal level;
- impaired ability to communicate which limits the child's ability to make independent choices about events and activities in his or her life;
- restricted movement which may serve as a barrier to the child's level of motivation to explore objects, people and places.

For children with such complex needs, learning will require close physical contact with adult partners. This contact may take several forms such as 'hand over hand' (or co-active) exploration of objects, or guidance from a sighted partner to move around the environment. Children who have severe physical impairments will be handled by different adults during the course of the day, and may often have very limited control over where, when and how they are touched by others.

In Figures 3.1 and 3.2 (pp. 26 and 28) we provided examples of different types of 'interactive' and 'non-interactive' touch and the wide range of ways in which touch is used during the course of normal daily activities. For children who have MDVI, interactive touch may consist predominantly of touch which is adult initiated and structured. For example interactive touch may be used:

- with a specific therapy goal, for example as in massage ('habilitative' touch);
- to convey information, for example finger spelling onto the child's hand or touch-speech cues ('informative' touch);
- to perform care-giving requirements, for example washing and dressing ('re-quisite' touch);
- to provide the child with opportunities to seek out and process information about objects and people through co-active interaction ('information-seeking' touch).

Indeed, because close and/or direct physical contact with different adults is fre-quently a defining feature of the learning environment of a child with MDVI, Brown *et al.* (1998) caution that:

> We shall need to rely upon personal contact, so we must be aware of the power of touch; that 'normally' personal touch is rarely used on another person with-out permission, that the learner may be able to find out more about us from the way we touch than can be gained through vision or hearing, that invasion of another person's close personal space can be very threatening, that touch should never be given suddenly or unannounced unless safety demands it. (pp. 34–5)

We will return to this issue in Chapter 8 when we consider the role of touch in communication.

Active and passive touch

We have made a distinction on a number of occasions between 'active' and 'passive' types of touch. Active touch implies independent activity, and we know that this type of touch has generally been found to be superior to passive touch in experi-mental studies where subjects are required to identify objects in the absence of vision.

This distinction is useful when considering how touch is used by, and with, children who have multiple disabilities. Best (1992) suggests that passive touch results from tactile experiences which are performed on children by others, for example massage, while active touch refers to those instances where children are able to use their touch to gain information independently, for example when reading a tactile code. A summary of this distinction is provided in Figure 6.1.

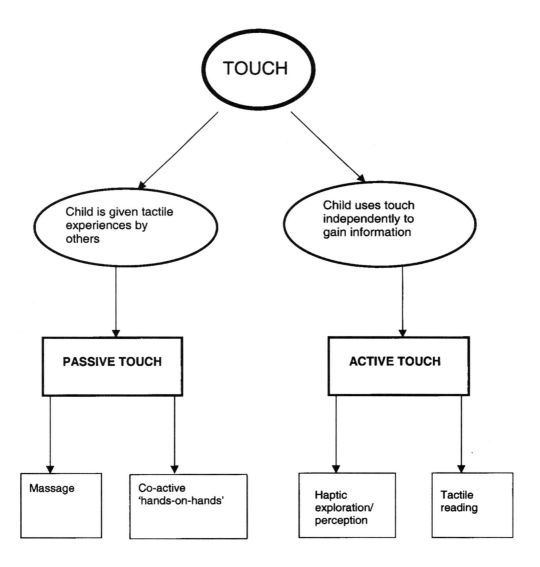

Figure 6.1 Examples of 'active' and 'passive' forms of touch for children who have a visual impairment (adapted from Best 1992)

Given the importance of touch in the lives of children with MDVI, Best suggests that touch experiences need to be defined within a framework of 'tactile environments' which incorporate five stages of expanding space within which the child is able to find out about the world (Figure 6.2).

Stage 1: Face space The focus of children's interest is mainly on their face and tactile experiences will involve the tongue, lips and the hands near the mouth.

Stage 2: Body space The child's world expands to include the whole body. This is the space where different types of massage activities can be used to create awareness that something is happening to the body.

Stage 3: Personal space The child's awareness of the world expands to include the space around the body and people and objects within that space. An element of manipulation of these will emerge as an increasing feature of the child's activity.

Stage 4: Social space This refers to a wider area around the child and may include the whole room.

Stage 5: Group Space The child may start to share an activity under direction, with another child and then take part in group activities.

Figure 6.2 Stages of expanding space (adapted from Best 1992)

Best proposes that this framework of spaces or zones can form a basis for work on the development of touch with children who have MDVI, and suggests that the first two spaces are more likely to entail passive touch activities such as massage.

However, as we saw in Chapter 3, the distinction between 'passivity' and 'activity' in touch is not as clear cut as we might suppose, and with respect to the learning opportunities of children with complex needs it is useful to think in terms of a continuum. For example, if we want to introduce an object to a child with the purpose of helping the child to explore it, we can approach the activity in a variety of ways. If we manipulate the child's hand in order to draw attention to particular sensory features of the object then this would be an activity that draws on only 'passive' touch. However if we move our hands to the child's wrist, we can still support and guide the child's hand but we are providing opportunities for the child to use more 'active' touch to manipulate the object independently. If we then move our hands to the child's elbow, we are providing the child with an even greater element of independent control in the manipulation of the object. This sequence is summarised in Figure 6.3.

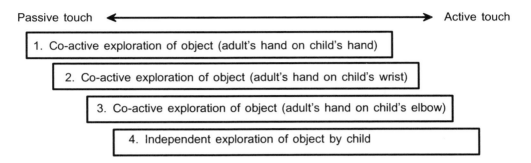

Figure 6.3 Levels of relative activity/passivity in co-active exploration of object by adult partner and child

Tactile strategies

The broad term 'tactile strategies' is applied to the range of approaches used to support the learning through touch of children with complex needs, such as hand-over-hand guidance and touch-speech cues. In the sections below we consider briefly some of the strategies in common use, with a particular focus on hand-over-hand and hand-under-hand guidance. However, we need to bear in mind that, as Chen *et al.* (2000) note, although a variety of tactile strategies are used with children, there is little research-based evidence that validates their use.

Hand-over-hand guidance

We have seen that hand-over-hand guidance involves adults placing their hand (or hands) over the child's to assist the child to manipulate an object or to make a gesture or sign. A number of variations of this technique are illustrated in Figure 6.4.

Chen *et al.* (2000) suggest that this strategy should be used cautiously. 'This "hand-over-hand" strategy should only be used when necessary and with sensitivity to the child's reactions. Some children dislike having their hands manipulated and feel threatened by the lack of control. Others become passive and prompt-dependent. They learn to wait for an adult's hand on their own as a prompt to initiate an action' (p. 2).

This sentiment is shared by Bridgett (1999), who notes that there is a 'fine line' between establishing awareness of the environment and 'coercively manipulating a

Figure 6.4a Hand-over-hand guidance. The adult partner sits behind the child. The adult's right hand is used to help guide the spoon of food held in the child's right hand to her mouth

Figure 6.4b Hand-over-hand guidance. The adult partner sits behind the young child. The adult's right hand helps to guide the spoon of yoghurt held in her right hand to her mouth. The adult's left hand is placed over the child's left hand to prevent her from knocking the pot of yoghurt off the table.

Figure 6.4c Hand-over-hand guidance The adult sits to the left side of the child at his table. The adult's right hand is used to help guide the spoon held in the child's left hand to his mouth.

Figure 6.4d Hand-over-hand guidance. The adult sits on a chair on the right side of the child at his wheelchair tray. The adult's right hand is used to guide the spoon in the child's right hand to his mouth. The adult's left hand is placed under the child's right arm to enable greater independent movement of his arm.

child through an experience that they may be unable to assimilate' (p. 184). Similarly, Nielsen (1996) remarks that inappropriately guiding a child's hands can disturb or interrupt their early development. 'Whenever a sighted person guides or leads the hands of the blind child, it will be the sighted person's strategy for tactile search that will be used. The strategy of the sighted person is influenced by the ability to see as well as by the degree of comprehension of how a blind person experiences surroundings' (pp. 29–30).

Indeed, Nielsen goes so far as to suggest that . . . 'it would be of benefit to the visually impaired child if his teachers would exclude from their educational methods the approach of guiding his hands. The only strategy for tactile search which is of value for the child who is visually impaired is his own' (p. 31).

Hand-under-hand guidance

'Hand-under-hand' guidance may be used as an alternative to hand-over-hand guidance and involves adults placing their hands underneath the child's as they manipulate and explore objects. There is no single established technique for hand-under-hand guidance, and as Chen *et al.* (2000) note, a number of variations of this method may be used:

- the adult may rest a hand underneath the child's and wait for the child to initiate an interaction;
- the child's hand is placed on top of the adult's hand while the adult grasps an object. The adult then rotates his or her hand so that the child is gradually introduced to the shape of the object;
- the adult gradually withdraws his or her hand until the child's fingers touch the surface of the object or texture being manipulated.

A number of variations of this approach are illustrated in Figures 6.5 and 6.6.

Although we have addressed them separately, as these illustrations demonstrate, supporting a child's learning through touch will usually involve a combination of tactile strategies. For example, the co-active exploration of an object with a child might start with the adult partner using 'hand-under-hand' guidance as a way of ensuring that the child understands the nature of the activity, and then change to either hand-over-hand (or indeed, hand-next-to-hand) exploration in order that the child has direct contact with the object. In the next section we present a summary of a hierarchy developed for children who are multi-sensory impaired, which offers useful indicators about the levels of support that adults can offer to children during a given interaction.

Figure 6.5 Hand-under-hand guidance. The adult sits on the left side of the child at his table. The adult's right hand holds the spoon. The child's left hand is placed on top of the adult's hand while the adult guides the spoon towards his mouth.

Figure 6.6a Hand-under-hand guidance. The adult sits on a chair alongside the child in her wheelchair. The child's right hand is on top of the adult's left hand. The adult plays with the beans in the plastic plate.

Figure 6.6b Hand-under-hand guidance. The adult then gradually moves his hand away allowing the child's fingers to touch the beans.

Hierarchy of adult support

McInnes and Treffry (1982) outlined a hierarchy of adult support ranging from 'co-active' through to 'cooperative' and 'reactive' in relation to activities with children who are multi-sensory impaired (Figure 6.7).

Co-active: in co-active activities the adult and child act as one person and the child is provided with a high level of physical prompting.

Cooperative: during cooperative activities the adult provides the child with sufficient support and guidance to achieve success.

Reactive: at the reactive level the child completes the activity independently and has learnt to imitate the adult's actions through being provided with appropriate experiences.

Figure 6.7 Levels of adult support (adapted from McInnes and Treffry 1982)

Central to this principle is the notion of the adult partner creating a 'reactive environment' which McInnes and Treffry propose is characterised by:

- emotional bonding and, as the child grows and develops, social responsiveness;
- problem-solving to reinforce the development of a positive self image;
- utilisation of residual vision and hearing and the integration of input with that from other sensory modalities;
- communication, with an emphasis on dialogue.

The reactive environment involves each of the child's adult partners who, it is stated, must constantly strive to provide situations which will 'stimulate the child to interact with the environment, solve problems, and attempt to communicate' (McInnes and Treffry 1982: 34). An important aspect of the reactive environment is the use of 'dialogue' which involves 'doing with' rather than 'doing for' the child. A key consideration within this environment is the notion of control:

> Any program which concentrates on increasing a child's awareness, mobility, and communication skills but does not provide a reactive environment designed to foster social and emotional growth can lead only to the child developing severe emotional problems because of the frustrations involved in living in a directive, restricting environment over which he has no or little control. (McInnes and Treffry 1982: 35)

McInnes and Treffry have also outlined a stages of interaction framework which is commonly used when working with children who have multi-sensory impairment. Of particular importance for our purposes in this chapter is the role that McInnes and Treffry assign to the adult in providing support to the child during each of the stages of interaction in order to minimise potential barriers to learning (see Figure 6.8).

Stage	Summary of adult's role
Stage 1: **Resists**	Adult works co-actively with child with the aim of forming an emotional bond. Child should be relaxed and secure when the new activity is introduced. If child resists an activity the adult does not insist but changes to a related activity which the child enjoys.
Stage 2: **Tolerates**	Adult support continues to be co-active. Child begins to tolerate the introduction of new activity. Child participates in the activity for short periods of time because of the rewarding, warm contact with the intervenor, not because of the satisfaction from attempting to complete the activity successfully.
Stage 3: **Cooperates passively**	Transition stage from the co-active to the cooperative mode. Adult partner may make a corresponding change in the method of interaction, i.e. change from a 'hand-on-hand' approach to a 'hand-on-wrist' approach, whilst not rushing to withdraw the support and guidance between sessions or between individual attempts.
Stage 4: **Enjoys the activity** **because of the** **intervenor**	The adult partner reduces the physical level of support further although he or she may still work from behind for most activities, and will gradually withdraw guidance to a finger-thumb touch on the wrist and then eventually to an elbow-touch signal to begin and sustain the activity.
Stage 5: **Responds** **cooperatively**	The child follows the adult lead with little direction or need for encouragement from the adult, although still working in a cooperative mode. The adult may now work alongside or in front rather than behind the child.
Stage 6: **Leads**	The child is able to take the lead in the activity and while physical contact is still essential it is minimal and may include occasionally directing the actions of the child to the activity.
Stage 7: **Imitates**	Stages 7 and 8 are part of the reactive mode. The child will go through the sequence of the activity independently when given the appropriate communication. The role of the adult partner now becomes one of working reactively with the child. Activities should pose a 'problem' which needs to be solved by the child, e.g. cover a toy which has until this point been explored co-actively and cooperatively, with a cotton handkerchief and observe how the child reacts to this task when locating the toy independently.

Stage	Summary of adult's role
Stage 8: Initiates	This stage is considered to be reached when the child demonstrates that he or she has integrated the response required by the activity by initiating the sequence independently to solve problems or for personal enjoyment.

Figure 6.8 Summary of adult's role within the 'Stages of Interaction' framework (adapted from McInnes and Treffry 1982)

In order to work effectively with the adult partner McInnes and Treffry note that the child needs to feel relaxed and secure enough to develop an emotional bond with the adult partner. They recommend that during interactions the adult carefully positions his or her body to limit superfluous sensory input. For example, during the early stages of interaction a young child may sit on the adult's lap or perhaps lie in a prone position between the adult's legs. These positions provide the child with a feeling of security and warmth while at the same time affording the child the opportunity to experience the movements of the adult as they work through a particular action sequence. It is worth remembering that in situations of such close contact the child's attention may be drawn to unintentional sensory stimuli. For example, the strong smell of perfume or aftershave, or the sound made by dangling jewellery each time the adult moves his or her head may serve to distract the child from the task in hand. The adult partner will need to be aware of the other potential distractions such as watches, bracelets or brooches and it may be necessary to provide the child with opportunities to explore them prior to the co-active interaction.

A summary of how the stages of interaction framework can be of value when determining the nature of the adult support required when exploring a novel toy with a young child who has MDVI is shown in Figure 6.9.

Although the stages of interaction offer a valuable framework for understanding the role of the adult in supporting a child's learning experiences, it is important to recognise that it was developed for children considered to be dual sensory impaired (i.e. deafblind). These children would not necessarily have had the range of additional impairments commonly found within the broader population of children who have MDVI. Children who have severe physical impairments which restrict their fine motor abilities will be even more reliant on the adult partner to structure their learning through both co-active as well as cooperative support, and may not be able to progress to the later stages of the framework which involve independent function. Further, the type of physical contact McInnes and Treffry advocate as being so important for developing an emotional bond between the

CO-ACTIVE MODE

Stage	Mode	Physical guidance provided by adult partner
1. RESISTS	Co-active mode: Adult partner works co-actively behind child to hold novel toy.	Works behind child with child on lap using hands-over-hands guidance.
2. TOLERATES	Co-active mode: Adult partner works co-actively behind child to hold toy.	Works behind child with child on lap using hands-over-hands guidance.
3. COOPERATES PASSIVELY	Transition from co-active to cooperative mode: Adult partner works cooperatively behind child to hold and manipulate toy.	Works behind child. Change from hands-on-hands to hands-on-wrist guidance.

COOPERATIVE MODE

4. ENJOYS	Cooperative mode: Adult partner works cooperatively behind child to hold and manipulate features of toy.	Mainly working behind child using finger-thumb touch on wrist and elbow-touch signal to begin and sustain activity.
5. RESPONDS COOPERATIVELY	Cooperative mode: Adult partner works cooperatively beside or in front of child to hold and manipulate features of toy.	May work beside or in front of child.
6. LEADS	Cooperative mode: Adult partner works cooperatively in front of child to hold and manipulate features of toy.	Physical contact is essential but minimal.

REACTIVE MODE

7. IMITATES	Reactive mode: Adult partner works reactively in front of child. Physical guidance provided to initiate and end contact with toy.	Minimal physical contact required.
8. INITIATES	Reactive mode: Adult partner works reactively in front of child. Child able to independently locate, grasp, manipulate and replace toy in tray.	No physical contact required.

Figure 6.9 Using the stages of interaction framework to determine the level of adult support when exploring a novel toy with a young child who has MDVI (adapted from McInnes and Treffry 1982)

child and the adult partner during the early stages of interaction may not be appropriate or practical if the child has a severe physical impairment such as spastic quadriplegia.

Flo Longhorn (1988) acknowledged therefore that some children may *always* require physical assistance and guidance from an adult in order to access their environment. In addition to the co-active, cooperative and reactive stages outlined by McInnes and Treffry, Longhorn proposed a fourth stage for supporting a child's learning which she termed 'preference learning'. This stage has particular relevance to children who have more severe and complex needs and she described it as the stage at which children who for the most part are dependent on adult support, may learn independently in *some* areas, and can begin to enter learning experiences selected by themselves: 'They may always need the physical help and guidance, described as co-active learning. However, they may well be able to show preference learning and the observation skills of the staff in recognising the child's potential are essential' (Longhorn 1988: 31).

Even very severe physical disabilities do not mean that children with a visual impairment cannot benefit from a reactive environment within which tasks are provided to challenge the child and opportunities offered for developing control over it. However, for children who have physical impairments so complex that they are unable to manipulate objects independently, such an environment will need careful planning. Of particular relevance to these children is the work of the Danish therapist Lillie Nielsen, who has been highly influential in our understanding of how barriers to learning can be minimised through appropriate structuring of the learning environment.

Lillie Nielsen

Lillie Nielsen has been closely involved in working with children who have MDVI for over 30 years. During this time she has developed a wide range of resources and materials designed to provide children in this population with appropriate opportunities for independent learning. We have included a number of her publications in the Recommended Reading at the end of this chapter.

During the course of her early work with children who have multiple disabilities, Nielsen observed that when surrounded by a range of objects in their immediate environment the children acted on toys in different ways. She noted, for example, that some children turned their activity to stereotyped behaviour:

> Touching and pushing seemed to be unconnected with grasping, or rather, an object which could be pushed was different from one which could be grasped .... Instead of exploring the toy by rattling or touching, some of them began

to throw the toy and became in some way arrested in this behaviour, they did not try to get hold of specific objects. Even if they were helped to get the same object once more, they only seemed to be interested in it for the purpose of throwing it, continuing such behaviour for months or even for years. (Nielsen 1988: 14)

Nielsen concluded that the development of purposeful hand movements was of 'decisive importance' in determining the future of children who are blind, and she proposed that activities at all age stages needed to contain possibilities for the development of such hand movements. She argued that a child who is blind and who cannot grasp and hold objects will be 'unable to make full or sufficient use of the impressions he is experiencing and the weaker the degree of receptivity, the more important it is that the stimuli which the child is capable of registering are reinforced' (1979: 5–6).

Nielsen proposed that as children develop an awareness of their own 'personal space', the tactile environment on which they lie or sit becomes increasingly important. To exploit the sensory experiences available in the child's immediate environment she developed a wooden resonance board – a plywood board raised above the ground on wooden supports. When the child makes a movement, or when an object is dropped onto or moved across the board, the vibrations are amplified and felt through the board.

The resonance board is used extensively with children across the spectrum of special education and a range of activities has been developed to go with it. For further information on how the board can be used effectively with children who have MDVI we recommend that you read the relevant publications by Nielsen listed in the Useful Resources section at the end of the book. You can experience for yourself the principle upon which the resonance board is based by placing your ear onto a wooden desk or table top. If you scratch the surface of the desk with your fingernail the sound becomes magnified. Now explore what happens when you scratch or tap the table top using a pen, as well as a range of other objects.

The resonance board offers a useful means of providing children with increased awareness of their body space in relation to the surface underneath them, but as Best (1992) notes, it is 'uni-dimensional' in that 'it is only a floor, and the walls and ceiling of the room are too far away to be understood by the child' (p. 120). Nielsen overcame this shortcoming by developing a 'Little Room' in order to offer an enclosed space within which the child could be placed. The Little Room consists of textured panels made of wood, material, plastic and rubber which can be attached to a metal frame in various combinations.

As part of her doctoral research, Nielsen investigated how the environment within this room could be organised to encourage children to perform 'preliminary movements' through which they could get feedback about 'success' and 'failure' in connection with objects and spatial relations. The activities were compared with measurements of the children's activity inside a control 'frame' from which the panels had been removed, and it was found that time spent in the Little Room could benefit the children by 'facilitating their ability to perform spatial related activities and to improve within this field of development' (Nielsen 1988: 83).

Nielsen reported that the children were particularly interested in touching objects with acute points or irregular surfaces while tactile search of objects with a smooth surface was discontinued very quickly. Further, tactile search seemed to be encouraged by a high degree of 'tactile discrepancy' within a single object, e.g. a rattle with a range of distinctive tactile properties.

A number of other similar resources are now commercially available (e.g. Be-Active box), details of which are included in the Useful Resources section at the end of the book. In addition to the Nielsen publications, we also recommend the work of Pagliano (1999, 2001), who discusses in greater depth the role of Little Rooms within the range of multisensory environments (MSE) that are used in the education of children who have learning difficulties.

Selective responses to touch

When we were considering the possible barriers to independent learning through touch, we noted that restricted physical movement can be a formidable barrier to the child's learning opportunities and that particular care will be needed to structure the learning environment. We also noted that children with MDVI may be *selective* in the types of sensory information that they will respond to. In Chapter 2 we saw how tactile defensiveness may have a physiological basis and may be linked to damage to the DCML system. However, selective touch may sometimes also be directly linked to an impairment of tactile sensation, for example hypersensitivity of the skin, which can serve as a barrier to the child's participation in, and enjoyment of, certain types of tactile experiences. McInnes and Treffry (1982) observed that without appropriate intervention, in some cases children who are multi-sensory impaired may be 'unable to learn to tolerate being touched, wear clothing, or accept cuddling' (p. 155). For children who have severe visual impairment, selective responses to touching, or to being touched, may also be a learnt response and may be the product of an inappropriate learning environment within which there is limited appreciation of the situation created by the child's particular combination of sensory needs.

Charlotte Royeen and Shelly Lane, occupational therapists from the USA, have written extensively on the subject of children's resistance to different types of tactile experiences. They make a clear distinction between 'poor tactile discri-mination' and 'tactile defensiveness,' a term that was coined by the Australian occupational therapist Jean Ayres within her theory of 'sensory integration'. Roy-een and Lane (1991) define poor tactile discrimination as an 'inability to opti-mally perceive and organise incoming discriminative touch information for use' (p. 113), and they consider it to be a disorder of tactile perception. They propose that this disorder includes:

- difficulty in discriminating where and how many times a person is touched;
- impaired ability to recognise the shape of an object through active manipula-tion;
- inefficiency in exploring an object to gain cues which provide meaning about that object through haptic or active touch;
- impaired awareness of self (i.e. body scheme).

On the other hand, they define tactile defensiveness as:

> observable aversive or negative behavioral responses to certain types of tactile stimuli that most people would find to be non-noxious (nonpainful). Simply stated, tactile defensiveness is the inability to interpret appropriately the affec-tive (rather than the perceptual) meaning of touch or touch experiences within the context of the situation and in a way meaningful for use by the organism. (Royeen and Lane 1992: 112)

Royeen and Lane propose that tactile defensiveness is characterised by three main types of behaviours:

1. Avoidance of touch
2. Aversive responses to non-noxious touch
3. Atypical affective responses to non-noxious tactile stimuli.

Examples of behaviours within each of these categories are given in Figure 6.10.

Since interactive types of touch are so important to a child's ability to bond and form relationships with others, Scardina (1986) suggested that resistance to tactile experiences may result in a range of additional 'secondary' deficits which can influ-ence the very foundations upon which human intimacy is based. Thus children with MDVI who show an aversion to being cuddled or held may provoke feelings of inadequacy in adults whose attempts at physical interaction are consistently rejected.

We discuss issues to do with assessment of touch in the next chapter but for now you may want to look again at the 'stages of interaction' framework we sum-marised earlier in the chapter, and consider how it might be used to monitor a child's selective responses to tactile experiences. By way of example McInnes and

Category of behaviour	Examples of behaviour
1. <u>Avoidance</u> of touch	a. Avoidance of certain styles or textures (e.g. scratchy or rough) of clothing, or a preference for certain styles of clothing (e.g. soft materials, sleeves).
	b. Tendency to pull away from anticipated touch or from interactions involving touch, including avoidance of touch to the face.
	c. Avoidance of play activities that involve bodily contact, possibly manifested by a tendency to prefer solitary play.

Category of behaviour	Examples of behaviour
2. <u>Aversive</u> responses to non-noxious touch	a. Aversion or struggle when picked up, hugged or cuddled.
	b. Aversion to certain daily living tasks, including baths or showers or face washing.
	c. Aversion to art materials, including avoidance of finger paints, paste or sand.

Category of behaviour	Examples of behaviour
3. <u>Atypical</u> affective responses to non-noxious tactile stimuli	a. Responding with aggression to light touch to arms, face or legs.
	b. Increased stress in response to being physically close to people.
	c. Objection, withdrawal or negative responses to touch contact, including that encountered in the context of intimate relationships.

Figure 6.10   Examples of behaviours which characterise tactile defensiveness (adapted from Royeen and Lane 1991)

Treffry outline a sequence for encouraging a child to progress from 'resists' tactile experiences (i.e. Stage 1) to 'tolerates' (i.e. Stage 2) these experiences (see Figure 6.11).

1. Child and adult place themselves in a secure position

2. Object is warmed to body temperature if possible

3. Object is introduced between adult and child

4. Object is removed once child resists and 'favourite calming activity' is introduced

5. Object is reintroduced and co-actively explored together

6. Adult conveys to child that she or he likes the child and likes the object

Figure 6.11   Supporting the learning experiences of a child who resists tactile experiences (adapted from McInnes and Treffry 1982)

Structuring the learning environment

Bell (1993) reported that if the information a child with MDVI receives is not complete, the child will have difficulty in achieving a balanced understanding of the environment. The task of those supporting the child will be to 'manipulate' the variables within an educational context in order to maximise the opportunities for developing this understanding. To achieve this, Bell recommends that when working with a child who has MDVI an important aim should be to ensure that their incidental learning is SOS, namely, 'Structured', 'Orderly' and 'Significant'. If we apply this recommendation to a child's learning through touch, then we must give careful consideration to the whole learning process within which tactile experiences are structured for each individual child. A number of these principles are illustrated in Vignette 6.1, which focuses on Nadia, a 9-year-old child who is blind and attends a school for children who have severe learning difficulties.

Vignette 6.1   Nadia

Nadia is reluctant to reach out and independently hold objects presented to her when seated at her desk, invariably withdrawing her hand on contact with objects or knocking them to the floor and occasionally throwing them across the room. Nadia's teacher notes that in general Nadia appears to resist new tactile experiences, particularly those which involve her holding an object. Her teacher has therefore developed an individual learning routine for her which includes daily opportunities to explore co-actively different objects with an adult partner, with the initial aim that Nadia will tolerate a novel object placed in her hand for a minimum of five seconds.

Supported by bean bags, the teacher sits on the floor with Nadia in her lap. After explaining to her what is about to happen, the teacher places a small wooden tray which has a raised edge surround (referred to as Nadia's 'special' tray) gently onto Nadia's lap and she is invited to reach out and find the tray. Nadia then spends some time co-actively feeling the features of the tray with her teacher. Following a verbal explanation, a toy rabbit containing a squeaker is placed into the tray. Nadia's teacher 'squeaks' the rabbit and Nadia is invited to find the rabbit 'hiding' on her 'special tray'. Although Nadia reaches out towards the tray and accurately locates the rabbit, she is reluctant to hold it and rapidly withdraws her hand. Her teacher utilises a number of strategies for encouraging her to tolerate the toy. For example, she places the toy rabbit on Nadia's lap and asks Nadia if she can find the lonely rabbit on her lap and put it back into the special tray. Nadia reaches to the rabbit on her lap and makes contact with it. She is still however reluctant to hold it, withdrawing her hand upon making contact.

The teacher informs Nadia that the rabbit is going to jump off her lap into its box and that her favourite dolly Michaela is going to climb onto the tray. Nadia's plastic dolly is then placed onto the tray and Nadia is invited to reach out to find it. Nadia locates Michaela and brings her towards her body, hugging her tightly with both hands. After approximately two minutes Nadia's teacher tells her that the rabbit is lonely in his box and is going to jump onto the tray again. She places the rabbit on the tray squeaking it three times. The teacher then invites Nadia to hold Michaela in one hand, and reach out with her other hand to find the rabbit sitting on the tray.

This short sequence highlights a number of important points about the individual learning routine which has been structured so as to be significant for Nadia. The main purpose of the session described here is to encourage Nadia to reach out independently to a range of objects and begin to tolerate holding them. This function is initially undertaken co-actively as Nadia is reluctant to hold objects independently. By sitting Nadia on the adult's lap the teacher is providing a safe and secure environment within which Nadia can learn (an example of nurturing touch). Further, this position prevents Nadia from throwing objects and potentially harming herself or others (an example of 'protective' touch). Nadia's partner will continue with this routine over a period of time, but will provide increased opportunities for Nadia to hold independently and manipulate different types of objects. As a number of people work with Nadia during the course of a week at school, each stage of the sequence is carefully documented so that all her adult partners are consistent in their approach in order that Nadia is able to anticipate what will be happening at any point in the learning routine.

Summary

Although children who have MDVI constitute a significant proportion of the population of children with a visual impairment, only a relatively narrow body of research exists on the role of touch in their learning. Children without sensory impairment who follow normal patterns of development become less dependent on others to structure their learning opportunities through direct physical contact with the environment. They become adept at using their distant senses in combination with their haptic abilities to make autonomous discoveries about their world. Children with severe visual impairment who are reliant on haptic information as a major source of sensory input, may aquire imprecise information about the world if their experiences do not continue to be structured by others at a level appropriate to their needs, especially if the child is resistant to tactile experiences. This reliance can have an important bearing on children's knowledge and understanding of the world at critical stages in their early development and it is necessary to consider carefully the structure of the learning environment. The implications for assessment in this area are explored in the next chapter.

Recommended reading

Longhorn, F. (1988) *A Sensory Curriculum for Very Special People: A practical approach to curriculum planning.* London: Souvenir Press.

McInnes, J. M. and Treffry, J. (1982) *Deafblind Infants and Children: developmental guide.* Toronto: University of Toronto Press.

McInnes, J. M. (ed.) (1999) *A Guide to Planning and Support for Individuals who are Deafblind.* Toronto: University of Toronto Press.

Nielsen, L. (1991) 'Spatial relations in congenitally blind infants: a study', *Journal of Visual Impairment and Blindness*, **85**, 11–16.

Nielsen, L. (1992) *Space and Self: Active learning by means of the Little Room.* Copenhagen: Sikon.

Nielsen, L. (1993) *Early Learning Step-by-Step.* Copenhagen: Sikon.

Pagliano, P. (1999) *Multisensory Environments.* London: David Fulton.

Pagliano, P. (2001) *Using a Multisensory Environment: A practical guide for teachers.* London: David Fulton.

CHAPTER 7

Principles Underpinning the Assessment of Touch

Introduction

Our assessment of children with multiple disabilities and a visual impairment needs to be an ongoing process of discovery about the child which guides our intervention and shapes our planning. As assessors we need to have an appreciation of the range of sources that can provide information about the child and a framework in which to analyse that information.

We have seen a shift of emphasis in recent years in the assessment of children who have special educational needs (SEN), and this is particularly apparent in relation to children with severe and complex learning difficulties. Traditionally, assessments were carried out by visiting professionals whose concern was to measure the child's abilities through formal psychometric testing. Today, however, assessment is more likely to be based on the observations of those with an in-depth knowledge of the child (Hogg and Sebba 1986) and parents and teachers are now seen as central participants in this process. Informal observation schedules or checklists are now commonly regarded as more appropriate methods for capturing the individual nature of the behaviour of children with severe and complex SEN. In this chapter we provide an overview of the assessment of children who have MDVI, focusing particularly on the role of touch. We begin with an overview of the assessment of sensory function and then consider some of the formal and informal methods which are used to assess how children use their haptic abilities.

Assessment of sensory function

For the purpose of this discussion we describe 'sensory function' as being concerned with how a child receives, interprets and consequently acts upon different types of sensory information in the course of a given task. Assessments of sensory function often attempt to make clear distinctions between the input of the various senses but in practice it is often difficult for the observer to work out what degree of sensory input each receptor is providing. As Brown *et al.* (1998) note, it is relatively rare for an individual to experience no sensation at all from a sensory organ which is impaired. For example, many people described as being 'deafblind' have some residual hearing and some degree of residual vision. Attempts to maximise the efficiency of each sense in isolation can sometimes be counter-productive:

> the teacher may overlook which sensations are most powerfully affecting the learner, for example, touch, while searching to maximise use of the recognised impaired sense, for example, vision. Additionally, it might also be falsely assumed by the teacher that, for example, because a visual impairment has been identified, all the other senses are fully intact. (Brown *et al.* 1998: 33)

In our own practice we have seen children being actively prevented from exploring objects by touch because the teacher has been advised that the child needs to be encouraged to 'develop their residual vision'. In reality, for children with low vision, touch may be required to complement or clarify the imprecise information that reduced vision provides. While some children will need encouragement to make best use of their vision, it should not be at the cost of reducing the use of other senses.

Observing sensory function

We can obtain information about children's sensory function by carefully observing the way they use their senses to perform actions. However, it can be difficult to identify the role each of the senses plays at different stages in any sequence of action. As an example let us think about the type of information that different senses provide us with in the course of a daily activity such as when we brush our teeth with a new flavoured toothpaste. Initially we may make use of vision to inspect the novel packaging of the container as it lies on the shelf. We will also use our vision to locate the toothbrush and our vision in combination with our proprioceptive abilities to squeeze the toothpaste onto the brush. We will then rely on smell and taste to make comparisons with our regular toothpaste. Information from proprioceptive receptors enables us to locate our mouth to begin the process of brushing, and the sensory information from our tongue and lips offers us a way of monitoring the temperature of the water and finding out whether we like the new taste and texture of the paste. When we have finished cleaning our teeth we might use our tongue to check we have removed every last trace of the plaque which coated our teeth.

In this sequence we are not concerned with the relative *importance* of each of the senses. Even if we were would it be possible, for example, to rate vision as being of greater importance than touch or smell in the above sequence? What we would want to observe, and begin to understand, is the precise role of each sense at particular points within the sequence of activity. Careful analysis of how we make use of our senses in everyday activities can help us to develop skills in observing how children with MDVI interpret different types of sensory information, as well as how they might compensate for reduced vision by using alternative sensory information.

Consider cleaning your teeth without the benefit of any visual information (you may wish to try doing this tonight!). You will, in all probability, still be able to complete the task, although it will probably take you more time. Further, you may find that in the absence of visual information you use your senses in different ways, for example to check that there are no traces of toothpaste left around your mouth you may lick your lips with your tongue.

As we saw in earlier chapters we use vision to coordinate or integrate a wide range of sensory information and vision is therefore often referred to as the 'unifying' or 'integrating' sense. Accurate visual information allows us to interpret events in the world, to link cause and effect and, crucially, vision enables us to anticipate what is about to happen next. In the absence of consistent information through the distance senses of vision and hearing, the immediate environment becomes increasingly significant. However, the effects of the wider environment also become exaggerated because we cannot so easily apprehend, alter or allow for them by personal initiative (Brown *et al.* 1998). In order to appreciate how children use information from their close senses we will need to be able to interpret their responses to a range of stimuli. In Figure 7.1 we provide a summary of a useful framework which is used in the assessment procedure *Vision for Doing* (Aitken and Buultjens 1992) to interpret sensory responses. Figure 7.2 shows how this framework has been incorporated into a recording sheet which can be used to assess how a learner uses his or her 'sense of touch'. The use of this framework is considered further in Vignette 7.1 at the end of the chapter. We have included details of a number of other procedures used for the assessment of sensory function in the Useful Resources section.

As Brown *et al.* (1998) note, functional assessment involves the systematic collection of information in relation to both 'input' and 'output'. In carrying out a functional assessment we need to record carefully both the characteristics of the sensory input and the nature of the child's response to it (the output). We also need to be informed enough to apply flexible interpretations to children's responses. For example, Best (1994) describes behaviours in children with a visual impairment which have a 'functional equivalence' to behaviours that we are more familiar

Awareness: at an awareness level learners show a 'simple' response to indicate that they are aware that the stimulus is present, for example blinking or change in breathing rate.

Attending: attention to a stimulus may be demonstrated in a number of ways, for example by learner 'stilling' to listen or an increase/decrease in vocalisation.

Localising: localisation occurs when the learner can identify where the stimulus came from. The learner may move a part of his or her body towards (or away from) the source of stimulation.

Recognising: recognition may be revealed by the learner's selective response to particular stimuli, for example a familiar voice or an object.

Understanding: understanding may be demonstrated by the learner's ability to relate different types of stimuli to particular events, thereby demonstrating anticipatory behaviour. An example might be the increased vocalisation and body movement shown by a child when putting on his or her coat in anticipation of going outside at breaktime.

Figure 7.1   Assessment framework used in *Vision for Doing* to record and interpret a child's responses (adapted from Aitken and Buultjens 1992 and Brown *et al*. 1998)

with in children who are fully sighted. He defines functional equivalence as referring to 'different' behaviours that can have 'identical' meaning, or 'identical' behaviours that can have a 'different' meaning. This has been supported by Murdoch (1997), who stresses the importance of the 'acceptance' and 'interpretation' of functionally equivalent behaviours in the process of recognising the implications of multi-sensory impairment.

A common example of a behaviour which has functional equivalence is the 'stilling' that parents observe in young children who are blind as they go to pick them up. Whereas children who are fully sighted may become animated as the parent comes closer, children who are blind might instead sit very still as they direct their concentration to the approaching voice. This stilling behaviour may be misinterpreted by the parent as apathy or even rejection, when in reality the child is actually listening attentively and creating the best possible conditions to gather auditory information about the event he or she is eagerly anticipating. Parents need an appreciation of the differences between the use of vision and hearing to realise that this stilling behaviour may be a natural means for the child to 'show' interest.

Selection of assessment procedures

Before we choose an assessment procedure to assess a child, we need to have a clear idea of its nature and its purpose. There are a number of considerations here:

SECTION 5
LEARNER'S SENSE OF TOUCH

	Consistently	Occasionally	Never
Learner shows awareness of touch by:			
startling:	☐	☐	☐
withdrawing:	☐	☐	☐
other:	☐	☐	☐
Learner attends to touch by:			
exploring by hand:	☐	☐	☐
exploring by mouth:	☐	☐	☐
exploring by other means:	☐	☐	☐

Learner localises by touch:
(draw on diagram positions
touched by learner)

30cm to 1m
10cm to 30cm
1cm to 10cm

	Consistently	Occasionally	Never
Learner recognises by touch:			
familiar objects:	☐	☐	☐
familiar person:	☐	☐	☐
Learner understands uses of objects by touch:			
appropriately:	☐	☐	☐

Figure 7.2 Recording sheet from *Vision for Doing* used to assess learner's sense of touch (reproduced from Aitken and Buultjens 1992)

- *standardisation*   if the procedure has been standardised, has it been standardised against the population of children with a visual impairment? Do the 'norms' refer to those of children with a visual impairment?
- *age appropriateness*   is the procedure appropriate for the chronological age of the child?
- *reliability*   can similar results be expected if the same procedure is performed again with the child?
- *validity*   does the test measure what it claims to measure?

Given the low incidence of MDVI and the diverse nature of these children it is not surprising that there are no standardised tests for comparing this population with the wider population. One of the few that seeks to offer age-equivalent scores for young children who have a visual impairment is the Reynell–Zinkin Scales, although even the co-author of this procedure, Joan Reynell, suggested that the measurement of children with a visual impairment by comparison with sighted norms is unrealistic. She claims that in areas such as understanding the permanence of objects, the relationship of 'object to object' is very dependent on visual perception, suggesting that the

> age scores for normal sighted children should be regarded as only an approximate guide ... the order and time intervals of the developmental stages is slightly different with sighted and visually handicapped children, particularly in the early months. This all makes direct comparison of progress difficult. (Reynell 1981: 36)

In Figure 7.3 we list a selection of assessment procedures which are used in education to assess children who have MDVI, and which can be of use when assessing how a child uses his or her haptic abilities. Further information about each of these procedures is given in the Useful Resources section.

Developmental approaches

A number of the procedures in Figure 7.3 (e.g. the OSPD) are based on a developmental approach, in other words they are based on the sequences of development observed in children without disabilities which are arranged into a linear progression, usually around themes. Although a developmental approach can be useful, Ware (1994) advised caution suggesting that progress should take account of the individual nature of the child's development rather than assuming that the child's progress will follow a linear sequence to a predefined endpoint. This view is supported by Stillman and Battle (1986) in relation to the developmental assessment of children who are deafblind. They argue that the behaviours among this group may differ considerably in both 'quality' and 'quantity' from those observed

Assessment procedure	Author and year of publication
Ordinal Scales of Psychological Development (OSPD)	Dunst, C. J. (1980)
Object Related Scheme Assessment Procedure (ORSAP)	Coupe, J. and Levy, D. (1985)
Reynell-Zinken Scales (R-Z scales)	Reynell, J. (1981)
Callier-Azusa Scale (C-A scale)	Stillman, R. D. (1978)
Functional and Instruction Scheme (FIS)	Nielsen, L. (1990)
Erhardt Developmental Prehension Assessment (EDPA)	Erhardt, R. P. (1994)
Affective Communication Assessment (ACA)	Coupe, J. et al. (1985)
Assessing Communication Together (ACT)	Bradley, H. (1991)
Behaviour Assessment Battery (BAB)	Kiernan, C. and Jones, M. C. (1982)
Vision for Doing	Aitken, S. and Buultjens, M. (1992)

Figure 7.3 Selection of procedures used in education for assessing the haptic abilities of children who have MDVI

in normally developing individuals, and state that among individuals in this population 'physical maturation often exceeds cognitive development. Thus, the deaf-blind child's abilities may be expressed through behaviours of which the normally developing child, at the same cognitive level, is incapable' (1986: 333).

Pagliano (1999) noted that a weakness of the developmental approach was that it was built on the assumption that development patterns observed in children without disabilities apply to children with disabilities, and suggested that the more severe and complex the disabilities 'the more this simplistic assumption must be called into question' (p. 122). Further, Kangas and Lloyd (1988) warned of the danger of extending assumptions from normally developing children with normal experiences to 'learners with disabilities who may have very different experiential opportunities' (p. 214).

However, given the relative lack of research into children with severe/profound disabilities who are functioning at early stages of development we are to some extent bound to make use of what we know about the development of children without disabilities. A number of researchers have proposed that it may be feasible to use information relating to normally developing children/adults, and then to consider the implications for individuals with severe intellectual disabilities (Clark 1981; Coupe and Levy 1985; Musselwhite and Ruscello 1984). Nevertheless because so few procedures have been developed specifically for children who have visual impairment, the appropriateness of items in any assessment needs to be considered carefully.

The developmental models of haptic perception that we discussed in Chapter 4 (Bushnell and Boudreau 1991; Gibson 1966; Piaget 1953) made a number of assumptions about the development of early haptic exploratory behaviours during infancy. However, we cannot be certain that the behaviours of infants are a good guide for assessing the haptic function of *older* children with MDVI. Although these children may commonly be described as 'functioning at early stages of development', it is important to remember of course that they are not infants!

Criterion-referenced procedures

An alternative to the use of norm-referenced (or standardised developmental) tests which compare children's performance with their peers are criterion-referenced assessment procedures. These instruments are designed to obtain information about a child's performance in a particular area with a view to developing an appropriate teaching programme. Tobin (1994) notes the concern is not about the extent to which a child conforms to achievement levels found to be typical of his or her age group, but rather about whether the child can carry out a specific task such as pulling an arm through a coat or using a spoon for independent feeding. The *Behaviour Assessment Battery* (BAB) listed in Figure 7.3 is one example of a criterion-referenced procedure. Further details of this publication are included in the Useful Resources section. We recommend the work of Aitken (1995) for a more detailed discussion of issues relating to norm- and criterion-referenced assessment.

Process-oriented assessment

Process-oriented models can be particularly appropriate for children who display a limited range of behaviours. Within this approach the role of the observer is to attempt to record the responses of the child to stimuli and to note whether the stimuli produce a change in the child's behaviour. This allows the observer to determine how the child processes a range of information in different environments. As such it can provide an estimation of a child's potential to 'continue developing' rather than a list of behaviours the child is unable to demonstrate (Langley 1986). An example of a process-oriented procedure listed in Figure 7.3 is the Affective Communication Assessment (ACA) (Coupe *et al.* 1985). The 'Touch Grid' included in *Assessing Communication Together* (ACT) (Bradley 1991) provides a further example of how a process-oriented model can be used to assess a child's responses to a range of tactile experiences using the sequence of responses to interaction outlined by McInnes and Treffry (1982) (see Figure 7.4).

As Bradley (1998) notes, any type of tactile experience may be entered on the left-hand column and its effects recorded easily using the sequence of responses along the top row. Through careful monitoring of a child's responses to different tactile experiences, this same record sheet may also be used to record progress over time. Further details of the ACA and ACT procedures are provided in the Useful Resources section.

NAME .... DATE...

TYPE OF TOUCH	BODY PART	VERY RESISTANT	ACCEPTS PASSIVELY	ENJOYS	SIGNALS FOR MORE	INITIATES
Stroking	Right hand	✓	✗	✗	✗	✗
	Left hand	✓	✗	✗	✗	✗
Stroking	Head	✓	✗	✗	✗	✗
Stroking	Right leg	✗	✓	✗	✗	✗
	Left leg	✗	✓	✗	✗	✗
Stroking	Stomach	✗	✓	✓	✓ Put hand back	✗
Stroking	Back	✗	✓	✓	✗	✗
Pouring warm water slowly onto:	Right hand	✗	✓	✓	✗	✗
	Left hand	✗	✓	✓	✗	✗
Pouring warm water slowly onto:	Right arm	✓	✓	✗	✗	✗
	Left arm	✓	✓	✗	✗	✗
Pouring warm water slowly onto:	Right foot	✗	✓	✗	✗	✗
	Left foot	✗	✓	✓	✓ wiggled feet	✗

Figure 7.4 Format for assessing a child's responses to different types of tactile experiences (reproduced from *Assessing Communication Together*, Bradley 1991)

Informal assessment methods

Tobin (1994) suggested that because of the difficulty of applying formal assessment procedures to the diverse needs of learners with MDVI, teachers often feel obliged to construct their own checklists and observational methods for assessing needs and progress of these children (p. 65). These informal procedures include structured checklists and daily diaries. It now seems clear that assessment of touch in children with MDVI is generally most effectively achieved by carefully observing how they use their touch in naturalistic or functional situations. As Curtis and Donlon (1985) note 'Observation is the major source of information about the severely multi-handicapped child. These observations, as soon as they are formulated, are undoubtedly the primary determinants of the teacher's attitude toward a work plan for the child' (p. 2). This is done best in a structured way over a period of time by people who work with the children regularly and know them well. This approach can identify functional abilities which may have been overlooked in more formal assessments, and as such can form part of an 'ecological' approach to assessment. Goold and Hummell (1993) recommend the use of such an ecological approach which they propose allows for the careful observation, documentation and interpretation of an 'individual's responses to tactile stimuli across a wide range of stimuli, environments and personnel' (p. 48).

An example of how a more informal approach to assessment can inform practice is presented in relation to Nadeen, a child with profound and multiple disabilities and with limited independent upper limb movement. As part of a functional assessment of his haptic abilities, a learning support assistant (LSA) notices that Nadeen regularly 'scratches' the plastic surface of his wheelchair arm with a fingernail. By placing different textures over the arms of Nadeen's wheelchair she is able to observe his haptic activity closely and record her observations. She notices that he only uses the forefinger of his right hand for the scratching activity and no similar movement is observed with his left hand. Further, the scratching activity appears to intensify when he is in contact with surfaces which produce distinctive sounds, for example a piece of bubble wrap. The LSA makes a recommendation that careful consideration should be given to the texture used to cover the arms of the child's wheelchair, and suggests that cloth hoods should be made onto which interesting tactile surfaces can be attached and altered at regular intervals.

As this example illustrates informal assessment requires sharp observation skills. Indeed, Nadeen's haptic behaviour might never have become apparent if he had been presented with a range of 'test' materials as part of a more formal assessment procedure. Tilstone (1998) warns, however, that much of what is observed in the classroom environment is the result of 'casual, non-directed activity' and without systems, information gained in these activities may go unrecorded. What we observe and record depends to some extent on what we are trying to find out. For example, a general question which asks 'How does Jessie make use of touch during the course of the day?' will demand a different framework for observation from the question 'Does Jessie show consistent hand preference when holding an object?' In general the more focused and specific the question, the easier it will be to develop a framework for observation. We recommend that you refer to the texts by Tilstone (1998) and Tobin (1994) for further information on how such frameworks might be constructed.

Assessment of children who demonstrate tactile defensive behaviours

We considered the term 'tactile defensiveness' in Chapter 6, and noted that rather than being a blanket aversion to touch, it is more likely to take the form of selective responses to specific learning experiences which the child finds unpleasant. For example, Lee and MacWilliam (1995) note that many children who have MDVI 'will habitually startle when touched or lifted if they are not given consistent and appropriate warnings of forthcoming events. The nappy change, the bath or being picked up, all of which should be fun, confidence building, social events can become frightening and confusing' (p. 6).

It is rare for a child to demonstrate tactile defensive behaviours to *all* objects, people or sensory experiences in *all* places at *all* times. In some respects therefore it might be more productive to think of a child's responses as tactile 'selectiveness' to different types of experiences, with the onus being on the adult partners to carefully document these responses. Indeed, Royeen and Lane (1991) argue that the identification of tactile 'defensiveness' should be based on patterns or clusters of behaviours that indicate possible dysfunction and that the identification of a problem should not be based on data from a single source. Further, they note that the identification of tactile defensiveness depends primarily on informal, non-standardised approaches based upon observation and enquiry, and suggest that it is useful to compile a 'sensory history' of the child which explores 'the developmental history of an individual in relation to how the individual responds to sensory stimuli' (p. 127). Sample questions which they recommend be used as part of the sensory history include:

Does the child:

- Seem to avoid using his or her hands?
- Mouth objects or clothes excessively?
- Seem overly sensitive to food or water temperature?

Did the child:

- Cry excessively during infancy?
- Have difficulty establishing sleep/wake cycles during infancy?

Following an assessment of the child's responses to different types of tactile stimuli, the levels of adult support outlined in Chapter 6 (Figure 6.7) offer a useful framework within which to plan an intervention programme, and as Best (1992) suggests this framework enables us to 'monitor the development of responses to a particular tactile experience and use this information to judge how much to repeat experiences and when to introduce new ones' (p. 120).

In addition to the levels of adult support framework, McInnes and Treffry (1982) have outlined four levels within which to assess a child's use of touch, noting that the child's ability to 'alert to', 'tolerate', 'facilitate' and 'integrate' tactile inputs should be considered. They propose that the act of touching includes at least four main components (i.e. duration; strength; area; stability) and that each of these components will be important to consider in designing a programme to support a child's learning through touch (see Figure 7.5).

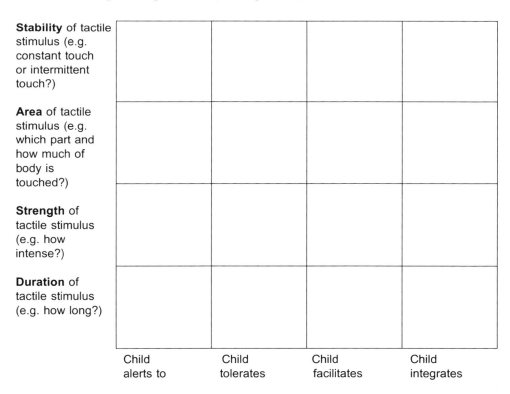

	Child alerts to	Child tolerates	Child facilitates	Child integrates
Stability of tactile stimulus (e.g. constant touch or intermittent touch?)				
Area of tactile stimulus (e.g. which part and how much of body is touched?)				
Strength of tactile stimulus (e.g. how intense?)				
Duration of tactile stimulus (e.g. how long?)				

Figure 7.5 Framework to assess a child's responses to different dimensions of touch (adapted from McInnes and Treffry 1982)

McInnes and Treffry (1982) caution that because a child 'alerts to' or 'tolerates' a particular stimulus, this does not mean that he or she will automatically be able to utilise this new source of information for the purpose of perceiving his or her environment, and they suggest that many practitioners 'have foundered on the assumption that to tolerate means to utilise' (p. 154). Further, McInnes and Treffry stress that it is difficult to make an effective evaluation of the child's responses until the child begins to 'cooperate passively' with an adult partner and suggest that evaluations made before this stage 'will not lead to the setting of realistic goals or objectives' (p. 26). Children need to be able to 'tolerate' being touched and manipulated before we can introduce a more formal programme of activities and McInnes and Treffry give the example of dressing and undressing as a valuable opportunity for this type of interaction to take place.

A list of publications which can be of value in assessing and developing the use of touch in children described as being 'tactile defensive' is included in the Useful Resources section.

Social context of development

We noted earlier that a significant feature of children who have MDVI is their continuing dependency on other individuals to structure their learning experiences, including their interactions with people, objects and different types of sensory experiences. In assessing how a child who has MDVI uses touch in his or her learning, we need to take account of the wider context within which any given interaction takes place, and in particular, acknowledge that effective learning through touch rarely takes place within a social vacuum.

Glenn *et al.* (1996) divide theories of child development into those which are primarily concerned with an infant's understanding of the 'non-social environment' and those which emphasise the 'social context' of learning. The theories of both Piaget and Gibson, as well as Bushnell and Boudreau's model of early haptic development that we looked at in Chapter 4, are predominantly 'non-social' in their approach. However, Glenn *et al.* (1996) note that there has been a strong move in recent years to 'incorporate into educational programmes theories which emphasise the social context of development' (p. 69). The ideas of Vygotsky, the Soviet theorist, have become increasingly influential in exploring the role of the adult in structuring a child's learning experiences. Central to Vygotskian thought is the idea that 'infants do not develop in isolation, but through interaction with more competent others ... The theory argues that learning is first achieved via social mediation, with the child subsequently internalising what has been learned in a social context' (Glenn *et al.* 1996: 69).

Vygotsky proposed the concept of the 'Zone of Proximal Development' (ZPD). The 'Zone' marked the distance between the level of development in a particular domain that the child can achieve *alone* and the level that the child could reach in *cooperation* with others. The notion of the ZPD implies that the child is able to 'tackle a certain group of tasks under adult guidance and in cooperation with cohorts who know more than he does but which he cannot tackle on his own' (Daniels 1996: viii).

Vygotsky proposed two levels of development: 'the actual developmental level as determined by independent problem solving, and the level of potential development as determined through problem solving under adult guidance or in collaboration with capable peers' (1978: 86). Bozic and Murdoch (1996) suggested that 'from this viewpoint, assessment of children's abilities requires more than the measurement of their actual (or current) developmental level . . . There is also a need to identify what children are able to achieve with support' (pp. 5–6).

Wood *et al.* (1976) used the notion of 'scaffolding' to explain how a more competent adult is able to support a child's achievement within a task by structuring activities so that they prop up and build on each other. A useful example of how scaffolding can be used to structure early literacy activities through specialist ICT (i.e. a tactile overlay on a concept keyboard in combination with auditory feedback) is given in Douglas and Dickens (1996).

To illustrate the importance of acknowledging the social context during assessment, and in particular the role of the adult partners in supporting a child's learning experiences, Vignette 7.1 describes the assessment of Baylie, a 7-year-old girl who is registered as educationally blind and attends a school for children with severe learning difficulties.

Vignette 7.1 Baylie

Baylie has a visit from the advisory teacher of the visually impaired. The teacher has come to assess how Baylie uses touch when playing with different types of objects. The assessment takes place in a small observation room adjacent to Baylie's classroom just before lunch. Baylie is informed by the advisory teacher that she has some 'special' toys for her to find on a tray which is placed on her desk. A toy is tapped three times on the tray and Baylie is asked if she can find the toy on the tray in front of her. Baylie moves her right hand towards the toy but withdraws it once she makes contact with the lip of the tray. The advisory teacher repeats the activity two more times and each time Baylie displays a similar response. There are a number of possible explanations for Baylie's response. It may be that:

- The routine of the assessment setting is unfamiliar to her (including the use of a tray which the QTVI has introduced for presenting objects).
- She may not find the activity sufficiently motivating.
- Other competing stimuli are more relevant to her.

Baylie's advisory teacher should be able to acknowledge, explore, and perhaps dismiss each of these (as well as other) possibilities through further functional assessments during subsequent visits. These visits will include observations of the sounds, people or objects that Baylie does respond to in the classroom. The functional assessment might seek to confirm that there is no impairment in her ability to hear sounds as well as to identify whether there are particular sounds that encourage her to reach towards a sound source. The assessment process will allow additional time for Baylie to process and respond to different sounds and might incorporate the use of video recording.

As Brown *et al.* (1998) acknowledge this is a difficult process. Careful analysis is required to determine which particular sensory stimulus is being responded to. It may be sound, smell, vibration or a combination of them all. They suggest that the three key questions are:

- What equipment/activities/people does the child show an interest in?
- What senses do they stimulate?
- Under what conditions, or in what context does the pupil respond?

By widening the scope of her assessment to other environments, the advisory teacher discovers that in other contexts there is evidence that Baylie can in fact *consistently* reach out to, locate, manipulate and explore different types of objects. The advisory teacher observes Baylie participating in a daily literacy session with two peers which is taken by the class Learning Support Assistant. The session relates closely to the current class topic on holidays and opportunities are provided for the three children in the group to participate in different types of sensory experiences which relate to this theme. Within the group routine Baylie is observed reaching out to a plastic tray placed onto her lap and, in response to a verbal prompt, she locates each of the objects which are presented separately to her in the tray (e.g. a small towel, an arm band, a sun hat). She is then observed independently manipulating each object with her hands, performing an action with the object in response to a verbal request (e.g. putting the sun hat onto her head) and then placing the object back onto the tray.

Baylie's responses to these particular types of sensory information are interpreted by the teacher using the levels outlined in *Vision for Doing* (see Figure 7.1 and Useful Resources section). In interpreting Baylie's responses, the advisory teacher observes that she appears to respond at a different level in different settings. She notes that Baylie responds at a higher level in a familiar situation with a group of peers and a known adult, than she does in an unfamiliar situation where novel sensory input is introduced by a relatively unknown adult.

Although this observation in itself provides interesting information about the child's performance in different types of environment, it also highlights the importance of ensuring that the nature of the social context is accounted for when interpreting assessment findings. The assessment of Baylie's responses suggests to the advisory teacher that with appropriate guidance from a familiar adult who supports her learning, Baylie can be assessed as functioning at the 'understands' level within the literacy activity, but when working with a less familiar adult who does not offer a similar level of support she is assessed as functioning at a lower level. The advisory teacher discusses her findings with the LSA and class teacher, and explores how her assessment of Baylie's use of touch can be incorporated within more meaningful contexts.

Summary

Assessment of children who have MDVI can be viewed as a means of trying to comprehend better how learners come to understand the world (Aitken and Buult-jens 1992). Practitioners working with children who have MDVI will need to understand the different approaches to assessment, and be able to select and use the types of assessment appropriate for each individual. Given the diverse range of needs in the population of children with MDVI a variety of procedures and approaches are required for accurately determining the developmental performance of a learner – no single assessment procedure is appropriate for every situation.

Observation provides a valuable tool for unlocking the potential of children who have MDVI and it is important to have a framework within which to observe behaviours and to interpret them appropriately. Each of a child's adult partners will need therefore to develop appropriate skills in observing and recording behaviours, as well as sharing their observations with others.

Recommended reading

Aitken, S. (1995) 'Educational assessment of deafblind learners', in Etheridge, D. (ed.) *The Education of Dual Sensory Impaired Children: recognising and developing ability.* London: David Fulton.

Buultjens, M. (1997) 'Functional vision assessment and development in children and young people with multiple disabilities and visual impairment', in Mason, H., McCall, S., Arter, A., McLinden, M. and Stone, J. (eds) *Visual Impairment Access to Education for Children and Young People*. London: David Fulton.

Douglas, G. and Dickens, J. (1996) 'The development of early tactile reading skills', in Bozic, N. and Murdoch, H. (eds) *Learning Through Interaction*. London: David Fulton.

Langley, M. B. (1986) 'Psychoeducational assessment of visually impaired students with additional handicaps', in Ellis, D. (ed.) *Sensory Impairments in Mentally Handicapped People*. London: Croom Helm.

McLinden, M. (1998) 'Assessment of children with multiple disabilities and a visual impairment', Supplement in *Eye Contact*, **21**, Summer.

Stillman, R. D. and Battle, C. W. (1986) 'Developmental assessment of communicative abilities in the deaf-blind', in Ellis, D. (ed.) *Sensory Impairments in Mentally Handicapped People*. London: Croom Helm.

Tilstone, C. (ed.) (1998) *Observing Teaching and Learning: principles and practice*. London: David Fulton.

Tobin, M. J. (1994) *Assessing Visually Handicapped People: an introduction to test procedures*. London: David Fulton.

Tobin, M. J. (1996) 'Optimising the use of sensory information', in Bozic, N. and Murdoch, H. (eds) *Learning Through Interaction*. London: David Fulton.

CHAPTER 8

Interpersonal Communication Through Touch

Introduction

Touch has been described as 'our first language' because it serves as the primary system for our earliest contacts with the world (Royeen and Lane 1991). Touch continues to play a role in the development of receptive and expressive communication throughout infancy, but its role changes as vision, hearing and language develop. For some children however, sensory, physical and/or cognitive impairments can render conventional methods of interpersonal communication inaccessible and touch continues to play a key role in communicative acts (Hendrickson 1997).

Of all the modalities that are used in communication it can be argued that touch is the most intimate. Huss (1977) illustrates the power of touch in communication:

> Touching involves risk. It is a form of non-verbal communication and, therefore, may be misunderstood by one or both parties involved. It invades intimate space and may be a threat. If we are not in tune with ourselves and the one we touch, it may be inappropriate. However, non-touch may be just as devastating at a time when words are insufficient or cannot be processed appropriately because of disintegration of the individual. (p. 305)

The purpose of this chapter is to explore how touch is used in communication with and by children who have MDVI. We begin with a discussion of the potential impact of visual impairment on the early development of communication, then review the role of the adult as a communication partner in supporting the learning experiences of children with multiple disabilities, and conclude with a discussion of a number of tactile systems which are used to develop children's early communication.

Early communication and visual impairment

Communication may be regarded as a two-way process that is reliant on at least one of the communication partners recognising the communication attempts of the other, assigning meaning to them, and responding to their behaviours 'as if' they had communicative value (Dunst and Lowe 1986). For children who are fully sighted, vision usually plays a central role in establishing early communication signals such as facial expressions and body gestures. As we have already discussed, much of a sighted child's learning and interaction with the world is based on visual cues, and studies of early non-verbal interactions between mothers and sighted babies consistently emphasise the importance of eye contact and facial expression in developing communication.

Hendrickson (1997) notes that the extent of the impact a visual impairment has on early communication will be influenced by a number of factors including the

- degree and type of visual impairment;
- degree and type of additional disabilities;
- knowledge, skills and attitudes of communication partners;
- structure of the learning environment.

Children who are blind need a carefully ordered and structured environment based upon non-visual references. When considering differences in the environment in the early stages of communication development, Warren (1994) suggests that while the environment for the blind child is not completely different, it is significantly different from that of the sighted child, and can serve to influence the communication exchange.

Adult partners working with children who have MDVI will need to be aware of the importance of non-visual responses, such as the use of touch and voice. Indeed, Best (1992) argues that any *physical* contact with a child who has MDVI may constitute an act of communication:

> When facial expression and tone of voice are too sophisticated (through learning difficulties) or inaccessible (through sensory impairments), then touch is the primary channel of communication for the children. Information and emotions will be conveyed through touch and so the adult will need to ensure that the intended message is being conveyed. It is easy, for example, for an uneducated, dithering touch to express uncertainty and lack of interest. Communication through touch can express patience, tolerance, affection, impatience and firmness as well as specific requests for actions. Effective communication requires careful thought as to how the child is held, pushed, guided, pulled, manipulated and it also requires careful observation of the child's responses. (p. 119)

Miles (1998) highlights the importance of the hands in the development of communication for children who are deafblind. She proposes that an adult working with these children will need to become especially sensitive to hands, learning how to 'speak the language of the hands to the hands' as well as 'read the language of the hands from the hands' (p. 1). We consider the role of the hands in supporting a child's communication through touch later in this chapter.

Role of communication partner

The role of the adult as a child's communication partner assumes greater significance in enabling the child to make sense of the world in the absence of consistent information through the distant senses of vision and/or hearing. One function of the communication partner might be, for example, to increase the tactual and auditory experiences available to the child to provide a 'joint experience' (Warren 1994). The adult needs to recognise that any behaviour can be *potentially* communicative and part of the role of the communication partner will be to help shape communicative behaviours. Thus communication partners can help to transform behaviours which are *responses* to experiences into actual *communications* about those experiences (Goldbart 1988).

Hendrickson (1997) notes that a skilled partner is one who can adapt and switch modes and techniques according to the context of the communication. This is supported by Siegel-Causey and Downing (1987), who suggest that a skilled partner can:

- develop nurturance by becoming aware of the child's needs and preferences;
- enhance sensitivity through recognising and responding to non-symbolic behaviours;
- sequence experience by establishing routines and providing turn taking opportunities;
- increase opportunities by creating needs and choices;
- utilise movement by responding to body movement and using movement as a form of communication.

We know that many children who have multiple disabilities may not be able to access 'formal' communication systems such as speech or manual signing. The onus is then on the child's communication partner to recognise and accurately interpret the meaning of unconventional messages from the child. For example, when pushing Chloe, a young girl who has MDVI, on a swing, the teaching assistant observes Chloe tapping her hand on the chain. The tapping action may be described as a form of 'unconventional' communication, which is 'intentional' in that it might indicate that Chloe wants to continue being pushed. The skill of the adult will be to observe and respond to such intentional communications. However, it is important to recognise that Chloe's tapping may also be non-intentional and as such have no communicative intent. A further skill of the adult will be to observe repeated non-intentional actions and seek to give these communicative value. In this particular example the teaching assistant could interpret this repeated tapping action as Chloe wanting 'more swinging', and consistently feed this interpretation back to her verbally (e.g. 'Chloe, do you want *more* swinging?') followed by a push on the swing.

Given the challenges that accurate interpretation of early communicative acts can pose to a child's communication partner it will be helpful to have a framework for the collation and sharing of information. Useful protocols are provided in *Assessing Communication Together* (Bradley 1991) and the 'Affective Communication Assessment' (ACA) (Coupe *et al.* 1985), each of which were discussed in Chapter 7.

The development of symbolic communication

The expression 'non-symbolic communicative behaviours' usually refers to our use of gesture, facial expression, body movement, tone of voice and vocalisation in interpersonal exchanges. 'Symbolic' communication differs in that it enables us to refer to events or objects that are not physically present and so symbolic communication is not 'context-bound' (Rowland and Schweigert 1989: 226). Symbols may take the form of spoken or written words, sign language or pictures and so they provide the communicator with access to a much wider range of communication options.

Research relating to pupils with MDVI highlights the challenges some children face in progressing from pre-symbolic communication to formal symbolic systems but suggests that with an appropriate communication system and consistent support such a transition is possible. For the purpose of this discussion we have broadly divided symbols into those which are *permanent* (i.e. exist in a tangible form) and those which are *transitory* (i.e. exist in a temporary form). Examples of different types of these symbols are presented in Figure 8.1.

Some of these symbol systems can be readily designed or adapted to incorporate a tactile component. For example, a 'sign' can be made on a part of the child's body, or a picture symbol can be raised to allow the child to feel it. In the next section we provide a summary of a number of different tactile systems which are used with individuals who have multiple disabilities. We begin with a discussion of 'tactile cues' and consider their role in supporting a child's learning.

Permanent symbols	Transitory symbols
Pictures, photographs, drawings *Tactile diagrams/drawings* 'Pictorial' symbol systems (e.g. Bliss, Makaton symbols, Rebus, Picture communication symbols, Compics, Sigsymbols) Print letters *Tactile codes (e.g. braille, Moon)* *Object symbols (e.g. objects of reference)*	Manual sign language (e.g. BSL, Makaton signs) *Deafblind manual alphabet* *Co-active signs (e.g. hand-over-hand Makaton signs)* *Body signs (e.g. Canaan Barrie)*

Figure 8.1 Examples of 'permanent' and 'transitory' symbols (symbols in italics incorporate a tactile component)

Tactile cues

As we noted in earlier chapters, one defining feature of children who have MDVI is their dependence, to a greater or lesser degree, on others to structure their learning experiences. Children with MDVI will often rely on direct physical support from an adult before they can achieve a task such as manipulating an object. The terms 'cues' and 'prompts' are frequently used interchangeably when describing the support provided by a child's partner within an interaction. However, each term does have a specific meaning, and a useful distinction is made by Goold and Hummell (1993), who note that whereas cues 'suggest' the learner's course of action, prompts are used to 'direct' a specific course of action. They propose that prompts can be divided into:

- **response prompts**, which *direct* the learner's behaviour through, for example, the use of modelling or physical guidance, and the use of verbal prompts;
- **stimulus prompts**, which are props used by the adult to encourage the desired response, for example a picture of a person cleaning their teeth can be used as a stimulus to prompt the child to clean his or her own teeth.

Different types of cues are used when working with children who have learning difficulties, and a range of examples is provided in Figure 8.2.

In practice, the cues that appear in Figure 8.2 can be employed in a variety of ways during the course of interactions with a child and in various combinations.

Type of cue	Description/example
Auditory cue	Communication partner activates the auditory association for the activity or event, for example: partner *jangles car keys* as asks 'Do you want to come for a *drive in the car*?'
Gestural cue	Communication partner pairs speech with natural pantomime, for example: partner *holds out arms and leans forward* as asks 'Would you like to *come up*?'
Olfactory cue	Communication partner ensures the individual has the opportunity to detect odours associated with an activity, for example: partner gently *waves Marmite under nose* as says 'Mmmm, how about some *Marmite toast*?'
Routine cue	Learner had her communication partners move through a 'set' timetable of meaningful activities/events that are repeated daily with minimal change to assist memory and anticipation. If the individual has representation or symbolisation, the instructor may use object or pictorial timetables to heighten the individual's awareness, anticipation and comprehension of the day's activities.
Tactual cue	Communication partner gently places the object of direct meaning to the activity onto the learner, for example: partner *places spoon gently on lower lip* while saying 'Here's some *soup*.'
Verbal cue	Communication partner's speech and intonation suggest individual's course of action, for example: partner suggests 'Let's go for a walk' (cue to stand up).
Visual cue	Communication partner *displays the real object associated with the activity, for example: partner displays swimming costume* as suggests 'Want to go *swimming*?'

Figure 8.2 Natural cues used by adult partner whilst supporting a child's learning (adapted from Goold and Hummell 1993)

Informal (i.e. non-standardised) tactile or 'touch' cues are often accompanied by verbal cues. For example, the adult partner might touch a child lightly on the shoulder whilst using the key words SIT DOWN each time he or she wants the child to sit down. Buekelman and Mirenda (1992) propose that touch cues should routinely be accompanied by spoken words at each step in an activity. They stress the importance of a consistent approach, suggesting for example that when greeting the child, all partners should touch the child on the same shoulder in the same manner and that touch is paired with speech.

As we saw earlier any form of touching has the potential to be a communicative act but we have to realise that the same *form* of touch might serve a range of different *functions*. If we silently take a child's hands into ours we can be giving:

- reassurance (don't worry, everything is OK);
- confirmation of presence (I'm sitting here);
- a cue to begin an activity (let's start a game);
- feedback to child (well done);
- admonishment (don't hit).

The meaning will vary according to a number of factors such as the location of the touch, how the child is touched (e.g. softly or tightly) and the context of the touch. There is plenty of room for confusion here and this confusion can be amplified if different types of tactile information are presented to the child simultaneously, for example, if the adult places one hand on the child's shoulder and holds the child's wrists with the other (you may wish to try this on a willing colleague or friend!).

The need for a more consistent approach to providing touch cues led to two therapists working with individuals who have multiple disabilities in Australia, to develop a system of 'Touch-Speech Cues' (Goold and Hummell 1993), a summary of which is presented below.

Touch-Speech Cues

Touch-Speech Cues are defined as 'a simultaneous touch-speech production in which the communication partner pairs a target word for comprehension with a specific touch signal on the individual's body or limb to provide a multi-sensory cue' (Goold and Hummell 1993: 6).

An example is given of the child's teacher using the word 'handcream' as a 'target word' in combination with a touch cue (gently rubbing the child's hand in circular motion) to alert a child to a forthcoming activity which the child enjoys, i.e. having handcream rubbed into his or her hand. The target words for inclusion in a programme are words that the child's partners feel are important ones in the child's environment but ones which the child does not yet understand. In this sense, target words are selected as desirable key words for the child to learn to recognise and understand (examples include 'lunchtime', 'sit down', 'stand up', etc.).

Goold and Hummell (1993) propose that Touch-Speech Cues be considered as a possible strategy for assisting individuals with multiple disabilities to comprehend target words or key phrases, and recommend they are used when one or more of the groups of characteristics summarised in Figure 8.3 is evident.

However, the authors of this approach warn that Touch-Speech Cues will not be appropriate for all individuals with multiple disabilities, and consider Touch-Speech Cue programmes to be inappropriate if:

---

1 Individual is 'non-symbolic'. He or she:

- has limited recognition of voices;
- does *not* appear to differentiate intonation patterns;
- does *not* appear to respond to own name;
- does *not* demonstrate understanding of frequently occurring words or phrases.

---

2 Individual is 'non-symbolic'. He or she:

- recognises familiar voices;
- differentiates intonation patterns;
- recognises own name;
- does not demonstrate understanding of frequently occurring words and phrases.

---

3 Individual who has emerging symbolisation. He or she:

- recognises familiar voices;
- differentiates intonation patterns;
- responds to own name;
- inconsistently demonstrates an understanding of frequently occurring words and phrases.

Figure 8.3 Characteristics used to determine suitability for a programme which incorporates Touch-Speech Cues (adapted from Goold and Hummell 1993)

- the individual is responsive to *natural* cues which can be better utilised for the activity/action/event;
- touch of all types and forms has been demonstrated in assessment to be *distressing* to the individual;
- communication partners are unable to implement Touch-Speech Cues *consistently*;
- the individual is unable to *attend* to a Touch-Speech Cue. 'Protective' and/or 'nurturing' touch may be used instead to assist the learner to gain control over the behaviour prior to use of a Touch-Speech Cue.

Goold and Hummell (1993) note that a Touch-Speech Cue programme is but one of a range of receptive communication strategies which may be used by a communication partner to 'facilitate an individual's attention to, recognition and comprehension of spoken language' (p. 43). They recommend, therefore, that prior to the introduction of such a programme an assessment is carried out of the child's performance across a wide range of environments and activities that are meaningful to the child and his/her partners:

Such detailed information is essential to determine the suitability of Touch-Speech Cue programmes. If Touch-Speech Cues are suitable, this information is used to develop that programme. If Touch-Speech Cues are viewed as unsuitable, this information provides the basis for developing alternative communication programmes. (Goold and Hummell 1993: 45)

For a more detailed discussion of the use of Touch-Speech Cues, you should refer to the work of Goold and Hummell (1993).

Tactile sign systems

A significant restriction in the sense of vision can sometimes make it difficult for children to differentiate the finer distinctions in more 'formal' signing systems (i.e. systems which follow recognised conventions). Makaton, for example, is a system widely used in special schools for children with severe learning difficulties. It was developed originally to provide communication for 'deaf, mentally handicapped hospitalised adults' (Walker 1985: 1) but has since been revised and adapted to cover the needs of children and adults with a wider range of special needs. As well as signs Makaton also incorporates a system of graphic symbols, a useful summary of which can be found in Detheridge and Detheridge (1997).

The standard signs used in Makaton were selected from British Sign Language (BSL) but their appropriateness for children who have MDVI has at times been questioned. Some practitioners argue for example that as Makaton signs draw upon a visual frame of reference there is potential for confusion between a number of the signs. For example, the Makaton sign for GOOD (as well as OK and HELLO) is a 'thumbs up' gesture. The sign for BAD (as well as NAUGHTY) is a raised little finger. To a child who has a visual impairment the distinction between the raised thumb and the little finger may be difficult to spot.

This is one reason why alternative or modified systems incorporating a distinct *tactile* component have been developed for children who have a visual impairment. The criteria for selecting a particular system are complex and outside the remit of this text. Needless to say, they include a variety of factors, including the traditions and practice of the school, the child's level of receptive and expressive communication, as well as the nature and degree of the sensory impairment. Although a variety of tactile systems are currently used when developing the communication of children who have multiple disabilities (Chen *et al.* 2000), we consider briefly below three commonly used techniques, namely 'hand-on-hand', 'co-active' (or 'hand-over-hand') and 'body signs'.

Hand-on-hand techniques

'Hand-on-hand' techniques (also referred to as 'hand-under-hand') are used to encourage both receptive and expressive communication. To receive meaning the child may place his or her hand on or under the partner's hand and the partner signs onto the child's hand. The child then expresses meaning by signing onto the partner's hand. An example of this type of technique is the manual alphabet used for communicating with individuals who are deafblind (Figure 8.4).

Co-active signs

In a 'co-active', or 'hand-over-hand' approach, the child's partner physically guides the child's hand/s to help the child to produce a sign. This type of co-active signing can be particularly useful during the early stages of signing, as well as with children who have restrictions in their manual abilities. A number of the Makaton signs have been adapted so that they can be performed co-actively using a hand-over-hand technique. An example is given in Figure 8.5 in which the adult partner verbally informs the child that the handwashing activity is finished, and augments this with the Makaton hand-over-hand sign for the keyword FINISH.

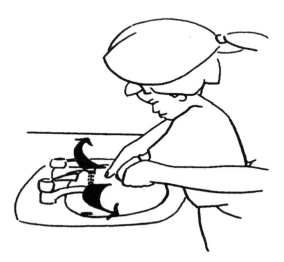

Figure 8.5 *We've finished washing our hands.* In this example the child's partner verbally informs the child that the hand-washing activity is finished and augments this with the Makaton hand-over-hand sign for the keyword FINISH

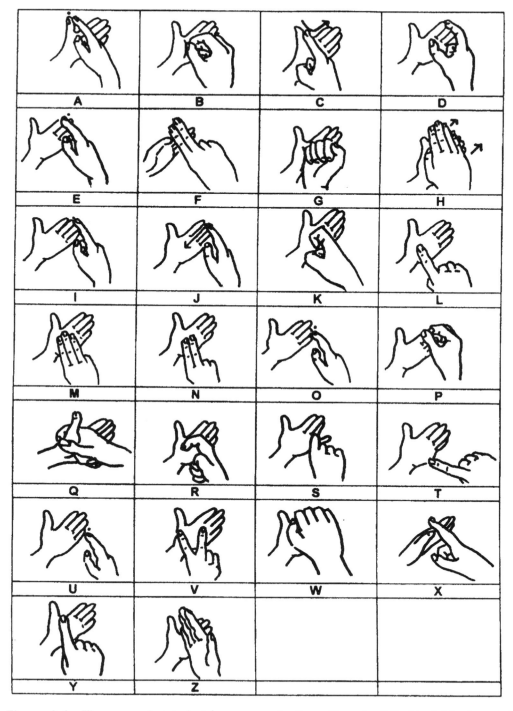

Figure 8.4 The manual alphabet for communicating with a deafblind individual – adult 'signs' onto child's hand (adapted from RNIB publicity leaflet 1995)

Body signs

Body signs are generally signed on areas of the body other than the child's hands. 'Canaan Barrie Signs' are a relatively recent development and include a number of body signs. They were originally designed as part of a broad interactive communication programme at a special school for children with MDVI in Scotland. The authors (Lee and MacWilliam 1995, 2002) based their approach on the observation that children who have MDVI find it difficult to construct signs which are 'made out in space':

> The main thing they seem to require is a point of contact on the body, and most of the signs we have adapted have taken this into consideration. Even children at a more advanced stage of communication when inventing their own signs, nearly always require a reference point on the body. (1995: 29)

British Sign Language (BSL) is used as the basis for the system, but the signs have been adapted to provide maximum tactile feedback and the authors advocate a 'multi-sensory' approach to maximise the use of the child's unimpaired sensory channels. The initial vocabulary comprises approximately 50 signs relating to the needs and activities that arise in the child's daily routine. The programme is based on three main stages, although the authors stress that these are not sequential and, depending on their level of communicative understanding, some children may be able to use elements from different levels of the programme out of sequence. Further, it is argued that once a child has acquired a number of signs, then it might be possible to consider transferring the child to a standardised sign system:

> Whether a child progresses to a standardised signing system like Makaton or British Sign Language, or whether he will continue to need an adapted sign vocabulary, depends very much on the child's communicative ability and degree of sight ... it is our experience that even children with some vision still seem to need the kind of additional tactile and auditory feedback that these adapted signs offer. (Lee and MacWilliam 1995: 31)

This approach has recently been updated (Lee and MacWilliam 2002) and further details are provided in the Useful Resources section.

Summary

The child with multiple disabilities and a visual impairment will have difficulty in influencing the environment and so will be more reliant on others to provide changes in activity and stimulation. The overall aim of the child's communication partner will be to ensure that appropriate and structured stimulation is provided within an interactive context. It is not possible to develop a single strategy suitable for use by all children who have MDVI and therefore the communication system which is selected should be one that will encourage interactions which are consistent, safe and reliable and which provide the child with opportunities to respond appropriately. In providing a structured system of communication a range of different approaches will be incorporated within a programme. We have discussed in this chapter a number of 'transitory' symbols and cues which incorporate a tactile component. The use of more 'permanent' tactile symbols is considered further in Chapter 9.

Recommended reading

Coupe, J., O'Kane, J. and Goldbart, J. (1998) *Communication Before Speech: development and assessment.* London: David Fulton.

Detheridge, T. and Detheridge, M. (1997) *Literacy Through Symbols.* London: David Fulton.

Goold, L. and Hummell, J. (1993) *Supporting the Receptive Communication of Individuals with Significant Multiple Disabilities: selective use of touch to enhance comprehension.* North Rocks, Australia: North Rocks Press.

Hendrickson, H. (1997) 'Development of early communication', in Mason, H., McCall, S., Arter, A., McLinden, M. and Stone, J. (eds) *Visual Impairment Access to Education for Children and Young People.* London: David Fulton.

Lee, M. and MacWilliam, L. (1995) *Movement Gesture and Sign: an interactive approach to sign communication for children who are visually impaired with additional disabilities.* London: RNIB.

Lee, M. and MacWilliam, L. (2002) *Learning Together.* London: RNIB.

Miles, B. (1998) 'Talking the language of the hands to the hands', Monmouth, OR: *DB-Link.* The National Information Clearinghouse on Children who are Deafblind (www.tr.wou.edu/dblink).

Miles, B. and Riggio, M. (1999) *Remarkable Conversations: a guide to developing meaningful communication with children and young adults who are deafblind.* Watertown, MA: Perkins School for the Blind.

Pease, L. (2000) 'Creating a communicating environment', in Aitken, S., Buultjens, M., Clark, C., Eyre, J. and Pease, L. (eds) *Teaching Children who are Deafblind.* London: David Fulton.

For further information on Makaton, contact:

Makaton Vocabulary Development Project (Registered Charity No. 287782), 31 Firwood Drive, Camberley, Surrey GU15 3QD. Tel: 01276 61390; Email: mvdp@makaton.org; Website: www.makaton.org

CHAPTER 9

Tactile Symbols and Early Literacy

Introduction

In Chapter 8 we looked at a range of symbols which are used to develop communication in children who have MDVI, making a broad distinction between those which are transitory in nature and incorporate a tactile component (e.g. tactile signs such as 'hand-over-hand' Makaton signs), and those which exist in a permanent form (e.g. object symbols). We considered the relevance of a number of types of systems to children who have MDVI and noted that the approach that is selected will be influenced by a range of factors including the type of the school the child attends as well as the abilities of the individual learner.

Depending on the degree of their visual impairment, in the course of a school day children with MDVI might encounter a range of 'permanent' symbols within their environment including pictures, drawings, photographs, print letters, tactile letters as well as signs on doors. In this chapter we develop our discussion of the use of these symbols with a particular focus on those which incorporate a tactile component such as object symbols, tactile pictures and tactile codes. Following a general discussion of the nature of such symbols we consider their relevance for children who have MDVI. We then explore the process of developing literacy through touch and consider how children with a visual impairment come to find out that symbols carry meaning and can be used to represent people, objects, places or events as part of the emergence of literacy. Within this discussion we consider in some detail the role of the adult partner in relation to the emergence of literacy for children who have MDVI.

What are symbols?

Symbols form an important part of our daily lives and we use them in a variety of ways to help us to access different types of information. For example, consider the range of different symbols that we use when attempting to find a particular house in an unfamiliar town a long way away. If we are using a road map we will need to be able to recognise the numbers and letters that tell us which motorway we need to go on and then be able to match them up with the overhead signs when we are on the road. We will need to recognise the representations of a bed, knife and fork and understand that they signify the travel lodge where we want to break our journey. We'll need to understand how motorway junctions are indicated so we take the correct turn off. When we reach the town we will need to be able to read street names and when we reach the street we are looking for we will need to be able to identify the right name or number of the house. An important feature of all these symbols is that they all 'stand for' or 'represent' particular types of information. As such, symbols have been defined as 'an internal re-enactment (re-presentation) of the activities originally carried out with objects or events' (Bates 1976: 11).

When reviewing the use of symbols such as pictures, photographs and objects with pupils with limited communicative abilities, Karlan and Lloyd (1983) summarised their main advantages as follows:

- they are permanent;
- they only require the pupil to 'recognise' and not to 'recall';
- they can be manipulated and so can be used in a variety of situations;
- they can be used to reduce demands on motor skills;
- they are 'iconic' and have an obvious relationship to their referents.

The iconic relationship between a symbol and its referent is a key element in the successful selection and use of symbols and so we will look at it in more detail.

Symbols and iconicity

'Iconicity' is a term used to describe the nature of the relationship between a symbol and its 'referent' (what the symbol is referring to). Iconicity can occur at a number of levels. For example, a photograph of a real cup may be described as having a *higher* iconicity than a line drawing of a cup. Look at the line drawing of a cup in Figure 9.1.

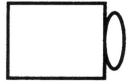

Figure 9.1   A simple line drawing of a cup used as a pictorial symbol to represent a real cup

This symbol of a cup is no more than a crude representation of those visual features which we commonly associate with a cup. Cups come in a multitude of shapes, sizes and textures and are used in a range of different contexts, but our symbol 'works' because we have a collective or shared understanding about what it represents. Another example of this shared understanding is found in the symbols of 'boys' and 'girls' used on the toilet doors of a school for children who have severe learning difficulties (Figure 9.2).

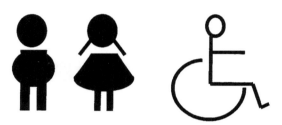

Figure 9.2   Examples of pictorial symbols used on toilet doors

These representations actually bear only a limited resemblance to the outfits worn by boys and girls in the school. However, the consensus about what these symbols stand for, or *re-present*, forms the basis for their use (with variations of course!) on toilet doors throughout the world.

However, Rowland and Schweigert (1989) make the important point that ultimately 'iconicity is in the eyes (or hands) of the beholder' (p. 228), noting that what may seem like an obvious relationship between a symbol and a referent to one person may not be so obvious to another, particularly if that other person has impaired vision and is more reliant on touch to process information.

Musselwhite and St. Louis (1982) used the terms 'representational' and 'abstract' to define the iconicity of a symbol:

- 'representational' describes symbols which are predominantly iconic and bear an obvious perceptual relationship to a referent, e.g. a picture of a drink or an object of reference (perhaps a real cup) to represent DRINK;
- 'abstract' is used to describe symbols where there is no obvious relationship to a referent and an artificial association has been developed, e.g. an abstract shape such as a triangle to represent DRINK. Formal symbolic language codes such as print or braille would be classified in this category. The written word CUP could be described as a collection of three individual abstract symbols each with low iconicity.

For someone who relies upon touch, tactile symbols which are adapted from visual symbols (e.g. raised Makaton symbols, raised line pictures, etc.) may have very low iconicity. For users who are fully sighted, the symbols in these systems bear an obvious relationship to their referents (consider for example, a line drawing of a house). However, when visual symbols are raised into tactile form and processed through touch, we can no longer assume this relationship holds true. On the contrary, symbols considered to be 'representational' when accessed through vision, may indeed become 'abstract' when accessed through touch!

Symbol systems

When grouped together in systems, symbols can be used to develop early communication. Communication systems can be used either to support speech (Augmentative Communication Systems), or in place of speech (Alternative Communication Systems). Collectively these systems are commonly termed Augmentative and Alternative Communication or 'AAC'. Lloyd and Blischak (1992) define augmentative communication as 'an approach which is clearly an addition to speech or writing' whereas alternative communication is used to refer to 'an approach that is clearly a substitute for (or alternative to) natural speech and/or handwriting' (p. 106). Hendrickson (1997) notes that these systems may include the use of manual signing systems (such as Makaton signs discussed in Chapter 8) and objects of reference, as well as other types of tactile symbols such as braille or Moon. If the child does not then go on to use spoken language effectively, the same forms may later provide a main means of expression, or may be used to support the child's attempts at spoken communication.

All AAC systems employ a system of representation. This may be composed of letters, words, pictures, graphic symbols, objects or speech units (which are commonly recorded and activated through an electronic device).

As already noted, a broad distinction can be made between visual and tactile symbols used in these systems. Whereas visual symbols exist in a pictorial or written form, such as a photograph, drawing, or a printed word, tactile symbols incorporate a third dimension enabling them to be processed through touch. Tactile symbols can be used to help individuals with a visual impairment in a number of ways including:

- enabling access to low and high tech communication aids;
- as an aid to mobility, e.g. environmental markers and tactile maps in both school and residential settings;
- as part of daily living skills providing access to menus, timetables, etc.

We now provide a brief summary of a number of the more common tactile symbols which have been used in the education of children who have a visual impairment, including those with multiple disabilities.

Braille

In developing the early literacy skills of children with severe visual impairments the emphasis has traditionally been placed on teaching children appropriate skills through the medium of braille. We have known for some time that a significant proportion of pupils who are educationally blind are unable to use braille at all or use it very ineffectively (Chapman and McCall 1989; Lorimer 1978). As a tactile symbol system with a complex set of rules, braille requires advanced skills in perceptual and cognitive processing and so for many children with multiple disabilities and a visual impairment braille will be an inappropriate goal (Figure 9.3).

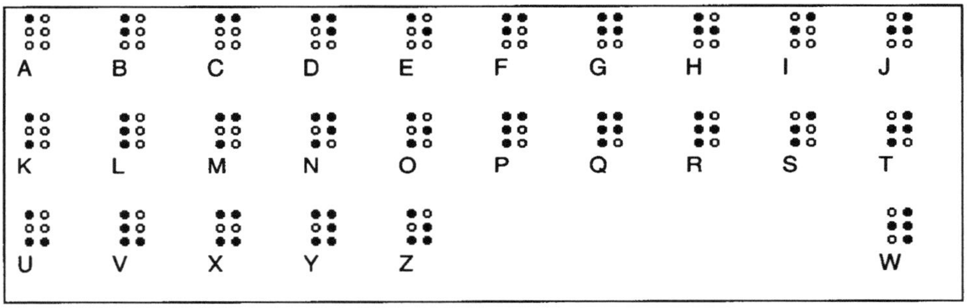

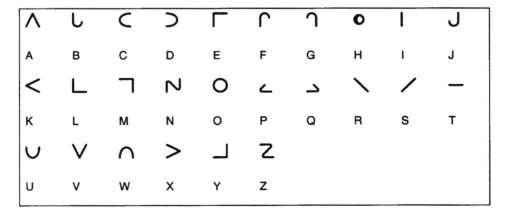

Figure 9.3   Grade 1 braille code

Moon

Moon is based on a simplified raised line version of the Roman print alphabet. It was devised in 1847 by Dr William Moon in Brighton and uses large and bold characters. Grade 1 Moon is presented in Figure 9.4.

Figure 9.4   Grade 1 Moon code

Despite the world-wide dominance of braille, Moon has survived partly because of its relative accessibility and simplicity. It found a valuable role among the elderly blind who lacked the agility of mind or hand to tackle the demanding task of learning braille. Moon is larger and bolder than braille and uses fewer contractions. As a result it takes up much more space than braille, and while its bulk makes Moon an inefficient medium for accomplished touch readers, for children and young people with a visual impairment and additional difficulties it can offer a number of distinct advantages:

- A Moon character presents a larger tactile stimulus than a standard braille cell and is therefore easier to feel. As Moon is a line-based code the characters can be enlarged without affecting their legibility (Figure 9.5).
- In comparison with braille Moon has relatively few rules and makes use of few contractions.
- Children who have once had vision or who have a deteriorating visual condition can utilise visual memory of print letters in learning the alphabet.
- Moon is an established code for blind adults which is supported by a number of national organisations for the blind, e.g. RNIB, National Library for the Blind.

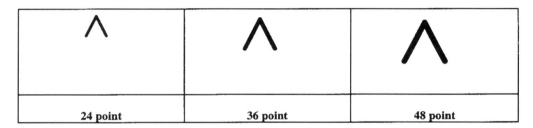

| 24 point | 36 point | 48 point |

Figure 9.5   Three different font sizes of the letter A in Moon

In the early 1990s research was conducted into the question of whether the Moon code could offer an alternative route to literacy for some children with a visual impairment and additional needs (McCall *et al*. 1994). The findings of this study suggested that while Moon could have an important role as a tactile medium in developing early literacy, the code also has a number of inherent disadvantages which may be particularly pertinent to children who have learning difficulties. For example the Moon alphabet is made up from a small number of basic shapes which rotate to provide different characters (i.e. the Moon letters L, E, Y, M). These rotations can lead to confusion when beginning to learn the code and suggest that a carefully structured teaching approach is required within which to introduce Moon letters (McCall *et al*. 1994).

In addition there is as yet no appropriate writing device which allows children and young people with additional difficulties to write Moon. Before embarking on a teaching programme, it is important to consider carefully the various methods available for the production of Moon and how accessible these are within the educational establishment. See the Useful Resources section for further information.

Parents and teachers need to be cautious and pragmatic about the potential of Moon for children. There is a wide range of children who are blind and who have learning difficulties. Their potential for achievement in literacy varies greatly according to the degree and nature of their abilities and disabilities. Moon has helped some of these children to develop their skills in communication by exploiting their ability to recognise a few raised symbols (McCall and McLinden 2001). This ability can be useful in simple activities such as making choices between items which have their first letter labelled on them in Moon (Figure 9.6).

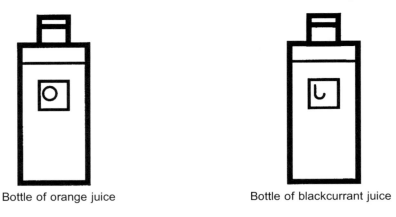

Bottle of orange juice   Bottle of blackcurrant juice

Figure 9.6   Moon letters used to label initial sounds of two types of juice in order for a child to make a meaningful choice

Many children will not, however, progress beyond this stage. A number of children may go on to develop the ability to recognise their own name in Moon. This can be useful for identifying personal belongings such as locating a coat on a rail. Only a very small number of children (most of whom already had spoken language skills) become able to recognise sufficient letters to 'read' basic words. Even so, most of these children will never become fluent readers and writers, but, as we consider later, Moon may help some of them to develop the early skills which are important in the emergence of literacy.

Object symbols/objects of reference

Object symbols (or objects of reference) have been defined as 'three dimensional iconic symbols that can be used to represent real objects or events' (Bloom 1990:

8), for example an armband may be used to represent the activity 'swimming'. If an object is consistently used in the context of a particular event, the child might learn to make an association between the object and the event. The object may also be presented with other objects of reference, for the purpose of making choices and requests. Despite a growing awareness of object symbols as a potential communication system for individuals with MDVI (Bloom 1990; Ockelford 2002), there is relatively little literature specifically concerned with their evaluation and use (Park 1995, 1997).

Object symbols have come to be seen as having particular relevance to children with multiple disabilities and a visual impairment and have proved useful in promoting communication skills because they can help reduce the cognitive demands in the communication process. For example, Bloom (1990) notes that object symbols have been found to be of particular value in developing the request function, which serves as a common starting point in the development of communication skills and involves the transition from non-symbolic to symbolic communication.

Murray-Branch *et al.* (1991) summarised the considerations that we should bear in mind when selecting object symbols including:

- tactile saliency (ease of recognition);
- types of objects preferred by child;
- whether the objects or tangible symbols can be reduced in size so that they are portable and can be used in a variety of settings;
- how easily the object or texture can be discriminated from others used in a group of tangible symbols.

However, as Millar and Aitken (1996) note, the intention in using object symbols is not to encourage 'a focus on the object per se but on the *representational* value conveyed by that object' (p. 122, italics added). Further information on the use of object symbols with children who have MDVI is provided in the Useful Resources section.

Tangible symbols

Tangible symbols were developed for use with individuals with 'multisensory impairments' (Rowland and Schweigert 1989) and are described as:

- permanent, i.e. requiring recognition rather than recall memory;
- manipulable, i.e. can be held by the user;
- requiring only a simple motor response, i.e. pointing or touching;
- tactually discriminable;
- iconic, i.e. bear an obvious perceptual relationship to a referent.

The terminology used to describe different types of tactile symbols can be confusing and in many respects tangible symbols are similar to objects of reference (or object symbols). However, applying the criteria presented above, the main distinction is their iconicity, i.e. while objects of reference *may* have a clear perceptual relationship to a referent, tangible symbols *must* have an obvious perceptual link (e.g. a front door key used as a symbol to represent the activity HOME). As with object symbols, research into the use of tangible symbols is limited, although work undertaken to date has demonstrated that they may have a role in helping individuals with multi-sensory impairments develop a viable communication system (Rowland and Schweigert 1989).

Raised pictorial symbols

Pictorial symbols, for example line drawings, have been raised and used on a largely ad hoc basis by practitioners working with children who have MDVI. An example is a black and white line drawing of a house to represent the activity HOME (Figure 9.7).

Figure 9.7   Raised pictorial symbol of a house to represent the activity HOME

As we noted earlier, as a visual representation the picture of the house can bear a clear iconic relationship to the referent, e.g. the house where the child lives. As a tactile representation, however, such a clear relationship may no longer be apparent and the individual may be confused by the tactile form which is basically a set of two-dimensional abstract shapes. As Best (1992) notes, any preparation and use of tactile material requires 'an appreciation of the process of tactile perception and a knowledge of the principles of tactile design' (p. 121). Before we incorporate a tactile component into a visual symbol, therefore, we will need to consider carefully the extent to which raised visual symbols relate to the particular needs of the child. We might also want to consider other types of symbols which have a more obvious iconic relationship with the referent. A simple example might be the use of real coins as a symbol on the front cover of a book about shopping rather than a raised visual representation of a shop.

Literacy through touch

Learning to recognise that symbols carry meaning and can be used to represent people, objects, places or events is an important stage in the emergence of literacy. Symbolic codes such as print, braille or Moon with a formal set of rules represent the summit of a range of symbolic systems. We need to be sure that the symbolic communication system we select is both relevant to the child's needs and compatible with the child's level of development.

It is useful to consider the development of literacy in children as part of a more general development of language and communication which encompasses reading, writing, speaking and listening and the development of a range of other skills. Recent research has given us a better understanding of the ways in which literacy develops in young children, and the view that literacy is simply concerned with the process of 'reading and writing' and involves learning skills of decoding symbols into recognisable sounds, is now seen as too narrow. Consider for instance the following sentence:

Bib had to rastile her shantles with the goosen in order to follise the liven.

Using your knowledge of syntax (described as the rules of grammar), it is possible to 'read' this sentence. However, your comprehension of the sentence will be limited by your lack of semantic awareness (described as meaning in language). Clearly, in order to make sense of this sentence you need not only to be able to decode each symbol in the form of a word and to be aware of the grammatical relationship between the symbols, but you also need to comprehend the meaning attached to each of these symbols. Adding meaning (see the 'dictionary' in Figure 9.8) will help the 'reader' to understand that, in order to make the dough, Bib first had to mix her ingredients with a whisk!

Meaningless word	Translation
rastile	mix
shantles	ingredients
goosen	whisk
follise	make
liven	dough

Figure 9.8   'Dictionary' to provide meaning to sentence '*Bib had to rastile her shantles with the goosen in order to follise the liven*'

Within a broad context, literacy can be viewed as beginning with the child's first interactions with the world and as continuing within the process of life-long development, similar in some respects to the process of walking and talking. The basic foundations of literacy are in place long before 'reading' and 'writing' take place and involve all aspects of the child's ongoing development. For example, we may not necessarily link movement with literacy, yet the development of both fine and gross motor skills allows children to explore and interact with the world, enabling them to build up a bank of experiences which in turn help them to understand stories (Stratton and Wright 1991).

The term 'emergence' is used by a number of authors to describe the way literacy emerges within certain contexts in young children. For example Hall (1987) notes that it is considered to be a useful description for a number of reasons:

- it implies that development takes place from within the child;
- 'emergence' is considered to be a gradual process and takes place over time;
- for something to emerge, there has to be something there in the first place, e.g. the abilities children have to make sense of the world;
- things usually only emerge if the conditions are right, e.g. in contexts which support, facilitate enquiry and provide opportunities for engagement in real literacy acts.

Stratton and Wright (1991) stress that literacy for a child with a visual impairment is the same gradual process of development as for the child who is sighted. It emerges from experiences which are relevant and meaningful to each child and begins as a general process of communication between adult and child. Children with a visual impairment need the same opportunities to learn as children who are fully sighted although for some children the 'emphasis or way of learning' may need to be different (Stratton and Wright 1999: xiii).

Although it can be argued that the learning processes are essentially the same for both fully sighted children and children with a visual impairment, there are additional, unique factors that must be taken into consideration when introducing literacy to this population (Rex *et al.* 1994). Thus, although a visual impairment need not necessarily affect *what* a child is taught, it may determine *how* something is taught. Olson (1981) stresses the need, therefore, for adults to make deliberate efforts to develop and refine sensory abilities in children with a visual impairment and suggests the following guidelines:

- the environment must be brought to the child in an organised, consistent and meaningful way;
- concepts must be taught in a similar fashion;
- understanding of basic concepts must stem from a child's personal interaction with the environment, rather than from rote memory (p. 33).

When we are considering a child's active engagement in literacy, it is useful to look at how we can arrange the environment so that the child's understanding about literacy can continue to emerge. Hall (1987) suggests the environment needs to meet three requirements if the emergence of literacy is to be continuous. It is an environment where:

1. Literacy has a high profile and status.
2. There is access to valid demonstrations of literacy.
3. There are opportunities to engage in purposeful literacy acts which are acknowledged as valid literacy behaviours.

To illustrate this final point consider a young child who brings to the attention of the adult a page of 'writing' produced on a braille machine which as yet does not resemble words. The adult may show his or her acceptance of the work by asking the child to read it aloud. The child's written work is, therefore, accepted as a valid demonstration of writing by the adult and this is clearly demonstrated to the child, highlighting the importance of the adult as a literacy partner in the early development of literacy. In developing this partnership it is helpful to have a clear description of:

- what literacy behaviours the child demonstrates to the adult;
- what literacy behaviours the adult accepts from the child, e.g. a consideration of the range of behaviours that might be acknowledged as 'valid' demonstrations of a child's literacy.

These points can be illustrated through Vignette 9.1 which focuses on Julie, a child of 11 years with a visual impairment and a range of additional disabilities, who is using Moon as a tactile medium to develop her literacy.

Vignette 9.1   Julie

Julie attends a school for children with severe learning difficulties. Using enlarged Moon letters (36 point) the teacher has been helping Julie to learn to recognise her own name and to distinguish this from the names of the five other children in the class. In describing Julie's literacy behaviours the teacher notes the following:

- she is consistently able to recognise the Moon letter 'J' in her name and in a range of other common words found in the classroom, e.g. JAM, JACK;
- she is beginning to learn that the letter 'J' makes a distinctive sound in her name which is different from the sounds made by other letters;
- she is beginning to understand that abstract symbols, in the form of Moon letters, have meaning and that each letter symbol has a specific sound associated with it;
- she can recognise that the first letter in her name is different from the first letter in other children's names.

In close partnership with her teacher Julie is using her emerging knowledge of letter symbols and sounds to begin recognising letters in her name. Although Julie might not yet be described as independently 'reading', she is clearly at an important stage in the process of developing her literacy and this is acknowledged by the teacher in recognising her literacy behaviours. Although still at an early stage in this process, Julie is beginning to learn that abstract symbols in the form of letter shapes can carry meaning in the form of sounds and that different letter shapes have different sounds. This knowledge can then be expanded upon by the teacher to help Julie to develop further her understanding of a range of symbols including letters and words.

The attainments of children like Julie in Vignette 9.1 can now be formally recognised as valid demonstrations of literacy within the National Curriculum. In 2001 the Department for Education and Employment (DfEE) and Qualifications and Curriculum Authority (QCA) (DfEE 2001) published guidelines which laid out Performance levels (P levels) to be used in planning, teaching and assessing the curriculum for children with learning difficulties. The P levels provide a framework which explicitly acknowledges behaviours such as: 'listen and respond to familiar rhymes and stories' (P4); 'select a few words, signs or symbols with which they are particularly familiar and derive some meaning from text, symbols or signs presented in a way familiar to them' (P5); 'select and recognise or read a small number of words or symbols linked to familiar vocabulary', as examples of reading.

Further, the recent guidelines for supporting the planning, development and implementation of the English curriculum for pupils with learning difficulties (QCA 2001b) define reading as:

> any activity that leads to the derivation of meanings from visual or tactile representations, *for example, objects, pictures, symbols or written words.* They may be accessed visually, aurally or through touch, *for example, looking at objects, pictures, symbols or words, feeling objects of reference, looking and listening to CD-ROMs or computer programmes, listening to an adult reading aloud or an audio tape.* (p. 7)

These developments offer a route to recognition for the hard-won attainments of children with MDVI against national standards within a more inclusive concept of literacy.

Summary

In this chapter we have explored the general nature of symbols and considered the relevance of a number of commonly used systems when developing programmes of literacy and communication for children who have MDVI. In general we have noted that the development of early literacy for this population requires a similar approach to that for sighted children although greater consideration will need to be given to the particular areas of development including perceptual skills and concept awareness as well as providing the child with opportunities for greater active exploration in the world. We can sum up the argument as follows:

- developing early literacy is broader than teaching a child reading and writing;
- literacy can be considered as an ongoing process of development and particularly within which the adult has a central role;
- the emergence of literacy in children with a visual impairment requires an emphasis on different skills and techniques when compared with sighted children.

The development of literacy offers an opportunity to engage with the child through active participation, to develop unique experiences and ideas which are relevant to each child's personal life and, therefore, has relevance to all children with a visual impairment. The main challenge for the adult working with the child as an effective partner will be to consider ways in which the emergence of literacy can be encouraged as part of an ongoing process which has relevance and meaning for each child.

Recommended reading

Bloom, L. (1990) *Object Symbols: a communication option*. North Rocks, Australia: The Royal New South Wales Institute for Deaf and Blind Children and North Rocks Press.

Detheridge, T. and Detheridge, M. (1997) *Literacy Through Symbols*. London: David Fulton.

DfEE (2001) *Supporting the Target Setting Process: guidance for effective target setting for children with Special Educational Needs*. London: DfEE.

Hendrickson, H. and McLinden, M. (1996) 'Using tactile symbols: a review of current issues', *Eye Contact* **14**, Spring, Supplement.

Koenig, A. J. (1992) 'A framework for understanding the literacy of individuals with visual impairments', *Journal of Visual Impairment and Blindness* **86**, 277–84.

McCall, S. and McLinden, M. (2001) 'Accessing the National Literacy Strategy: the use of Moon with children in the United Kingdom with a visual impairment and additional learning difficulties', *The British Journal of Visual Impairment* **19** (1), 7–16.

QCA (2001) *English: planning, teaching and assessing the curriculum for pupils with learning difficulties*. Sudbury, Suffolk: QCA Publications.

Rex, E. J., Koenig, A. J., Wormsley, D.P. and Baker, R.L. (1994) *Foundations of Braille Literacy*. New York: American Foundation for the Blind.

PART 3

FINISHING TOUCHES

CHAPTER 10
Mediating Experiences Through Touch

Introduction

At the start of this book we provided you with some simple activities to allow you to investigate your own use of touch. Since then we have taken you on a long journey. In the first part of the book we explored the nature of touch and the ways it provides us with information about the world, considering how the development of touch can be affected by loss of sight. In the second part of the book we examined techniques that adults can use to overcome the barriers to learning through touch in children with MDVI, and looked at issues such as communication, structuring the learning environment as well as assessment.

Inevitably, given the breadth of the topic our journey hasn't taken in all aspects of touch. For example, we have not considered to any great extent the role of massage, which is widely used as a technique with children who have profound learning difficulties. The role that Information and Communication Technology (ICT) can play in developing learning through touch for children with multiple disabilities is another important area that we have not looked at in detail (although we consider its broader implications in the next chapter). For those of you who wish to find out more about these and other areas we have not addressed in any depth, we have suggested some publications in the Useful Resources section.

In this chapter we are going to revisit the four themes we established in the Overview and review them in the light of what we have found out about touch, with a specific focus on the role of the adult partner who is central in supporting a child's learning. At the end of the chapter we will try to draw together these themes through their application to two short vignettes.

Theme 1   Sensory function

> The learning experiences of a child who has MDVI will incorporate a range of sensory information, some of which will be distorted in quality and/or quantity. In order to work effectively with the child, the adult partner requires knowledge and understanding of the child's level of sensory function, namely how the child receives, interprets and consequently acts upon different types of sensory information during a given task.

We began Chapter 1 by examining the question of which sense we would least like to lose. This question could be posed in another way – which of our senses is the most important? We have subsequently seen that this is a meaningless question. The processes through which we integrate and act upon sensory information are very complex and each sense has a unique role in providing us with different types of information about our functioning in the world. It can be argued, therefore, that no one sense is more or less important than another.

In the literature on visual impairment estimates can be found that suggest that 80–90 per cent of the information we receive comes through vision. However, even if this estimate is true (and it is hard to see how it can be proved) it must reflect the *quantity* rather than the *quality* of the information we receive. It is the reduction and the distortions in the *quality* of information that we receive from our senses that can also serve to create barriers to learning. By way of example, imagine you are in a very busy, noisy railway station and you are trying to listen for information about your train's departure time. Public address systems sometimes provide very loud information but it is often distorted and we can't make sense of the information. We are receiving sensory information which is 'high' in quantity but 'low' in quality and it actually serves to hinder rather than help us – a point we raised in Chapter 5.

We only need to think about how we use our senses in everyday situations to appreciate the complexity of the roles of the senses in relation to each other and to see why it is too simplistic to think of one as being more or less important in our learning than another. Our health and well-being often depends on non-visual information, for example our taste tells us that the milk has turned sour, our smell that there is gas leaking in another room, our hearing tells us that the fire alarm has gone off, our touch that the prickly label is scratching the back of our neck. Nevertheless we have seen that our vision does have a unique role in relation to our other senses, which is often referred to as an integrative role. We use it to check or make sense of the information we receive through our other senses, for example, we would look at the milk carton to check the sell-by date, or look for chafing on our neck in the mirror. Therefore it seems reasonable to conclude that children who have little or no vision will need additional input to link up the information they receive from their other senses, particularly if that information is distorted by additional disabilities. An important role of the adult partner can be considered as one of mediation, of helping the child integrate (i.e. link up and make sense of) the information that comes through the senses.

We have seen how multiple disabilities serve to restrict a child's independent exploration and understanding of the world. Children who are unable to gather sufficient quality of information from the environment to learn independently will consequently be more reliant on others to support their learning experiences. Further, we have argued that adults who work with children with MDVI need to understand the concept of sensory function, namely how the child receives, interprets and consequently acts upon different types of sensory information in a given task. Many children who have MDVI will have some functional vision (i.e. vision which can be used for doing things) and an accurate assessment of vision can help determine how this sense can be most effectively used to help them learn. However, in order to be really useful, we have seen how assessments need to take account of how children with MDVI use their senses in *combination* with each other to complete a task.

Sensory function is a complex concept and not all practitioners who support a child's learning will be familiar with it. However, all adults who work with the child have a responsibility to ensure that information of good quality is presented to the child in consistent ways that are relevant and have meaning to that particular individual. We have stressed how the combination of multiple disabilities affects each child differently and an obvious corollary of this is that those working with the child will need to know how to present information to the child of sufficient quality to optimise their sensory function.

Information about a child's sensory function can be presented to those who support the child's learning in a number of accessible formats. One example is through the use of 'Communication Passports' (Millar and McEwan 1993) which detail how the child can make best use of his or her different senses for communication and can be helpful for disseminating key information. Regularly updated 'Passports' are useful for all practitioners who work with children who have MDVI and provide a simple means of ensuring that information about the child is current and relevant.

Theme 2   Role of close and distance senses

In considering how a child processes and acts upon sensory information, a distinction can be made between information received from within the body and information which is external to the body. This external information can be broadly divided into information which informs us about the world which is relatively distant to our bodies (for example, through the distant senses of vision and hearing), and information which is close to the body (for example, through the close senses of touch and taste). In the absence of consistent information through the distant senses, the information received through the close senses increases in significance in a child's learning experiences.

Throughout this text we have made a broad distinction between the senses which provide us with knowledge about the world which is relatively 'distant' from our bodies, and senses which provide us with information about the world which is relatively close. Although this distinction is very simplistic (for example, smell, vision and hearing can provide us with information about *both* our close and our distant world) we have argued that it can offer a useful framework for understanding how a child interprets his or her sensory experiences through touch when the quality of information through the distance senses is distorted or when it is absent.

When information from vision (possibly in combination with hearing) is absent or reduced in quality, we become more dependent on the quality of information we receive through our close senses, including touch. We looked at some of the specific functions of touch in the early chapters of this book, and discussed their role in providing us with particular types of information about the world. As a further illustration of the increased significance that our close senses assume in the absence of vision, imagine that you have bumped your head hard on a rafter in a very dark attic. In the absence of visual information the information you receive through touch will increase in significance. After banging your head you might use your sense of touch to inspect your head for damage by feeling for lumps, or to see if it is wet with blood. You might also bring your hand to your mouth in order to taste whether there is blood on it. This is an unpleasant but valid example of the strategies we adopt to compensate for a temporary reduction in one or more of our senses.

Children who have little or no visual input also have to learn strategies which integrate the information from their remaining senses. This process is complicated by additional disabilities and we have argued throughout the book that the onus is on the child's partner to develop an understanding of how reliance on close senses affects children's access to the world. In part, this understanding comes from reading the literature and from professional practice, but we would argue that it can also be enhanced through an understanding of our own use of our close senses, and in particular our sense of touch. It is for this reason we have included so many opportunities for you to reflect on your own use of touch throughout this book. The adult's understanding of touch is a vital element in observing and correctly interpreting the child's responses in the learning environment. We will illustrate this idea in the vignettes at the end of this chapter.

Theme 3   Interpreting sensory experiences

For a child who is more reliant on information received through the close senses, his or her learning experiences can provide imprecise information about the world if they are not mediated at a level appropriate to the child's needs. This can have an important bearing on the child's knowledge and understanding of the world at critical stages in early development.

In the second part of this book we have been predominantly concerned with children who continue to operate at early stages of development throughout their school years. We looked in some depth at the development of children and considered the effects of the absence or the reduction in quality of visual information, and how this can be compounded by additional disabilities. Not least among the challenges that these children face is that the knowledge and understanding of the world that they have may not be recognised or understood, and that their attainments may go unnoticed.

Earlier in the book we discussed a number of frameworks for assessment which can provide valuable insights into a child's 'understanding' of the world. In Chapter 9 we also looked at National Curriculum documents for children with learning difficulties in relation to the issue of literacy. These documents include a framework for recognising attainment below Level 1 of the National Curriculum (Figure 10.1). This framework draws upon a number of the assessment procedures we introduced in Chapter 7 (Aitken and Buultjens 1992; McInnes and Treffry 1982), and offers a means of recognising and recording a child's attainment below Level 1 of the National Curriculum. As such, this framework can be of value in ensuring that the attainments of these children are recognised and recorded within a *national* structure that applies to all children, and may be an important step towards greater inclusive practice. We consider the use of this framework in helping to identify the role of the adult partner in supporting the child's learning experiences within Theme 4.

Level of attainment	Description
Encounter	Pupil is 'present' during experience. Encounters activities and experiences and may be passive or resistant. Any participation is fully prompted.
Awareness	Demonstrates 'awareness' that something has happened within an activity. May attend briefly to interaction with familiar person. May give intermittent reaction during experience.
Attention and response	Pupil attends and begins to respond – beginning of ability to distinguish between different people, objects, events and places.
Engagement	Demonstrates more consistent attention to, and is able to tell the difference between specific events in his or her surroundings.
Participation	Engages in sharing, taking turns and the anticipation of familiar sequences of events.
Involvement	Actively strives to reach out, join in or comment in some way on the activity itself or on the actions or responses of the other pupils.
Gaining skills and understanding	Gains, strengthens or makes general use of skills, knowledge, concepts or understanding that relate to experience of the curriculum.

Figure 10.1   Recognising attainment below Level 1 of the National Curriculum. Adapted from *General Guidelines* (QCA 2001a) and *Supporting the Target Setting Process* (DfEE 2001)

Theme 4   Mediating learning experiences

The child's adult partner will need to have knowledge and understanding of his or her role in mediating the child's learning experiences through each of the senses to ensure that these are appropriate to the child's individual needs.

We have argued throughout the book that a significant feature of children who have MDVI is their reliance on others to structure their environment in order to ensure *effective* learning experiences are provided. In mediating the child's sensory experiences each of the adult partners will require a clear understanding of his or her role in this process, and need to be able to work collaboratively to ensure that the child's learning experiences are consistent and meaningful. We discussed some of these issues in relation to a child's learning through touch when we looked at the use of Touch-Speech Cues in Chapter 8.

Although the focus of the framework presented in Figure 10.1 is very much on the responses demonstrated by the child, it also helps to identify the role of the adult partner in supporting the child's learning experiences. At the earliest levels the adult will have a major role to play in ensuring the child is able to physically participate in an experience. At the level of **encounter** all participation will need to be fully prompted and the adult will be required to employ a range of prompts (including physical, auditory, verbal, tactile and possibly visual prompts) to enable the child to participate in the activity. An example of this is the use of hand-over-hand activities to direct the child's attention to an object. At this level, described as P1(i) in the Performance Descriptions, responses from the child are considered to be mainly reflexive. As such the adult's hand may need to be in direct physical contact with the child's hand throughout the learning experience as they jointly examine the object.

At the next level, **awareness**, the child is described as demonstrating emerging awareness of activities and experiences. The child may have periods when he or she appears to 'be alert' or 'focus attention' on people, events, objects or parts of objects and may, for example, be able to attend briefly to interactions with a familiar person. Participation does not need to be fully prompted at this level, although the child will still be very dependent on the adult to structure his or her learning experiences. In terms of touch, the adult may be offering hand-over-hand support, possibly to direct a child's hand to an object (or indeed introduce an object to the child), but the child may be able to spend brief periods *independently* touching the object. During each successive level within the framework the child is described as demonstrating increasingly independent responses to events in the environment, including active participation in social activities, and the input from the adult will also need to shift to reflect this greater level of independence.

The introduction of the Performance Descriptions for target setting has not been without its critics, and particularly at the earliest stages of development, it has been argued that attempting to group highly complex behaviours into 'best fit' categories does not really do justice to, or acknowledge the independent learning styles of each child. However, the basic principle of a hierarchy of learning, within which there is progression from relative dependence on others to a greater degree of individual autonomy and independence within a learning experience, is one that is well established. It would be illogical to exclude children with MDVI from the National Strategies concerned with promoting excellence for *all* children and this attempt to link in children's learning to national frameworks is a desirable goal. As we have seen, frameworks adopted for assessment continue to evolve, but effective learning depends on the adults' knowledge of the child's individual needs and his or her ability to connect or mediate a given experience at a level which is appropriate to these needs.

Putting it together

In our final vignettes we use some of the ideas we have discussed here and in earlier chapters to consider how adults in a school setting might work together to respond to the challenge of optimising the learning environment. We begin with John, a 9-year-old who attends a day special school (Vignette 10.1).

Vignette 10.1   John

Originally designated as a school for children with physical disabilities, John's school now caters for children with a wide range of additional special needs including sensory impairments and severe learning difficulties. John has light perception, cerebral palsy which affects the use of his hands for grasping and manipulating objects, and is described as having severe learning difficulties. He is non-ambulant and uses a wheelchair for getting about within the school. Considering what we have learnt in the course of reading this book, in what ways can touch be used to help John to optimise his learning? We will begin with a focus on his close tactile environment and will pan outwards from John's worktop to his classroom, and then to the school and finally to the world outside of school.

John's worktop

We have seen that learning can be considered as an experience based upon social interaction and that adults play a vital role in structuring the environment to maximise learning opportunities. John is fortunate in that he has a learning support assistant (LSA) and a classroom teacher who are attuned to his needs. They receive regular support from an advisory teacher of the visually impaired who has based her approach on one outlined by Best (1992) to help structure John's tactile experiences. When the advisory teacher first arrived at the school she conducted (with the help of the headteacher, John's class teacher and his LSA) an environmental audit to determine how best to create an appropriate environment for learning. This audit focused on the 'visual', 'auditory', 'sound', 'tactile' and 'social' environment. As a result of the audit inexpensive changes were made to both the classroom and school environment.

One of the first changes in the classroom was to change John's worktop. John used to have objects placed straight into his hands and a hand-over-hand exploration technique was the only strategy the class teacher and the

LSA were aware of. Now learning materials are always presented to John on an adapted wooden tray. The tray can be attached to the wheelchair at a height which is comfortable for John. He can rest his forearms on the pad at the front of the tray so his body doesn't need to bear the weight of his arms unsupported – this allows him to move his hands more freely and makes it less tiring for him to explore objects. The two sides and the back of the tray have raised edges which serve to stop John accidentally knocking objects off the tray and they also provide a distinct boundary to his work surface which he can use as a point of reference in his exploratory movements.

Since the tray has been introduced, John's class teacher and LSA have noticed that John has been able to initiate a range of independent exploratory strategies when manipulating objects. After advice from the QTVI, the LSA began to incorporate hand-under-hand techniques when working with John, placing her hands in such a way as to allow John to slide his hands over hers to locate objects on the tray. Now she finds that it is only necessary to support John's upper arm if he needs help in locating objects. If there are a range of objects on the tray, the LSA will help John build a mental map of the tray, initially guiding his hands around the surface. She is trying to develop a structure for John's exploration so that he won't miss out areas of the tray's surface. He starts at the same place each time and locates objects in reference to the raised edges of the tray. His LSA tries to make the area a consistent one, and ensure that objects which John removes from the tray for more detailed exploration are returned to their original position.

In the early part of each day John is presented with a range of object symbols that represent the lessons of the school day. Using the object symbols the LSA goes through each of the lessons in sequence. The next lesson takes place in the school swimming pool so John is asked to find the symbol for swimming, which is a piece of an armband. To stop it slipping around, the armband, like the other symbols, is mounted on a small wooden tile which has a non-slip surface on the reverse. Using the search strategy he has been taught John locates the symbol independently and grasps it. None of the object symbols are larger than John's hand and each has distinct tactile features.

The school environment

John is taken by the LSA to the swimming pool. John is drawing on a range of sensory cues that his LSA has brought to his attention on previous trips to orient himself. He knows where the door is because he can hear the wind chime that has been placed over it. He can feel the change in vibrations as the wheelchair moves from the carpet around his working area to the lino. As they leave the classroom he notes the change in the acoustics as the classroom door opens and he moves into the corridor. He is aware of the increase in light as he passes each window, and notices the smells of food being prepared for lunch as he passes the dining room. The slope of the ramp tells him that they are nearing the swimming pool, and the heat, the bright light, the smell of chlorine and bumpy surface of the tiles at the entrance to the pool area confirm that he has arrived. His LSA directs John's attention to the symbol which is hanging on a cord from the door of the pool. John is able to grasp and manipulate the symbol to ensure it matches the one he has brought with him. Time for him to explore the symbol has been built into his lesson. Although each teaching area did have an object symbol at its entrance before the advisory teacher came to the school, the symbols were permanently attached to the door and John couldn't reach them.

The world outside the school

At the end of each school day John goes to the school entrance to catch the minibus home. He knows he is approaching the door because he feels a slight draught on his face and hands. It is a sunny day and as he leaves the building he can tell his LSA where the sun is from its brightness and the warmth of the sunrays on one side of his face. He says his goodbyes as his wheelchair is put on the ramp. Although he had been travelling to and from school for a number of years, it wasn't until his advisory teacher arrived that anyone realised that John had a very limited understanding of the features of the minibus.

He was provided with a number of opportunities to explore the minibus, including being wheeled slowly around the outside of the bus and being given time to inspect its various components. This was initially done as part of his weekly mobility lesson with the visiting rehabilitation worker and is now repeated every half term. He was also given a cane so he could feel how high the roof of the bus was, and was allowed to explore the driver's seat and feel the steering wheel. His class teacher tried to introduce a model of the minibus to John in the classroom but she isn't sure whether John was able to make the connection just yet so they are continuing to rely on his real life experiences to develop his understanding.

This vignette provides a brief example of how learning environments can be adapted to meet the particular needs of a child and how this in turn resulted in adaptations to the techniques used to support his learning. You may wish to use a similar approach to the one outlined in this vignette to help you analyse the environment of a child you are working with, and we provide further guidance in the Recommended Reading section at the end of the chapter.

It is important to recognise that a degree of subjectivity is involved in putting together an environment for a child who has MDVI. The task that faces professionals and parents alike is how to view the world from the unique perspective of the child. Our final vignette is based upon a short transcript taken from a classroom observation which records the conversation that takes place between Saheed, an 8-year-old child who is congenitally blind with additional learning difficulties, and his class teacher. We feel that this transcript illustrates nicely how it is possible to allow for this unique perspective when supporting a child's learning experiences.

Vignette 10.2 Saheed

After a morning break, Saheed is guided to the door of his classroom by his teacher. She asks him if he wants to play in the sand tray which is located by the window of the class. Saheed walks independently towards the window where the sun is streaming into the room. He reaches out to touch the glass window. After a few seconds of touching the window he says:

It's hot, very hot, hot sun.

Teacher: *That's right, Saheed, it is hot, the sun is shining on the window and it makes the glass feel warm to touch.*

Saheed: *Hot sun, hot window, hot, hot hand.*

Teacher: *Yes, Saheed, it is hot, the sun is hot and it makes the glass hot. When you touch the glass, your hand feels warm. Do you want to come over to the sand tray now?*

The teacher taps the sand tray three times. Saheed continues to stand by the window exploring different parts of the window frame and the glass panes. The teacher asks him again:

Saheed, I've got something that's hot over here in the sand tray. It's the sand. The sand is warm from the sun as well. Do you want to feel the warm sand?

The teacher taps the sand tray three times again. Saheed walks towards the tapping sound and reaches out to find the sand tray. He places his fingers in the sand.

Saheed: *Hot, hot sand, hot sun, hot sand, hot.*

Teacher: *That's right, Saheed, the sun is hot and it makes the sand feel hot when you touch it. Some of the sand is still cold, can you find the cold sand in the sand tray?*

This short description provides a powerful illustration of the role of touch in a child's learning experiences and the salient features which influence his understanding of the world. Fortunately in this case Saheed's teacher is sufficiently aware of his perspective to be able to tune in to his needs, and, in this example, to use his interest in temperature to help further his learning. All of us who have the privilege of working with these children need to ensure that we do not impose our own view of the world onto the child but rather seek to acknowledge and appreciate the child's unique perspective. This perspective can help us to see behaviours that we might otherwise consider irrational or outlandish for what they really are: logical and coherent adaptations to a world mediated predominantly through touch.

Recommended reading

Arter, C. (1999) 'Environmental issues', in Arter, C., Mason, H., McCall, S., McLinden, M. and Stone, J. *Children with Visual Impairment in Mainstream Settings*. London: David Fulton.

Best, A. (1992) *Teaching Children with Visual Impairments*. Milton Keynes: Open University.

Lewis, C. and Taylor, H. (1997) 'The learning environment', in Mason, H. and McCall, S. (eds) *Visual Impairment: access to education for children and young people*. London: David Fulton.

Lomas, J. and Ackerley, B. (1995) 'An environmental audit', in *Eye Contact*, 12. Pull out supplement. (A revised supplement is included in the VITAL pack *Approaches*, 1998, see Useful Resources for further information on this pack.)

McLinden, M. (1999) 'The child with a visual impairment in combination with additional difficulties', in Arter, C., Mason, H., McCall, S., McLinden, M. and Stone, J. *Children with Visual Impairment in Mainstream Settings*. London: David Fulton.

Millar, S. and McEwan, G. (1993) 'Passports to communication', in Wilson, A. and Millar, S. (eds) *Augmentative Communication in Practice*. Edinburgh: CALL Centre.

CHAPTER 11

Concluding Thoughts

Introduction

It is clear from the issues we have raised in this book that meeting the needs of children who have a visual impairment and additional difficulties poses significant challenges to those responsible for their education. With an increasing emphasis on inclusive practice, the needs of these children can no longer be considered the sole responsibility of specialist teachers and special schools. Changes in SEN legislation as well as new initiatives relating to national curriculum frameworks have led to a re-appraisal of what constitutes an appropriate education for all children with severe and complex needs.

Furthermore, there is a broad realisation that many of the traditional approaches (for example, the use of braille as a tactile medium for literacy) to the education of children who are blind or who have low vision do not meet the needs of this sector of the population. In this final chapter we offer our thoughts on a range of issues which have relevance to the role of touch in the learning experiences of children who have MDVI. We begin by revisiting the broad spectrum of need within the population and then consider briefly the implication of this heterogeneity for future teaching and research. This is followed by a short discussion of the potential impact for teaching and learning of developments in Information and Communication Technology (ICT). Finally we consider issues relating to the continuing professional development (CPD) of those supporting children with MDVI.

Spectrum of need

In the Overview we looked at some of the difficulties of defining the population of children this book is concerned with. We would agree with those (e.g. Lewis and Collis 1997) who question the value of grouping together children who are similar only in some respects. It is clearly possible, for example, to cluster children within the heterogeneous population of children with MDVI according to broad medical conditions such as physical disability. However, *within* a number of these clusters children can be further subdivided according to the type of their condition. For example, a significant number of children with multiple disabilities have a physical impairment arising from cerebral palsy, a general term which describes a disorder of movement and posture associated with damage to the motor area of the brain. Cerebral palsy is commonly classified according to the part of the body it affects: quadriplegia (all four limbs); hemiplegia (arm and leg on the same side); paraplegia (legs). It is also classified according to its effect on muscles, spastic (very rigid, hypertonicity in the affected muscles); athetoid (abnormal, involuntary motions in the affected muscles); ataxic (irregular muscle action and poor coordination) (Kelley 1998). Since each of these sub-groups of cerebral palsy has specific educational implications, we can begin to see how difficult it is to generalise characteristics even across cluster groups.

Given the wide spectrum of need within the population it is clearly not possible to be prescriptive about teaching methods or particular techniques suitable for every child. However, we would argue that the impact of reduced information through the distance sense of vision (frequently in combination with impairment in one or more senses) does have broad implications that both researchers and educators who work with children who have multiple disabilities need to appreciate.

Implications for research

We also noted in the Overview that research to date relating to the role of touch in optimising the learning experiences of children who have MDVI is limited. As we saw in Chapter 4, it is questionable whether the findings of research undertaken into the early haptic perception of infants who are fully sighted is directly applicable to older children who have a visual impairment and multiple disabilities. We would suggest that older children who do not have the means to engage with the world independently are involved in a learning process that is altogether different from that of infants who are following a conventional course of development. It is a process in which the child is (and, crucially, will probably continue to be throughout his or her educational career) reliant on others to a greater or lesser extent to provide meaningful opportunities to interact with the world.

Lewis and Collis (1997) report that research into children with disabilities has traditionally emphasised the ways in which individuals within a group are *similar* to one another, and little attention has been given to the ways in which children in a group may *differ* from each other. Indeed, the wide range of needs within the population presents those involved in conventional research with difficult challenges, and researchers in areas such as active touch are inclined to focus their attention on children who are following more conventional pathways in their development. To some extent this is not surprising. It is not always clear for example what should be the precise research focus when investigating children who have severe and complex needs. A scientific study of how a child with MDVI interacts with objects will also need to account for the role of the adult partners in providing and structuring learning experiences for the child, especially if the child is unable to hold and manipulate objects independently (McLinden 2000). This type of study requires different types of research methods and will in many respects be concerned as much with models of pedagogy (or teaching styles) as with the issue of how information is acquired through the sense of touch.

The research that *has* been conducted into the haptic perception of children who have a visual impairment has traditionally adopted what has been termed a 'domain comparison' approach in which the haptic abilities of children who are sighted are compared those of children who are blind. However, as Lewis and Collis (1997) point out, a significant drawback in this approach is that development in any one domain does not occur independently of development in other areas. Investigating one domain may simply highlight the developmental tasks that children with a disability *cannot* perform when compared to their 'normal' peers, rather than attempting to recognise the possibility that they may be following alternative routes of development. The studies of haptic activity in infants we reviewed in Chapter 4, for example, could not be easily replicated in children with MDVI since their haptic activity cannot be considered purely within the 'haptic domain'.

An additional complication is that there is a wide diversity in the haptic behaviours of children with MDVI and the nature of this haptic activity may not only be different from that observed in 'normal' child development, but equally significantly, it may differ greatly from one child to another. The developmental models we reviewed in Chapter 4 provide some points of reference for examining the haptic strategies of children with MDVI but none is sufficiently comprehensive to account for the range of factors that may influence the haptic interactions of a child with MDVI. In particular, difficulties arise in analysing those haptic behaviours that differ in both *quality* as well as *quantity* from those considered within a conventional developmental framework (for example, the continued mouthing of objects by older children who have MDVI).

Our knowledge and understanding of the developmental patterns followed by children who have MDVI over extended periods of time is very limited since few studies have adopted a longitudinal approach. Researchers who undertake investigations into the performance of older children with MDVI often have very little information about the types of approaches which were used to structure their early learning experiences and in general we have no evidence of the relative effectiveness of different approaches. We propose that the changing needs within the population of children who have a visual impairment demand a reappraisal of the research focus, with a view to establishing relevant methods of enquiry appropriate for children who have additional disabilities.

Developments in the use of ICT

The use of ICT to support the learning of children who have multiple disabilities is a rapidly developing area and a number of specialist publications have been published in recent years (see for example Bozic and Murdoch 1996). Although we have not directly addressed the issue of ICT in helping to support a child's learning experiences through touch, we believe that technology does offer some exciting possibilities both for teaching and research.

As Tobin (1996) notes, modern technology may be able to offer a means of improving the overlap in the information coming in through the defective sensory channels and may make possible the modulation of the quality or intensity of the stimuli arriving via a particular channel, thereby enhancing the learning environment for the child:

> It can be argued that this is really no more than an extension of what teachers of children with visual impairments and multiple disabilities do as a matter of routine, and that technology is, therefore, just an additional means of attaining long-standing objectives. Where it may be said to differ is in its precision and speed. (p. 64)

Clearly it is not possible to ignore the potential impact of new technologies in the education of children with special needs, from the development of touch-sensitive screens for computers, to the increasingly sophisticated equipment designed for use within multi-sensory environments. Further, most practitioners will be familiar with the wide range of switches that are available to provide children who have multiple disabilities with a concept of control within their environment (Reed and Addis 1996). However, as Millar and Aitken (1996) have highlighted, technology in itself is not necessarily helpful, but it is technology which is used to 'increase social interaction (not to replace it!) which should be the major focus with children who have complex multiple impairments' (p. 121).

In recent years there have been a number of exciting developments which can create opportunities for such interactions to take place. For example taction pads have the potential to enhance the motivation value of the environment for children with MDVI and can be useful for developing their early reaching and communication skills. The taction pad is a small plastic mat which can be attached to an object (for example, the child's plate). A short message can be recorded into its speech unit (the VoicePal), so that when the object is touched the message (e.g. 'This is Alice's plate') is heard by the child. The wider use of taction pads is described in some depth by Millar and Aitken (1996).

We have discussed the need for careful observation in order to monitor how a child uses his or her touch when acting on a particular object. Video is now widely used by teachers as a means of recording progress in children with multiple disabilities and the use of slow motion playback offers both teachers and researchers the possibility of capturing subtle nuances in haptic activity. A drawback with this technique for researchers is the level of subjectivity involved in interpreting a child's haptic activity. However, developments in technology in fields outside education generally offer researchers more objective means of recording and analysing human movements.

A particular type of technology, known as 'motion measurement', works by detecting the positions of reflective markers attached to the body, perhaps on the hands and arms, or down one side of the body. Several digital cameras are used to view the person performing a movement from different angles. This information is then relayed to a computer where the movements are recorded and can be played back and analysed. A Swedish commercial product known as the 'ProReflex' has been used for a wide range of applications, including analysis of gait and posture in adults with physical impairments, measuring and analysing the development of reaching and grasping movements, analysis of movement dysfunction in adults with cerebral palsy, as well as for analysing the movement patterns of top class athletes. We are not aware of instances where this technology has been used with children who have multiple disabilities, but it would seem to have the potential for exploring and coding, with a greater degree of accuracy and objectivity, the frequently complex and sophisticated ways in which children use touch when engaging with objects and people. It may have particular relevance for recording and analysing the *development* of reaching and grasping behaviours in children who have MDVI, particularly those with limited fine motor abilities which serve as barriers to independent manipulation of objects.

The work of the experimental psychologist Suzanna Millar (1994, 1997) has been influential in recording the haptic strategies adopted by blind subjects when reading braille through touch. While working at Oxford University Millar developed a system comprising a transparent worktop stationed above a video camera in order to monitor each subject's hand movements. The video tape is then analysed and the haptic movements coded using an appropriate classification system. This technology has obvious applications for children who have multiple disabilities. It might be feasible for example to use Millar's techniques (which would be significantly cheaper than the 'motion measurement' system described above) to analyse in some detail the haptic movements that are employed by children who read Moon or to explore the particular haptic strategies children with MDVI employ when manipulating different object properties (for example, surface textures, contours of objects, etc.).

Although this discussion has been brief, we would suggest that ICT can be viewed as a medium that not only is used to benefit the child directly, but also as one which can help teachers and researchers by improving the quantity and quality of the information we have about how these children learn.

Continuing professional development

Our own role in training practitioners who work with children with a visual impairment confirms that the significance of touch for children who have MDVI is an area that has not to date been given sufficient attention in programmes of professional development. The National SEN specialist standards (TTA 1999) which now form the basis of mandatory programmes for specialist teachers working with children who have a sensory impairment should serve to ensure that this oversight is corrected. Within the standards relating to 'Communication and Interaction' it is stated, for example, that teachers working with children with a visual impairment will need to demonstrate their knowledge and understanding of 'the principles of haptic perception' (p. 15). Although this standard is not linked directly to children who have MDVI, it has implications for course providers structuring programmes for teachers who work with children across the broad spectrum of visual impairment.

Given the relative dearth of teaching materials in relation to haptic function in this population we have devised a series of portfolio activities which relate to key issues in this text. A number of these activities cross reference with the specialist extension standards which we consider to have particular relevance to learning through touch for children who have MDVI (see the Appendix).

An increasingly wide range of professionals are now coming into contact with children who have MDVI. These will include learning support assistants, physiotherapists, occupational therapists, community paediatricians, psychologists as well as speech and language therapists. Their role in supporting these children requires an appreciation of how the child uses and responds to touch and this issue is one that should be addressed in their professional development.

In education the responsibility for ensuring consistency in the approach adopted by professionals from different disciplines perhaps ultimately rests with the school and clear policies need to be in place that address issues such as social touching and the handling of children. Although we have not addressed the ethical issue of what constitutes 'appropriate' or 'inappropriate' touch or issues of child safety, this area is likely to become one of increasing concern in the future. As well as the development of general policies relating to touch at a school level, parents and teachers will also need to collaborate in devising individualised approaches which can be applied consistently both at home and at school.

Final thoughts

Practitioners working with children who have multiple disabilities have at their disposal an ever increasing range of assessment tools and frameworks. At one level this means that we can describe more accurately than ever how a child responds to different types of sensory information, and we can structure and report our observations accordingly. These observations can then be reflected upon and shared with colleagues in an attempt to gain insights into the child's unique situation. However, we need to realise perhaps that we can never fully understand the world as it might be perceived by a child with MDVI. Perhaps the best we can hope for is that practitioners and researchers in this field will succeed, at least in part, in identifying some of the unique and distinctive perspectives of children with MDVI and continue to extend the knowledge base so that we can meet their needs more successfully. For children with MDVI, a strange world is one where the significance of touch in their learning has not been fully appreciated. We hope that this book goes some way to raising this level of appreciation.

Glossary of Useful Terms

The purpose of this glossary is to provide succinct definitions of terms which are commonly used when discussing the sense of touch in relation to children who have multiple disabilities and a visual impairment. Rather than present these terms in alphabetical order we have grouped terms according to use. For example, although the terms **haptic**, **tactual** and **tactile** do have distinct meanings, they are frequently used interchangeably (i.e. haptic-, tactile- *or* tactual-perception) and have, therefore, been presented together. This glossary is neither definitive nor exhaustive and you will need to refer to the references we provide at the end of each chapter if you wish to explore any of the terms in further depth.

Sensation – Perception – Cognition

Sensation generally refers to physical stimulation at the organs of sense, or the neural signals we receive from the sense organs (Gregory 1987).

Perception implies a conscious awareness of the information that comes through sensation. You are receiving many types of sensations at present, from within your body as well as from external sources, but you will not be consciously aware of them all. The process of perception of a sensory stimulus involves sensation, memory and motivation.

Cognition is a generic term which is broadly concerned with the mental processes by which we acquire, organise and use knowledge as we come to know and understand the world. It involves different levels of mental processing including problem solving, memory, attention and perception. Assessment of the development of cognitive abilities in young infants has traditionally been linked closely with their activities with objects.

Somatosensory

Somatosensory is derived from the Greek work *soma* meaning body. Somato-sensory is used to describe the particular sensations that are perceived by the receptors within the body. These receptors can be broadly divided into those which provide us with information about what is happening within our bodies and are therefore helpful in knowing about body space and move-ment (i.e. *proprioception*), and those which provide us with information about the world outside of our bodies, for example receptors located in the skin, eyes, ears, nose, etc. (i.e. *exteroception*). The somatosensory area of the parietal lobe of the brain is the area of the brain that receives input from the skin.

Kinaesthesia – Proprioception – Exteroception

Kinaesthesia derives from the Greek words *kinein* meaning to move and *aesthesia* meaning feeling or sensation. It can be translated therefore as move-ment feeling, movement sensation or sense of movement. Kinaesthesia (or kinaesthetic awareness) can be used as a term to describe how we sense the position of our body when *moving* through space, as well as to describe the *movement* of individual body parts in relation to one another.

Proprioception is used to describe the perception of sensations produced *within* the body. *Proprioceptors* are receptors located within particular parts of the body (e.g. muscles, tendons, joints, inner ear) which are used to inform us about the movement of our body and relative position of individual body parts.

Exteroception is a term used in biology to describe the perception of stimuli which are produced *outside* of an organism.

Exteroceptors are those receptors within the body through which the exter-nal stimuli are perceived, for example the receptors within the skin, eyes, lips, nose, etc. and through which we are able to know about the world outside of our bodies.

Haptic – Tactile – Tactual

Haptic is derived from the Greek word *haptikos* meaning able to touch. As an adjective the term can be used as relating to the sense of touch and is usually combined with the term perception i.e. haptic perception. *Perception* can refer to the conscious recognition of a sensation, whether this is auditory, visual or tactile. *Haptic perception* is used in this text to refer to perception which relates to the sense of touch. More particularly, it concerns the recognition of sensory information which is received through the manipulation and exploration of the object's properties, e.g. size, shape, weight, texture, etc. As such, the term **haptic** is sometimes described as *active touch*.

Tactile is commonly used to describe the qualities or properties of objects that are accessible through the sense of touch. Tactile is used within this book to refer to the physical features or properties of an object which can be detected through the sense of touch, for example its contours, surface temperature, texture and/or weight. This term is also commonly used as an adjective to describe how particular individuals make use of their sense of touch, for example, 'she strikes me as being very tactile', or 'he always seems to be tactile defensive when handling wet clay'.

Tactual has a similar derivation to the term *tactile* and is frequently used interchangeably in the literature with both tactile and *haptic* to refer to the sense of touch (for example 'haptic-', 'tactile-' or 'tactual-' perception). Within this book a distinction is made between the terms tactile and tactual; as noted above, tactile refers to the physical properties of objects and/or sensory features which can be perceived through the sense of touch (e.g. shape, size, temperature, etc.). Tactual is used in a similar way to the term *haptic* and refers to the exploratory and manipulative actions we perform on objects and sensory features to acquire information about these properties (e.g. grasping an orange and squeezing it to determine its softness).

Active – Passive touch

Active touch refers to touching, usually with the hands, which involves independent exploratory and manipulative use of the skin and therefore stimulation of receptor systems in the muscles, tendons and joints. It is commonly used to refer to independent activity on the part of the person who is doing the touching, for example when manipulating and holding an object. Active types of touch imply 'doing' or 'involvement' on the part of the child and are usually distinguished therefore from relatively *passive* types of touch.

Passive touch refers either to the actions involved in being touched either by an object or by another person (as in the act of massage), or to touching an object but with no independent exploratory and manipulative use of the skin. Passive implies therefore things being done to, or with, the child rather than the child 'doing' the doing. The distinction between active and passive touch is particularly pertinent to this book given that many children in the population are limited in their ability to actively manipulate objects, and are reliant on others to provide information to them through passive modes of touch. When structuring the learning environment it is important to consider how a child can be presented with greater opportunities to be involved in any given activity.

Anatomy – Physiology

Anatomy is concerned with the structure, form, and relationships of different parts of the body. As an example, a diagram of the cross-section of the skin presented in Chapter 2 describes the anatomy of the skin with a particular focus on the sensory receptors found within this particular section of the skin.

Physiology refers to the *function* of the parts of the body and how each of these parts works.

Exploratory strategies – Manipulation

Exploratory strategies (used interchangeably with the term *exploratory procedures*) are purposeful actions which are used to investigate or discover the properties of objects or sensory features. They can be described therefore as the particular types of movements which are used to find out about the properties of objects or sensory features, for example feeling the texture of cloth by rubbing it between your thumb and forefinger, squeezing a pear to find out how soft it is prior to eating it. In a young child, exploratory procedures will incorporate a range of actions on objects including grasping, shaking, stroking, squeezing, hitting, banging objects. Exploratory movements are distinguished from random movements or repetitive movements that have no exploratory intent. Banging an object, therefore, may or may not be an exploratory strategy.

Manipulation refers to the handling of an object or part of an object and performing an act on or with it, for example holding a spoon and bringing it to your mouth. Although manipulatory acts can be distinguished from exploratory acts in that they are not intended to find things out about objects, in practice such acts can also be used to provide information about object properties. For example, when picking up a spoon from a dishwasher we may find that when grasping the handle the first thing we notice is that it still feels warm to touch.

Prehension/Prehensile

Prehension derives from the Latin word *prehendere* meaning grasp, and refers to voluntary grasping and manipulating of objects, usually with the hands. **Prehensile** is an adjective used to describe a limb or part of a body which is capable of grasping, for example our hands (although monkeys' tails are also described in similar terms!). The development of prehensile movements in the young child provides them with opportunities to independently manipulate and explore objects and thereby begin to act in increasingly sophisticated ways on the environment.

Tactile symbols

Tactile is derived from the Latin word *tactus* meaning touched. **Symbols** can be described as things which re-present or stand for something else, for example a picture of the sun on a weather chart to indicate a sunny day, a cup to represent the activity drink. **Tactile symbol** is used in this text as a generic term applying to a range of different symbols which incorporate a raised component in order that it can be perceived through touch. Tactile symbols include *object cues, objects of reference, object symbols* or *tangible symbols* and *raised symbols*. Although these different descriptions are often used interchangeably each of these terms has a slightly different meaning depending on the context within which it is used. The explanations presented below are not meant to be definitive but do provide a useful way of distinguishing between potentially confusing terminology. For a more in-depth discussion of a number of these terms you should refer to the SALUTE website, details of which are included in the Useful Resources section.

Object cue   An object or part of an object which is used to represent a person, place, object or event and which is used *within* the actual situation the object represents. An example is the use of arm bands as a cue for a child to inform him or her that the next lesson is swimming, and which are then used as part of the swimming activity itself.

Objects of reference   Objects described as tangible or material things that can be seen, heard, touched, smelt and/or tasted. When objects are used to stand for or represent a person, place, event or another object they are referred to as symbols. As with an *object cue*, an object of reference can also be used to represent a person, place, object or event. However, an important difference is that as a symbol the object of reference is not used in the actual situation. An example is the use of a cup which represents the activity DRINK for a child. As a *representation* of this activity however this cup is not the one from which the child actually drinks.

Object symbols are used interchangeably in the literature with the term objects of reference and again highlight the symbolic nature (representational) of the object selected to re-present or stand for a particular person, place, object or event.

Raised symbol   A raised symbol refers to a visual or pictorial symbol which has its contours raised in order that it is accessible through touch. Raised symbols may be used to provide additional sensory information to children with a visual impairment, allowing them to trace along the raised contours with their fingers. Examples include raised Makaton symbols, tactile pictures and tactile diagrams.

Cues – Prompts – Clues

Cues are commonly used as antecedents to inform a child of a forthcoming task or activity. A range of cues are used with children who have MDVI including auditory (shaking the chain of a swing for the child to hear); tactual (touching the cup onto a child's lips prior to a drink); verbal (telling the child what is happening next) and visual (holding up an object for the child to see).

Prompts are used to support a child's learning during a particular task. Prompts can take a number of forms including physical (hand-over-hand guidance); visual (pointing); verbal (talking) or auditory (making a noise to direct the child's attention). When supporting the learning of a child with multiple disabilities, a combination of different types of prompts will often be used which may then be reduced or altered as the child learns to complete tasks more independently. You should refer to Goold and Hummell (1993) for a more detailed discussion of prompts and cues.

Clues can take the form of natural or environmental sounds, smells, tactile or visual stimuli in the environment which can be used by a child to orientate him- or herself. Examples of commonly used environmental clues within a school are the smell of the swimming or hydrotherapy pool, the sounds of people eating in the dining room, the ticking of a clock on the classroom wall, the feel of the textured floor mat leading into the school corridor from the playground, etc.

Sensory receptors of the skin

Layers of the skin

Dermis   The inner layer of the skin that contains sensory receptors and nerve endings.

Epidermis   The outer layer of the skin which contains dead skin cells.

Classes of receptors

Mechanoreceptors   Receptors that respond to indentations of the skin, for example when a finger touches the back of the hand. Two types of mechano-receptors have been identified: rapidly adapting (RA) and slowly adapting (SA) (Goldstein 1989).

Thermoreceptors   Receptors that respond to temperatures or changes in temperature, for example when picking up a hot saucepan handle (warm receptor) or when eating a cold ice lolly (cold receptor).

Noiceptors   Receptors that respond to stimuli which damage the skin, for example, the high heat which results in a burn on the skin.

Skin receptors   Many of these receptors were named by anatomists in the nineteenth century. Although early experimental studies suggested a direct relationship between different sensations and particular skin receptors, more recent studies have not always supported these findings, suggesting more tenuous links.

Free nerve endings   Nerve endings in the skin which have been linked with the sensation of pain and temperature.

Meissner's corpuscle   A receptor in the skin which has been linked with the sensation of edges as well as the location and timing of tactile stimuli. A rapidly adapting (RA) mechanoreceptor which responds best to slower movements (Goldstein 1989).

Merkel disc   A receptor in the skin with a distinctive disc shape which has been linked with the sensation of pressure and direct impact. A slowly adapting (SA) mechanoreceptor (Goldstein 1989).

Pacinian corpuscle   A receptor in the skin with a distinctive elliptical shape. The Pacinian corpuscle is activated only at the beginning or end of a pressure stimulus, for example when an object touches the skin and when it is removed from the skin. As such it has been linked with the sensation of pressure and vibration. A rapidly adapting (RA) mechanoreceptor (Goldstein 1989).

Ruffini endings   Receptors in the skin which have been linked with the sensation of skin stretch. A slowly adapting (SA) mechanoreceptor (Goldstein 1989).

Supporting the Learning of Children Who Have Multiple Disabilities and Visual Impairment: Selection of National SEN Specialist Standards (TTA 1999) Which Have Particular Relevance to the Role of Touch

(i.) COMMUNICATION AND INTERACTION

Knowledge and Understanding

Teachers with additional specialist knowledge and understanding will show that they know and understand the following:

(i.) Communication and Interaction (Deafblindness)

ii. *the range and forms/modes of communication used by pupils who are deafblind;*

iii. *the roles of the different senses in combining to produce environmental awareness, and the kinds of sensory information potentially available to a pupil with auditory and visual impairments;*

iv. *the use of objects of reference.*

(i.) Communication and Interaction (Visual Impairment)

i. *the principles underlying the development of alternative and augmented communication systems, including Braille; and their appropriate application in providing a curriculum that utilises pupils' strengths;*

iv. *the principles of haptic perception.*

Skills

Teachers with additional specialist skills in this area will demonstrate them through one or more of the following:

Deafblindness

i. *providing opportunities for pupils to have increased tactile, proprioceptive and kinaesthetic awareness during daily routines and planned activities;*

ii. *using specific visual, auditory and tactile methods to help pupils understand the functional use of objects to gain information about the environment, and use visual, auditory or tactile cues to initiate and terminate interactions.*

(ii.) COGNITION AND LEARNING

Knowledge and Understanding

Teachers with additional specialist knowledge and understanding will show that they know and understand the following:

c. *the range of cognitive skills necessary for effective learning and the effects of single or multiple disabilities on functions such as perception, memory and information processing;*

d. *the range of visual, motor and linguistic channels available to promote cognitive potential;*

e. *the importance of assessing how pupils process auditory and visual information.*

(iv.) SENSORY AND PHYSICAL DEVELOPMENT

Knowledge and Understanding

Teachers with additional specialist knowledge and understanding will show that they know and understand the following:

c. *the anatomy and physiology of sensory and/or physical functions and their role in normal development;*

h. *how to use special equipment and technology to overcome or reduce the impact of physical and/ or sensory difficulties;*

i. *how to design and produce teaching and learning materials in an appropriate medium, and collaborate with others in their use and evaluation;*

l.   how to make optimal use of the residual and physical functions and where appropriate, how to retain such functions.

Skills

Teachers with additional specialist skills in this area will demonstrate them through one or more of the following:

a.   the sensitive use of appropriate assessment methods such as the focused use of observation, supported by developmental scales and skills checklists;

b.   using specialised assessment information provided by colleagues from other professional disciplines to assess pupils' functional use of sensory information;

d.   modifying and adapting resources and equipment, including ICT hardware and software, to make them accessible to pupils with wide and varied physical and sensory needs;

e.   using technology to support alternative and augmented communication and to minimise the adverse effects of physical disability on educational progress;

f.   working in co-operation with parents/carers and appropriate professionals to develop, implement and review programmes of support, remediation and treatment.

Portfolio Activities

Introduction

These activities have been designed to draw out key issues from chapters in the text and invite you to explore implications for your practice. We hope that they will enhance your knowledge and understanding of how effective learning opportunities can be provided through touch for children who have visual impairment and additional needs. These activities are designed to cross reference with a number of the 'extension' standards selected from the National Special Educational Needs Specialist Standards (TTA 1999) (see Appendix).

The extension standards define the 'additional specialist knowledge, understanding and skills that will be required by some teachers to enable them to teach pupils with more severe and/or complex needs' (TTA 1999: 6). Knowledge and understanding can be demonstrated in a number of forms including written and oral evidence, whereas 'skills' imply the *application* of knowledge and understanding through practical demonstration. You will need to consider therefore how your responses might also be demonstrated as 'skills' in relation to the relevant extension standards.

No single activity can demonstrate an appropriate level of knowledge and understanding of a particular extension standard. It is important to highlight therefore that these activities are intended to be used as only *one* source of evidence in a portfolio of professional development. In practice of course, evidence of your knowledge, understanding and/or skills in relation to particular standards will incorporate a range of sources arising from your own professional practice and you will need to consider carefully which of these you draw upon.

We have designed the activities to be relevant to supporting children's learning through touch. The selection of standards presented in the Appendix is not a definitive one and you will, in all probability, find that other extension standards have relevance to your professional role when supporting a child's learning in this area. We hope that our activities will give you ideas for demonstrating your knowledge, understanding and skills in relation to these other standards too.

Portfolio Activity 1: Exploring haptic perception

a. In your own words, write down a short description of your understanding of the term 'haptic perception'. You should support your description with at least three examples from your own experience.

Note down at least three ways in which information acquired through haptic perception is different to that acquired through visual perception. What implications might these differences have for structuring the learning experiences through touch for a child who has a visual impairment and additional needs?

b. Write a short account that demonstrates your knowledge and understanding of the terms 'passive' and 'active' touch. You should support your description of each term with at least three examples from your own experience or professional practice.

Note down in what ways an understanding of these types of touch can help you support the learning experiences of:

● developing infants following a normal pattern of development;
● children who have a visual impairment and additional needs.

c. With reference to a child with a visual impairment and additional needs provide an example of a learning experience predominantly based on *passive* forms of touch. Provide a brief summary of how opportunities might be provided to enable the child to have a more active and independent role within this experience.

Portfolio Activity 2: Roles of the senses

a. Note down in bullet point form at least three key differences in the roles of 'distance' and 'close' senses in providing a child, following a normal pattern of development, with sensory information.

Describe the potential impact of a reduction in the information received through the sense of vision in a child's early development. Note down what implications this reduction might have for an adult supporting the child's learning.

b. Provide a brief summary of the respective roles of vision and touch in a child's early interactions with objects during the first year. You may wish to refer to Chapter 3 to remind yourself of important milestones within this period.

Provide at least three examples of how a visual impairment and additional disabilities might affect this development. Relate these to a child known to you.

c. Write down three types of information that each of your different senses might provide you with during the course of a daily activity, for example finding the key for your front door in your pocket.

Consider the respective roles of each of your senses when you are:

- making a piece of toast in a toaster;
- brushing your teeth.

Consider the kinds of sensory information potentially available to a child who has a visual impairment and additional needs when performing the same, or similar, everyday activities.

Portfolio Activity 3: Communication and interaction through touch

a. With reference to a child with a visual impairment and additional needs, summarise at least three principles that you will need to consider when designing and developing an appropriate alternative and augmentative communication system. Provide a brief description of different types of symbols which might be included in the system and demonstrate how they can be used in order to utilise the child's strengths.

b. Provide a brief summary of how 'objects of reference' may be used to develop the communication of a child with a visual impairment and additional needs. Include in your summary a minimum of five potential advantages and five disadvantages of using objects of reference with a child.

Identify at least five factors which you consider to be associated with developing effective practice when using objects of reference with a child known to you. Your list should include reference to both the design and production of the objects of reference, as well as to the role of others in their use and evaluation.

c. In relation to the learning of a child with a visual impairment and additional needs, briefly describe how you might promote opportunities for enhancing tactile, proprioceptive and/or kinaesthetic awareness during daily routines or planned activities. Note down at least three factors which need to be considered when offering increased learning opportunities through each of these sensory channels.

Consider how you might demonstrate your specialist skills in this area to a parent seeking guidance about providing effective learning opportunities when supporting children with sensory impairments and additional needs.

d. In relation to a child with a visual impairment and additional needs whom you support, consider what tactile methods and/or strategies might best enable the child to learn about the functional use of objects. In particular, you should focus on the types of visual/auditory and/or tactile cues you can use prior to, during and after the child's engagement with an object. You might want to focus on particular examples from the child's daily routine, for example the child's engagement with a bath sponge as part of a class activity on 'Looking After Our Bodies'. The following framework might be helpful in structuring your response:

Approach/presentation: How are visual, auditory and/or tactile cues used to initiate interactions with the child? In the absence of consistent visual and/or auditory information how is the child made aware that the object is present in his or her environment? How are decisions made about appropriate methods of *presenting* the object to him or her within the activity?

Manipulation/exploration: What is the role of the adult partner in supporting the child's manipulation/exploration of the object? How are opportunities provided to maximise the child's *active* involvement in manipulating the object?

Termination: How are visual, auditory and/or tactile cues used to make the child aware that his or her interaction with the object is to be terminated?

---

e. With reference to a child with a visual impairment and additional needs note down at least two different types of 'tactile strategies' which are used to support the child's learning through touch, for example hand-over-hand or hand-under-hand guidance. Note down at least three advantages and three disadvantages of each of these strategies in supporting the child's learning experiences. The following website will be useful to refer to when completing this part of the activity: www.projectsalute.net

Portfolio Activity 4: Reducing barriers to learning

a. With reference to a child who has a visual impairment and additional needs, note down how one piece of specialist equipment has been used to support the child's learning through touch (for example a switch, a communication aid, a touch-screen). Consider to what extent this specialist equipment has assisted in reducing the barriers to learning arising from the child's particular combination of impairments.

---

b. Provide an example of specialist teaching materials incorporating a tactile component that you have been involved in designing and producing for a child who has a visual impairment and additional needs. Examples might include tactile books, objects of reference, tactile calendar, Moon or braille resources, raised diagrams, etc.

What collaboration with others was necessary at each stage in the *design, production, use* and *evaluation* of the materials to ensure that they were appropriate in meeting the child's individual needs? Note down which other people were involved at each of these stages.

c. You have been asked to offer some advice to a colleague about a child with a visual impairment and additional needs who is described as being 'tactile defensive'. Note down at least five additional questions you might ask your colleague prior to offering any advice or guidance.

Which assessment methods and/or procedures might you recommend in order to assess the nature of the behaviours described to you?

Which professionals might you recommend to be included in an assessment of the child?

Useful Resources and Further Reading

Literacy and touch

Mencap (1999) *Reading for All*. London: Mencap.

A resource pack containing ideas for stories and reading for children and young adults with severe and profound learning disabilities. The pack was developed with a grant from the National Literacy Trust as part of the National Year of Reading, a Government backed campaign to promote reading throughout the United Kingdom. Partners in the project were Mencap (The Royal Society for Mentally Handicapped Children and Adults), The Royal Schools for the Deaf Manchester, Widgit Software Ltd, The Royal National Institute for the Blind and The University of Birmingham. For further information or copies of the pack contact: Public Liaison Unit, Mencap on 020 7696 5593, www.mencap.org.uk

---

McCall, S. and McLinden, M. (1996) 'Literacy: a foot in the door?', *Eye Contact*, **16**, Autumn.

An *Eye Contact* supplement in which the authors examine the development of emergent literacy in children who are educationally blind with additional learning difficulties.

RNIB (1999) *Literacy for All? Improving literacy standards of visually impaired children*. London: RNIB.

A short leaflet setting out the action required to enable children with impaired vision, including those with additional needs, to benefit from

literacy activities. Further information about this leaflet, as well as more current literacy developments, products or training available from the RNIB is available from:
Policy Officer, Education and Employment Division, RNIB, 105 Judd Street, London WC1H 9NE. Tel: 0207 388 1266

Detheridge, T. and Detheridge, M. (1997) *Literacy Through Symbols: Improving access for children and adults.* London: David Fulton.

A helpful guide to the range of symbols currently in use with children and adults with learning difficulties to enhance literacy. Although not intended specifically for practitioners supporting learners with a visual impairment, the ideas are underpinned by a discussion of the educational and social issues that surround general use of symbols and their role in enhancing autonomy and independence.

Further reading for literacy and touch

Douglas, G. and Dickens, J. (1996) 'The development of early tactile reading skills', in Bozic, N. and Murdoch, H. (eds) *Learning Through Interaction: technology and children with multiple disabilities.* London: David Fulton.

McCall, S. and McLinden, M. (2001) 'Literacy and children who are blind and who have additional disabilities: the challenges for teachers and researchers.' *International Journal of Disability, Development and Education* 48(4), 354–75.

McCall, S., McLinden, M. and Stone, J. (1995) *The Mooncats Reading Scheme: Books A–C.* Peterborough: RNIB.

McCall, S., McLinden, M. and Stone, J. (1995) *Mooncats Teaching Guide: a guide to teaching Moon to pupils with a visual impairment.* Peterborough: RNIB.

Millar, S. (1997) *Reading Through Touch.* London: Routledge.

Olson, M. R. (1981) *Guidelines and Games for Teaching Efficient Braille Reading.* New York: American Foundation for the Blind.

Rex, E. J., Koenig, A. J., Wormsley, D. P. and Baker, R. L. (1994) *Foundations of Braille Literacy.* New York: American Foundation for the Blind.

Wormsley, D. P. (2000) *The Braille Literacy Curriculum.* Philadelphia, PA: Towers Press, Overbrook School for the Blind.

Wormsley, D. P. and D'Andrea, F. M. (eds) (1997) *Instructional Strategies for Braille Literacy.* New York: AFB Press.

Communication and touch

Bloom, Y. (1990) *Object Symbols: a communication option*. North Rocks, Australia: North Rocks Press.

A short monograph which examines in some depth issues to do with use of object symbols in the development of the request function for children with severe and multiple disabilities. The monograph is based on work undertaken at the Alice Betteridge School at North Rocks in Australia. Available from RNIB Customer Service (see p. 189 for details).

Ockelford, A. (2002) *Objects of Reference: promoting early symbolic communication*. London: RNIB.

This text provides a useful introduction to objects of reference and their role in promoting early communication in children with learning difficulties. Available from RNIB Customer Service (see p. 189 for details).

Hendrickson, H. and McLinden, M. (1996) 'Using tactile symbols: a review of current issues', *Eye Contact* **14**, Spring.

A short *Eye Contact* supplement in which the authors outline a number of tactile communication systems and review some of the issues that need to be considered when developing appropriate systems to meet the needs of children with multiple disabilities and visual impairment.

Goold, L., Borbilar, P., Clarke, A. and Kane, C. (1993) *Addressing the Communication Needs of the Individual with Significant Impairments: an ideas kit*. North Rocks, Australia: North Rocks Press.

A useful and concise summary of practical ideas that can be used to meet the frequently complex communication needs of children with multiple disabilities including visual impairment. Developed by speech pathologists working at the Alice Betteridge School at North Rocks, Australia this 'display kit' contains examples of different communication systems which have been used successfully with a range of children. The booklet includes examples of a range of symbols with a tactile component, including object symbols, braille and Moon. This text may be particularly valuable for practitioners seeking an overview of the range of symbols currently used to meet the wide spectrum of need within the population.

Available from RNIB Customer Service (see p. 189 for details).

Best, A. and Boothroyd, E. (1998) *Objects of Reference: report of the exploratory meeting.* (No publisher given)

This report describes the international exploratory meeting held at RNIB Condover Hall in June 1998 to discuss objects of reference and their role in teaching and learning of children and young adults with multiple disabilities and visual impairment. The primary objective of the meeting was to explore the current use of objects of reference in order to establish a research/issues 'menu' that could be used to identify developmental activities. Copies available from Sense (see p. 190 for details).

Lee, M. and MacWilliam, L. (1995) *Movement Gesture and Sign: an interactive approach to sign communication for children who are visually impaired with additional disabilities.* London: RNIB (out of print).

Lee, M. and MacWilliam, L. (2002) *Learning Together.* London: RNIB.

The 1995 publication provides a useful summary of a communication programme which develops from the child's early attempts to communicate through to the acquisition of a more formal sign system which is adapted for children with a visual impairment. A revised version was being published as this text went to print. The original version includes a useful chapter on the use of objects of reference to reinforce the understanding of language. Available from RNIB Customer Service (see p. 189 for details).

Goold, L. and Hummell, J. (1993) *Supporting the Receptive Communication of Individuals with Significant Multiple Disabilities: selective use of touch to enhance comprehension.* North Rocks, Australia: North Rocks Press.

A short monograph in the same series from North Rocks in Australia as the Bloom text on object symbols (see above). The purpose of this monograph is to explore how touch can be used to enhance comprehension with individuals who have multiple disabilities including visual impairment. Of particular relevance is the description of a selection and use of Touch-Speech Cues (pairing a target word for comprehension with a specific touch signal on the individual's body) which it is proposed can be utilised as a strategy to promote attention, recognition and comprehension of key spoken words. Available from RNIB Customer Service (see p. 189 for details).

TACPAC – Communication Through Touch (no date).

TACPAC (Tactile Approach to Communication) is a series of movement and sensory activities matched to specific music compositions devised by a music therapist and special educators of children with profound learning difficulties. The pack utilises 'tactile play' in combination with music and is based on the premise that for children with profound learning difficulties and additional sensory impairment, touch may be the primary means of contact. The pack consists of three half-hour tapes of music, three matching laminated cards and an accompanying booklet to set up tactile activities in order to encourage early communication. The pack has been used in specialist settings to promote sensory stimulation, body awareness, anticipation, communication as well as symbolic understanding, although the goals associated with TACPAC are personalised to meet each child's specific needs. The pack is available from TACPAC, Newdigate, Church Hill, Harefield, Middlesex, UB9 6DX. Further information on the use of TACPAC can be found in *Information Exchange*, Issue 56, Winter 2000, p. 24.

Miles, B. and Riggio, M. (1999) *Remarkable Conversations: a guide to developing meaningful communication with children and young adults who are deafblind.* Watertown, MA: Perkins School for the Blind.

Writing for families and teachers, the authors of this publication provide practical approaches for creating communication-rich environments and aim to address the needs of children with a wide range of abilities, from those with 'non-linguistic' forms of communication (e.g. objects or body movements) to those with 'linguistic' forms (e.g. sign language or writing). Of particular relevance to this section is Chapter 6: 'Assessment of Communication', which considers the child's available avenues for 'communication input and output', and presents a series of questions which can assist in finding out more about the child's use of: vision, touch, taste, smell, hearing, vocalisation, motor skills, perception and sensory integration. An in-depth case study then illustrates how this functional information can be of value when planning and developing a child's communication.

Bradley, H. (1991) *Assessing Communication Together (ACT) – A systematic approach to assessing and developing early communication skills in children and adults with multi-sensory impairments.* Penarth, Glamorgan: MHNA Publications.

Although published by MHNA (Mental Health Nurses Association), this publication is now available from APLD: Association of Practitioners in Learning Disability, PO Box 9, Whixley, YO26 8YP. Tel./Fax: 01423 331404

ACT is described as an 'assessment approach' that makes use of the observation and knowledge of adult partners who know the child well in order to plan intervention strategies. It is designed for use with children and adults with multi-sensory impairments who are at early stages of communication (i.e. little or no formal communication skills). In completing the Background Information section, the adult partner is required to find out information about the child's use of vision, hearing, touch and physical impairments and consider the implications of the information for communication. The Assessment and Progress Sheet provides a useful way of recording the child's responses to different types of communication (i.e. sign, gesture, symbol, etc.). The ACT is also of value in assessing a child who is resistant to touch.

Coupe, J., Barton, L., Barber, M., Collins, L., Levy, D. and Murphy, D. (1985) *Affective Communication Assessment.* Manchester: Melland School.

Although rather dated, the Affective Communication Assessment (ACA) is still used as an observation and intervention assessment procedure for children at an early stage of development who are not yet communicating intentionally. The procedure is designed for adults to carefully observe and interpret the child's behaviour in response to a variety of selected stimuli and events, thereby responding to the child in such a way as to increase the frequency and occurrence of these behaviours and enable the child to develop and strengthen potentially communicative signals. There are three components to the schedule: 'Observation'; 'Identification' and 'Intervention'. An Observation Recording Sheet is used to record the responses of the child to different types of sensory stimuli, for example a rattle being shaken close to his or her ears. The meaning of the behaviour thought to be conveyed by the child in response to each stimulus is then interpreted i.e. 'I want'/'I don't want' or 'I like'/'I don't like'. An Identification Recording Sheet is then used to gather further information about the consistency and type of behaviours which might form the basis of intervention, in which the adult can respond to the child in a consistent way, treating the behaviours as if they had communicative intent. Available from Melland High School, Holmcroft Road, Gorton, Manchester M18 7NG.

Further reading for communication and touch

Coupe, J., O'Kane, J. and Goldbart, J. (1998) *Communication Before Speech: development and assessment.* London: David Fulton.

Grove, N. (2000) *See What I Mean: guidelines to aid understanding of communication by people with severe and profound learning disabilities.* Wolverhampton: British Institute of Learning Disabilities.

Huebner, K. M., Prickett, J. G., Welch, T. R. and Joffe, E. (eds) (1995) *Hand in Hand: essential communication and orientation and mobility for young students who are deaf-blind.* New York: AFB Press.

Kearns, T. (1993) 'Communicating with signs and symbols', in Harris, J. (ed.) *Innovations in Educating Children with Severe Learning Difficulties.* Chorley, Lancashire: Lisieux Hall.

McLarty, M. (1995) 'Objects of reference', in Etheridge, D. (ed.) *The Education of Dual Sensory Impaired Children: recognising and developing ability.* London: David Fulton.

McLarty, M. (1997) 'Putting objects of reference in context', *European Journal of Special Needs Education* **12**(1), 12–20.

McLinden, M. (1995) 'Touching the moon', *British Journal of Special Education* **22**(2), 64–9.

Miles, B. (1999) 'Talking the language of the hands to the hands', Monmouth, OR: *DB-Link.* The National Information Clearinghouse on Children who are Deaf-Blind (www.tr.wou.edu/dblink).

Millar, S. and McEwan, G. (1993) 'Passports to communication', in Wilson, A. and Millar, S. (eds) *Augmentative Communication in Practice.* Edinburgh: CALL Centre.

Ockelford, A. (1994) 'In touch with their needs: can we help blind children who are struggling at a stage of pre-literacy to take the next step?', *Special Children* **78**, 27–9.

Park, K. (1995) 'Using objects of reference: a review of the literature', *European Journal of Special Needs Education,* **10**(1), 40–6.

Park, K. (1997) 'How do objects become objects of reference? A review of the literature on objects of reference and a proposed model for the use of objects in communication', *British Journal of Special Education* **24**(3), 108–14.

Pease, L. (2000) 'Creating a communicating environment', in Aitken, S., Buultjens, M., Clark, C., Eyre, J. and Pease, L. (eds) *Teaching Children who are Deafblind.* London: David Fulton.

Rowland, C. and Schweigert, P. (1989) 'Tangible symbols: symbolic communication for individuals with multisensory impairments', *Augmentative and Alternative Communication* **6**(4), 226–34.

Massage

Given the more specialist nature of 'massage' for children with a visual impairment and additional needs, this text does not address directly issues concerning how this technique should be used, although the main themes should be of value to those using massage with these children. A list of useful references is presented below for those seeking additional information in this area.

Longhorn, F. (1993) *Planning a Multisensory Massage Programme for Very Special People*.

Written by Flo Longhorn, who pioneered work on the sensory curriculum for children with special needs, this text explores the use of multi-sensory massage which aims to stimulate the senses in a meaningful way. This publication outlines the use of multi-sensory massage and aromatherapy in an educational context, and in particular links the use of massage with areas of the National Curriculum. Includes a useful collection of resources for developing a 'massage bank' as well as methods for assessment and recording children's responses. Available from Catalyst Education Resources Ltd, 35 Send Road, Send, Woking, Surrey GU23 7ET.

Sanderson, H., Harrison, J. and Price, S. (1991) *Aromatherapy and Massage for People Who Have Learning Difficulties*. Birmingham: Hands On Publishing.

This book is written by professionals with qualifications in massage and/or aromatherapy. It contains in-depth information on massage techniques and aromatherapy, as well as case studies of work carried out with individuals who have learning difficulties.

Further reading for massage

Barber, M. (1991) 'Massage and the multi-sensory impaired child', *Talking Sense* Summer, **22**.
Evans, P. and Theiss-Tait, K. (1986) 'Massage: an alternative starting point', *Talking Sense* **32**(1).
Hider, J. (2001) 'A loving touch', *Massage and Health Review* Summer, 12–13.
Hider, J. (2001) 'Massage, mobility and movement', *Eye Contact* **30**, Summer, 5-7.
Holden-Peters, P. (1993) 'The gentle touch', *Special Children* November–December, 28–9.

McConnell, A. (1994) *The Massage and Aromatherapy Guidelines: working with children and adults with learning difficulties*. The Jade College of Natural Therapy, 12 Jenkyn Road, Bedford, MK43 9HE. Tel: 01234 767619.

Information and communication technology

Bozic, N. and Murdoch, H. (eds) (1996) *Learning Through Interaction: technology and children with multiple disabilities*. London: David Fulton.

Written for teachers and other professionals who support the learning of children with multiple disabilities, the aim of this text is to explore and suggest ways of using different forms of technology including computers, communication aids, multi-sensory equipment and mobility aids. The main focus of the text is on the role of the adult partner in the successful use of technology with children who have multiple disabilities. A cyclical framework (Planning, Intervention, Review) is outlined which is based on the concept of the child, adult and technology forming functional systems, and which can be used to support a wide range of applications in order to meet individual needs.

RNIB (2001) *Accessing Technology: using technology to support the learning and employment opportunities for visually impaired users*. London: RNIB.

Provides information, case studies, and resources about the use of technology for individuals with a visual impairment in education, employment and at home. Although references to children who have additional needs is limited, this publication offers a helpful summary of the range of technology currently in use in education and provides a comprehensive section on where to go for further information, support and resources.

Further information for ICT and multiple disabilities

AbilityNet
Tel: 0800 269545
Email: enquiries@abilitynet.co.uk
www.abilitynet.co.uk

AbilityNet is a registered charity which offers impartial advice and information about appropriate computer technology for individuals with disabilities, including those with a visual impairment and additional needs.

ACE Centre, Oxford

Tel: 01865 759800

www.ace-centre.org.uk

ACE/ACCESS Centre, Oldham

Tel: 0161 627 1358

www.ace-north.org.uk

Each of these centres offers independent assessment, training, advice and information in the use of technology, with a particular focus on the needs of individuals with impaired communication, including those with sensory impairment and learning difficulties.

The Communication Aids for Language and Learning (CALL Centre)

Tel: 0131 651 6235

www.callcentre.education.ed.ac.uk

This centre provides support and information on technology for children who have speech, communication and/or writing difficulties in educational settings in Scotland. Staff at the centre have expertise in advising on appropriate technology to meet the needs of children with visual impairment and additional needs.

Functional sensory assessment

Aitken, S. and Buultjens, M. (1992) *Vision for Doing: assessing functional vision in learners who are multiply disabled. Sensory Series No. 2.* Edinburgh: Moray House Publications.

A popular assessment framework which is commonly used to assess sensory function in children with multiple disabilities and visual impairment. The hard copy version is out of print although a copy of the publication is available online for free from the Scottish Sensory Centre website (see p. 189 for details).

Pagliano, P. (2001) *Using a Multisensory Environment: a practical guide for teachers.* London: David Fulton.

This book is written for teachers and therapists and offers practical ideas and suggestions for using a multi-sensory environment with pupils who have profound learning difficulties. The publication includes a series of photocopiable forms which provide a useful means of assessing a child's functional abilities in the areas of: proprioception, taste and smell, touch, hearing, vision, engagement and communication.

Multi-Sensory Action Pack (no date)

The Action Pack was written and developed by a team of staff from Stallington Hospital in Staffordshire including specialists in psychology, speech therapy and physiotherapy. It is designed for use with individuals who have severe learning difficulties and multiple impairments and in particular those who demonstrate an aversion to physical contact. The pack may be used as a form of assessment whereby the adult partner learns through observations of the person's responses to a series of stimuli how he or she indicates likes and dislikes. The pack includes a brief but useful introduction to each of the senses, an individual profile sheet and a teaching plan to assist in planning and evaluating activities. Although designed predominantly for adults, the format of the pack will also be of value to those involved in assessing how children use their senses in response to different types of stimuli. The Action Pack can be obtained from: Broom Street Specialist Resources Centre, 41 Broom Street, Hanley, Stoke-on-Trent, Staffordshire ST1 2EW, Tel: 01782 425050.

Sensory Interactive Profiles (SIPS) (no date)

SIPS was devised by Lincolnshire County Portage Service in conjunction with Lincolnshire County Psychology Service. It was developed for use with young children with profound and multiple learning difficulties (PMLD) and provides a developmental checklist for finding out about how a child uses his or her senses to learn about the world. The profile is divided into five sections, each representing the senses of sight, touch, hearing, taste and smell. It is intended to be used as a tool for baseline assessment and recognition of progress, as well as providing a guide to long term goals when used in conjunction with Portage Long Term Goal Sheets. Responses of the child's behaviour to different sensory stimuli are recorded as either 'Resists', 'Tolerates', or 'Enjoys', and can, therefore, be used to determine progress over time. Although intended predominantly for pre-school children, the format of the profile means that it can also be used with older children who are functioning at 'early stages of development'. SIPS can be obtained from National Portage Association, P.O. Box 3075, Yeovil, Somerset BA21 3FB. Tel: 01935 471641.

Jones, L. (1994) *The Kidderminster Curriculum for Children and Adults with Profound Multiple Learning Difficulties.* Yeovil: National Portage Association.

Although designed as a curriculum to help meet the specialised needs of children and adults who have severe/profound learning difficulties in combination with additional sensory disabilities, this procedure also offers a useful framework for assessing which types of sensory stimuli are reinforcing to the individual. Through use of a 'Reinforcer Assessment List' the adult presents a range of stimuli (e.g. vibration, cold air, warm air, etc.) and records whether each can be considered to be 'aversive' (individual cries, withdraws, etc.), 'neutral' (i.e. no response) or is likely to be effective as a reinforcer (individual is very responsive). An Assessment Checklist is used to monitor and record progress as specific skills are developed in a number of core areas (i.e. Self-Help, Gross-Motor, Fine-Motor, Socialisation and Communication, Play/Leisure, Daily Living) with target skills and teaching suggestions provided in the Handbook.

Further reading for functional sensory assessment

Brown, N., McLinden, M. and Porter, J. (1998) 'Sensory needs', in Lacey, P. and Ouvry, C. (eds) *People with Profound and Multiple Learning Disabilities: a collaborative approach to meeting complex needs.* London: David Fulton.

Buultjens, M. (1997) 'Functional vision assessment and development in children and young people with multiple disabilities and visual impairment', in Mason, H. and McCall, S. (eds) *Access to Education for Children with Visual Impairment.* London: David Fulton.

Erin, J. (1996) 'Functional vision assessment and instruction of children and youths with multiple disabilities', in Corn, A. and Koenig, A. (eds) *Foundations of Low Vision: clinical and functional perspectives.* New York: American Foundation for the Blind.

McLinden, M. (1998) 'Assessment of children with multiple disabilities and a visual impairment', Supplement in *Eye Contact*, **21**, Summer.

Thies, L., Keeffe, J. and Clarke, G. (1998) 'Low vision', in Kelley, P. and Gale, G. (eds) *Towards Excellence*. North Rocks, Australia: North Rocks Press.

Tobin, M. (1996) 'Optimising the use of sensory information', in Bozic, N. and Murdoch, H. (eds) *Learning Through Interaction: Technology and Children with Multiple Disabilities*. London: David Fulton.

Tactile defensive behaviours

A summary of publications which have particular relevance to assessing and developing behaviours in children who are described as resistant to touch is included below. This list also includes a number of the sources which have been described in other areas of this section.

> Fink, B. (1989) *Sensory-Motor Integration Activities*. Arizona: Therapy Skills Builders.
>
> Although this pack is designed as a collection of sensori-motor integration activities for 'remediation of dysfunctions' found in early years children without sensory impairment, it offers some useful ideas for supporting a child's learning through touch. A 'tactile' section highlights the role of information received through touch as a basis for learning and offers a series of activities which aim to promote better tactile integration, thereby enabling the child to use the sense of touch in more effective ways to learn from body and environment. Available from Winslow, Telford Road, Bicester, Oxon, OX6 OTS. Tel: 01869 244733.

> *Assessing Communication Together (ACT) – A systematic approach to assessing and developing early communication skills in children and adults with multi-sensory impairments.* (Details given on p. 168)
>
> The use of touch in developing communication is considered in some depth and a touch-grid is included for assessing the child's responses to different types of touch (i.e. Very Resistant; Accepts Passively; Enjoys; Signals for More; Initiates). A more up-to-date summary by the same author can be found in Bradley, H. (1998) 'Assessing and developing successful communication', in Lacey, P. and Ouvry, C. (eds) *People with Profound and Multiple Learning Disabilities: a collaborative approach to meeting complex needs*. London: David Fulton.

The Kidderminster Curriculum for Children and Adults with Profound Multiple Learning Difficulties. (Details given on p. 174)

As noted above, the Reinforcer Assessment List provides a useful summary of a child's responses to sensory stimuli including a range of stimuli received through touch (e.g. vibration, cold air, warm air, etc.) and provides a basis for structuring the teaching curriculum. A number of specific skills within the component Sensory Stimulation are designed to increase the child's positive responses to different tactile stimuli, including vibration, warm/cold air as well as a range of different tactile substances.

McInnes, J. M. and Treffry, J. (1982) *Deafblind Infants and Children: Developmental Guide.* Canada: University of Toronto Press.

Although rather dated, this book still provides a useful source of information for those working with children who are deafblind. This book introduces the Stages of Interaction framework to which reference is made in this text and which provides the basis of other more current developmental frameworks (e.g. QCA/DfEE 2001). Includes a useful section on tactile development incorporating an evaluation checklist for assessing a child's responses to different types of tactile stimuli, as well as providing ideas for activities to develop a child's responses through touch.

Sensory Interactive Profiles (SIPS)
(Details given on pp. 173–4)

A detailed developmental checklist on 'touch' provides a useful tool for recording a child's responses to different types of tactile experiences. The achievements of the child are recorded as Resists, Tolerates and Enjoys, with the aim of an intervention programme being to work with a child in moving from 'resisting' a tactile experience (i.e. tactile defensive behaviour) to 'tolerating' it, and eventually 'enjoying' the experience.

Longhorn, F. (1988) *A Sensory Curriculum for Very Special People: a practical approach to curriculum planning.* London: Souvenir Press.

Although rather dated, the whole text is a valuable resource for those seeking detailed information on how to develop and use a 'sensory curriculum'. Of particular relevance to this section is Chapter 6 which examines in some depth the development of a Tactile Curriculum and Tactile Bank. A number of frameworks are included in this chapter which will be useful in developing a child's active participation in different types of tactile experiences.

Dale, F. J. (1990) *The Stimulation Guide: a sourcebook of suggestions and activities for multi-sensor impaired children and others with developmental difficulties.* Cambridge: Woodhead-Faulkner.

Written by a teacher of children who are deafblind, this practical guide is a useful sourcebook of suggestions and activities aimed at increasing the physical and psychological development of children who are multi-sensory impaired, as well as others with developmental difficulties. The book is divided into the areas of locomotion, occupation, person/social, self-care and communication/language. A number of these areas include the use of touch and suggestions are provided for activities to use if the child either does not appear to enjoy touching objects or people, or does not like to be touched by others.

Wyman, R. (2000) *Making Sense Together.* Guernsey: Guernsey Press.

A very practical text in which the author draws on her experience of working closely with parents to develop the abilities of children who have multisensory impairments. The text includes information on creating 'reactive' learning environments through the use of the Little Room and the resonance board, as well as a helpful summary on structuring learning through touch for children who are defensive to touching and being touched.

Allen, C. A. (ed.) (2001) *Framework for Learning: for adults with profound and complex learning difficulties.* London: David Fulton.

Although intended for practitioners supporting the learning of adults, this publication also has relevance to the needs of children and young people with complex learning difficulties. Of particular relevance is Chapter 3, which explores 'acceptance' of touch as a foundation skill to be developed when structuring a programme for an individual. Further references to the important role of touch when supporting learning experiences are included throughout the text. Chapter 11 offers a helpful summary of functional assessment of visual and/or hearing in older learners with complex learning difficulties and suggests how the information from this assessment can be used when planning a programme for the learner.

Ferrell, K. (1985) *Reach out and Teach*. New York: American Foundation for the Blind.

A helpful publication from AFB with particular relevance to supporting the learning of young children with a visual impairment. The text includes reference to children who are defensive to touch and offers a number of useful suggestions for supporting the child's learning experiences.

Selection of procedures which have relevance to the assessment of children who have MDVI

Dunst, C. J. (1980) *A Clinical and Educational Manual for Use with The Uzgiris and Hunt Scales of Infant Psychological Development*. Baltimore, MD: University Park Press.

Uzgiris, I. C. and Hunt, J. (1975) *Assessment in Infancy*. Urbana, IL: University of Illinois Press.

Although the 'Uzgiris-Hunt Scales' (also referred to as the *Ordinal Scales of Psychological Development* or *OSPD*) were originally standardised on normally developing infants, revisions were made to the scales by Dunst (1980), who developed a practical manual and scoring system to determine an individual's overall pattern of sensori-motor development that was intended to assess 'the development of infants and older retarded and handicapped children who are at risk for manifesting delays and/or deviations in their sensori-motor development' (p. 1).

The OSPD incorporates seven separate domains or branches of development (i.e. Object permanence; Means-ends abilities; Vocal imitation; Gestural imitation; Operational causality; Spatial relationships; Schemes for relating to objects). Within most of these domains, vision is central in order to record the progression of 'critical behaviours' outlined for each scale step, e.g. in 'Object permanence', 'Means-ends abilities', 'Gestural imitation', 'Spatial relationships.' The domains in which vision is not so crucial in describing such critical behaviours are 'Vocal imitation', 'Operational causality' and 'Schemes for relating to objects'. The domain 'Schemes for relating to objects' has particular relevance to assessing a child's haptic abilities with objects. The eliciting situations for assessing the child's schemes are grouped according to three types of behaviours:

- actions with simple objects;
- actions on several objects available together;
- actions on objects having social meaning.

The critical behaviours within this domain are determined in response to the child's spontaneous behaviours applied to objects within these three groupings. It is highlighted that a variety of different toys and materials from each group should be offered to the child during the course of assessment to ensure that the child's repertoire of 'scheme action' is adequately sampled.

Coupe, J. and Levy, D. (1985) 'The object related scheme assessment procedure: a cognitive assessment for developmentally young children who may have additional physical or sensory handicaps', *Mental Handicap* **13**, March, 22–4.

In an attempt to devise a 'simple but effective instrument' (Coupe and Levy 1985, p. 22) the ORSAP was developed, based largely on the sub-scale 'Schemes for Relating to Objects' from the OSPD. The procedure was designed to enable the educator to gain insight into a child's repertoire of schemes during interaction with an object. Information about the level of cognitive development is acquired through observation and recording the child's behaviours in response to object stimuli presented individually or in combination. Coupe and Levy (1985) reported that the aim of the assessment procedure was for the child to be able to 'apply a generalisation of patterns of behaviour, that is, schemes, and use them by discriminating the properties and functions of the object presented' (p. 22).

The situations for assessing the child's schemes for relating to objects are the same as described for the OSPD, i.e. actions with simple objects, actions on several objects together, actions on objects having social meanings. The 'critical behaviours' are determined in response to a child's spontaneous behaviours applied to objects within these groupings. The child is considered to have reached the highest performance level (scheme) when the same behaviour has been exhibited five times with at least three different objects. An assessment summary provides a profile of the child's functional cognitive process and indicates the direction for strategies of intervention.

Reynell, J. (1981) *The Reynell-Zinkin Scales Developmental Scales for Young Visually Handicapped Children, Part 1 Mental Development.* Windsor: NFER-Nelson.

In developing the R-Z scales, Reynell (1981) proposed that they would be useful for developmental assessment of babies and young children, including those who were likely to have additional handicaps. Five main areas of development were selected as those considered most important for the 'intellectual development of children with severe visual handicaps' including the sub-scale 'Sensori-Motor understanding'. It was reported by Reynell and Zinkin that 'sensori-motor understanding' indicated the level of learning in relation to concrete objects. Reynell (1981) emphasised that during assessment it was important to study the ways in which children with congenital visual impairment learnt and made sense of their world, rather than attempting to compare them with sighted children 'minus the visual component' (p. 5). It is stressed that there were no attempts to standardise the scales, 'partly because there is no "standard" blind population, but mainly because the aim is to use them as a basis for planning a programme of help for individual children rather than for comparing the child to a "standard" population' (p. 67).

However, approximate age levels are provided, 'so that relative strengths and weaknesses' could be assessed in the different learning areas, 'and so that rate of progress could be estimated' (p. 67).

Stillman, R. D. (ed.) (1978) *Callier-Azusa Scale* (G). Dallas: University of Texas.

The Callier-Azusa scale is described as a 'developmental' scale specifically to aid in the assessment of children considered to be 'deaf-blind as well as those who are profoundly handicapped' (Stillman 1978: 2). The aim of the scale is to provide the assessment information 'necessary to synthesise developmentally appropriate activities for a child' rather than to 'tell the user what activities to carry out with the child' (p. 2). Although the stated purpose of the procedure is to be comprehensive particularly at lower stages of development, Stillman (1978) acknowledges that since 'the example behaviours take into account the specific sensory, motor, language, and social deficits of some deaf-blind and severely and profoundly impaired children, the behaviours sometimes differ from behaviours typically observed among normal children at the same developmental level' (pp. 2–3).

The scale comprises 18 sub-scales in five areas (i.e. 'Motor Development', 'Perceptual Development', 'Daily Living Skills', 'Cognition, Communication and Language' and 'Social Development'). Within these areas the sub-scales

'Development of Fine Motor Skills' (in the area Motor Development) and 'Cognitive Development' (in the area Cognition, Communication and Language) have particular relevance to assessment of a child's haptic activities. Administration of the scale is in accordance with the 'Criteria for Assessing Developmental Level' given in the procedure.

Nielsen, L. (1990) *Functional and Instruction Scheme: the visually impaired child's early abilities, behaviours, learning.* Copenhagen: Sikon.

The FIS (Nielsen 1990) is an observation checklist of 27 areas designed to observe and record progress made by young children with a visual impairment. It was developed 'on the basis of the problems which have emerged during pedagogical work with 400–500 visually impaired children, and partly on the basis of a scientific study on spatial relations in congenitally blind infants' (Introduction to FIS). The FIS was based on a series of questions, which it was claimed, 'make it possible to find inspiration and ideas' about activities which can be included in 'the programme for educational treatment of the child' (Introduction to FIS). The questions are answered using the categories, 'Yes', 'No', 'Don't know', 'Has been able to', 'Learning has begun', 'Learned in learning situation', 'Used spontaneously'. Nielsen commented that as 'knowledge is so far not available about the time when a visually impaired child can be expected to perform certain tasks, the assessment of the child is made on knowledge about a normal child's development' (Nielsen 1990, Introduction to FIS).

Although the FIS has been described as a 'comprehensive observation checklist' (Pagliano 1999: 31), the absence of criteria for administration of the scheme together with lack of operational definitions describing how particular terms should be interpreted may limit the value of the scale for assessment purposes.

Erhardt, R. P. (1994) *Erhardt Developmental Prehension Assessment (EDPA).* Tucson, AZ: Therapy Skill Builders.

The EDPA was designed to assess hand function with a particular focus on 'atypical variations' in prehension in children with cerebral palsy. Within the procedure, Sections 1 and 2 were designed to measure prehension from the early days of development to the 15 months level which, it was proposed, could be considered 'the maturity of prehension' and, therefore, an 'approximate norm for assessing older children and adults' (Erhardt 1994b: 2).

Kiernan, C. and Jones, M. C. (1982) (2nd Edition) *Behaviour Assessment Battery*. Windsor: NFER-Nelson.

The Behaviour Assessment Battery (BAB) was designed for use by teachers and psychologists to evaluate the behaviour of children with severe and profound learning difficulties as well as to develop targets for educational programmes. The Battery describes procedures for assessing the cognitive skills, including play and social behaviour, communicative and self-help skills. The Battery incorporates criterion-referenced test items with the child being required to demonstrate the 'criterion behaviour' in order to achieve the test item. The BAB was not developed for use by children who have a visual impairment and vision is implicit in many of the test items. However a number of test items within the section 'Exploratory Play' have relevance when assessing the haptic abilities of children with MDVI and may provide ideas for further assessment and target setting.

Play

RNIB (1994) *Look and Touch – Play activities and toys for children with visual impairments*. London: RNIB.

A 20-page booklet produced jointly by RNIB and the National Association of Toy and Leisure Libraries. The booklet describes how children with visual impairments can develop through play with helpful suggestions for toys and activities. Available from RNIB Customer Service (see p. 189).

RNIB *The Toy Catalogue* (updated annually). London: RNIB.

A 48-page catalogue produced jointly by RNIB and the British Toy and Hobby Association. The catalogue lists over 100 toys selected for their suitability for children with a visual impairment. Available from RNIB Customer Service (see p. 189).

RNIB (1995) *Play It My Way: Learning through play with your visually impaired child*. London: HMSO.

This publication is aimed at parents of children with a visual impairment including those with additional needs, and is intended as a resource book containing practical ideas for day-to-day routines to enable children to find out about their world through play. This publication is available from HMSO Publications Centre (020 7873 9090) or RNIB Customer Service (see p. 189).

Lear, R. (1990) *More Play Helps: Play ideas for children with special needs*. Oxford: Heinemann Medical Books.

An A–Z guide of inexpensive and easy to make toys and activities for parents as well as practitioners. Although this publication does not deal solely with children who have a visual impairment, it does address the needs of children with a wide range of disabilities including those with additional needs. A number of sections have particular relevance to children with a visual impairment including 'Ways of Hanging Toys'; 'Ways of Keeping Toys to Hand'; 'Feely Toys'; 'Hands' and 'Visual Stimulation'.

Action for Leisure (2000) *To Infinity and Beyond: Age-appropriateness in play and leisure activities*. Moreton Morrell: Action for Leisure.

Action for Leisure is a registered charity promoting play and leisure with and for adults and children who have disabilities including sensory impairments. It produces a range of publications on different issues relating to play and leisure, including posters and training handbooks. This short leaflet outlines issues concerning age-appropriateness for people with learning difficulties with a particular focus on play and multi-sensory environments. See below for details of Action for Leisure.

Useful contacts for play and leisure

PLANET
(Play Leisure Advice Network) Cambridge House, Cambridge Grove, London W6 0LE. Tel: 020 8741 4119.

Action for Leisure
c/o Warwickshire College, Moreton Morrell Centre, Moreton Morrell, Warwickshire, CV35 9BL
Tel: 01926 650195
Fax: 01926 650104
www.actionforleisure.org.uk

Curriculum materials and resources

DfEE/QCA (2001) *Supporting the Target Setting Process – Guidance for effective target setting for pupils with special educational needs* (revised edition). Nottingham: DfEE
Reference: PP47/031/64
Contact: DfES Publications Centre, PO Box 5050, Sherwood Park, Annesley, Nottingham NG15 ODJ
Tel: 0845 602 2260, Fax: 0845 603 3360
Also available at: www.standards.dfes.gov.uk/otherresources/publication/targetsetting

Equals (1999) *Baseline Assessment and Curriculum Target Setting*. North Shields: Equals
Contact: Equals (Entitlement and quality education for pupils with severe learning difficulties)
PO Box 107, North Shields, Tyne and Wear, NE30 2YG
Tel: 0191 272 8600

SCAA (1996) *Planning the Curriculum for Pupils with Profound and Multiple Learning Difficulties*. London: School Curriculum and Assessment Authority.

QCA (2001) *Planning, Teaching and Assessing the Curriculum for Pupils with Learning Difficulties*. London: Qualifications and Curriculum Authority.
Reference: QCA/01/736-750
Contact: QCA Publications
PO Box 99, Sudbury, Suffolk CO10 2SN
Tel: 01787 884 444, Fax: 01787 312 950
www.qca.org.uk

The full range of the curriculum subject materials in this set is available on the National Curriculum website: www.nc.uk.net/ld

TTA (1999) *National Special Educational Needs Specialist Standards*. London: Teacher Training Agency. Publication number 91/12-99.
Contact: TTA Publications
Portland House, Stag Place, London SW1E 5TT
Tel: 0845 606 0323
This publication is available on the TTA website: www.teach-tta.gov.uk

Further reading for the curriculum

Aird, R. (2001) *The Education and Care of Children with Severe, Profound and Multiple Learning Difficulties*. London: David Fulton.

Lawson, H. (2002) 'Effective target setting', in *Special*, Spring, 18–21.

Lawson, H., Marvin, C. and Pratt, A. (2001) 'Planning, teaching and assessing the curriculum of pupils with learning difficulties: An introduction and overview', *Support for Learning* **16**(4), 162–7.

Further reading – children with multiple disabilities

Aitken, S., Buultjens, M., Clark, C., Eyre, J. and Pease, L. (eds) *Teaching Children who are Deafblind*. London: David Fulton.

Chen, D. (ed.) (1999) *Essential Elements in Early Intervention: visual impairments and multiple disabilities*. New York: AFB Press.

Gibson, J. and Cronin, P. (1990) *Designing Programs for Children with Multiple Disabilities and Severe Vision Impairment: A Step by Step Approach*. Victoria, Australia: RVIB.
Contact: Royal Victoria Institute for the Blind
Education Centre, 333 Burwood Highway, Burwood, Victoria 3125, Australia
Tel: (03) 9808 6422, Fax: (03) 9808 2194.

Lacey, P. and Ouvry, C. (1998) *People with Profound and Multiple Learning Disabilities: a collaborative approach to meeting complex needs*. London: David Fulton.

McInnes, J. M. (ed.) (1999) *A Guide to Planning and Support for Individuals who are Deafblind*. Toronto: University of Toronto Press.

Orelove, F. and Sobsey, D. (1996) *Educating Children with Multiple Disabilities: a transdisciplinary approach*. Baltimore: Paul H. Brookes.

Rogow, S. M. (1988) *Helping the Visually Impaired Child with Developmental Problems*. New York: Teachers College Press.

VITAL/RNIB (1998) *Approaches . . . to working with children with multiple disabilities and a visual impairment*. London: RNIB.
An educational pack published by the RNIB on behalf of VITAL (Visual Impairment Touches All Learning), a non-affiliated organisation which consists of professionals who support the learning of children with MDVI. This pack contains key articles explaining how visual impairment affects all aspects of learning and contains useful ideas and ways of working with children. Sections in the pack include Population; Communication; Sensory Stimulation; Environmental Clues and Curriculum. Available from RNIB Customer Service (see p. 189).

Further reading – Lillie Nielsen (Little Room and Resonance Board)

Lillie Nielsen has published a range of texts which have relevance to supporting the learning of children with multiple disabilities. The following have particular relevance to the themes of this text. Information on the design and use of the 'Little Room' for children who have MDVI is given in Nielsen (1991) and (1992).

Details of the 'Be Active Box', an alternative to the 'Little Room', can be found in the catalogue produced by Rompa (see below for details). Ideas for use of the resonance board when supporting a child's learning are included in a number of the publications listed below. The Family Centre at SENSE has produced a fact sheet giving details on the design of a resonance board as well as ideas for equipment to use with the board (see below for further details).

Nielsen, L. (1979) *The Comprehending Hand*. Copenhagen: Socialstyrelsen.

Nielsen, L. (1990) *Are you Blind? Promotion of the Development of Children who are Especially Developmentally Threatened*. Copenhagen: Sikon.

Nielsen, L. (1991) 'Spatial relations in congenitally blind infants: a study', *Journal of Visual Impairment and Blindness*, **85**, 11-16.

Nielsen, L. (1992) *Space and Self – Active Learning by Means of the Little Room*. Copenhagen: Sikon.

Nielsen, L. (1993) *Early Learning Step by Step*. Copenhagen: Sikon.

Further reading for multi-sensory environments

Glenn, S., Cunningham, C. and Shorrock, A. (1996) 'Social interaction in multi-sensory environments', in Bozic, N. and Murdoch, H. (eds) *Learning Through Interaction: Technology and children with multiple disabilities*. London: David Fulton.

Gray, M. and Hirstwood, R. (1995) *A Practical Guide to the Use of Multi-Sensory Rooms*. Available from TFH (Toys for the Handicapped), 5–7 Severnside Business Park, Stourport-on-Severn, Worcestershire DY13 9HT. Tel 01299 827820 Fax 01299 827035 Email mail@tfhuk.com Website: www.tfhuk.co.uk

Hirstwood, R. and Smith, C. (1996) 'Developing competencies in multi-sensory rooms', in Bozic, N. and Murdoch, H. (eds) *Learning Through Interaction: Technology and children with multiple disabilities*. London: David Fulton.

Pagliano, P. (1999) *Multisensory Environments*. London: David Fulton.

Pagliano, P. (2001) *Using a Multisensory Environment – A Practical Guide for Teachers*. London: David Fulton.

Further reading for haptic perception and children with multiple disabilities

Davidson, P.W. (1985) 'Functions of haptic perceptual activity in persons with visual and developmental disabilities', *Applied Research in Mental Retardation* **6**, 349–60.

McLinden, M. (1999) 'Hand on: haptic exploratory strategies in children who are blind with multiple disabilities', *British Journal of Visual Impairment* **17**(1), 23–9.

McLinden, M. and Douglas, G. (1999) 'Developing haptic perception', *Eye Contact*, **22**, Spring.

McLinden, M. and Douglas, G. (2000) 'Haptic exploratory strategies in blind children with multiple disabilities: preliminary case study findings', *Journal of the South Pacific Educators in Visual Impairment* **1**, 5–10.

Nielsen, L. (1996) 'How the approach of guiding the hands of the visually impaired child can disturb his opportunity to build up strategies for tactile orientation', *British Journal of Visual Impairment* **14**(1), 29–31.

Rogow, S. M. (1987) 'The ways of the hand: a study of hand function among blind, visually impaired and visually impaired multi-handicapped children and adolescents', *British Journal of Visual Impairment*, Summer, **2**, 59–61.

Rowland, C. and Schweigert, P. (2001) 'Assessment and instruction of hands-on problem solving and object interaction skills in children who are deafblind', *British Journal of Visual Impairment* **19**(2), 57–68.

Commercial distributors of specialist sensory products and services

Rompa International
Goyt Side Road
Chesterfield
Derbyshire
S40 2PH
Tel: 0800 056 2323
Fax: 01246 221 802
Email: sales@rompa.com
www.rompa.com

Suppliers of a wide range of products for education and care provision.

The Sensory Company
Broad Lane Business Centre
Westfield Lane
South Elmsall
WF9 2JX
Tel: 01977 646414
Fax: 01977 646416
Email: sales@sensoryco.com
www.sensoryco.com

Manufacturers and suppliers of innovative sensory products specifically created for individuals with special needs.

SpaceKraft Limited
Crowgill House
Rosse Street
Shipley
West Yorkshire
BD18 3SW
Tel: 01274 581 007
Fax: 01274 531 966
www.spacekraft.co.uk

Manufacturers and suppliers of resources for multi-sensory environments.

Kirton-Healthcare Group Ltd
23 Rookwood Way
Haverhill
Suffolk
CB9 8PB
Tel: 0800 212 709
Email: info@kirtonhealthcare.demon.co.uk
www.kirton-healthcare.co.uk

Suppliers of Sensory Concepts which include switching systems, mobile sensory units and multi-sensory environments, designed to meet a range of individual needs.

SEMERC
Tel: 0161 827 2719
Email: sis@granadamedia.com
www.semerc.com

Offers individual assessments, consultancy and advisory support, presentations, demonstrations, as well as training in the use of ICT for children with SEN as part of the Special Needs Learning Network Programme.

QUALISYS MEDICAL
Tel: 00 46 31 336 9400
Email: sales@qualisys.se
www.qualisys.se

Swedish medical company and suppliers of the ProReflex 'motion capture system' described in Chapter 10 for recording and analysing body movements.

Useful services and sources of further information

Scottish Sensory Centre
Tel: 0131 651 6501
www.ssc.mhie.ac.uk

RNIB Customer Service
Tel: 0845 702 3153
www.rnib.org.uk/wesupply/publicat/booksales.htm

RNIB Education and Employment Information Service
Tel: 0845 766 999
www.rnib.org.uk

RNIB Technology Information Service
Tel: 0870 013 9555
www.rnib.org.uk/technology

RNIB Research Library
Tel: 0207 391 2052
www.rnib.org.uk

SENSE
The National Deaf-Blind and Rubella Association
11–13 Clifton Terrace
Finsbury Park
London N4 3SR
Tel: 0207 272 7774
www.sense.org.uk

The Family Centre
SENSE
86 Cleveland Road
Ealing
London W13 OHE
Tel: 020 8991 0513
Fax: 020 8810 5298

Soundabout

A non-profit making Charitable Trust which aims to provide training in the use of interactive music techniques to enable young people with disabilities, who might otherwise be excluded from making music, to enjoy communicating through music and sound. The 'standard' piece of equipment around which most 'low-tech' sessions are based is the *resonance* board (which can be purchased from the company). High technology methods include use of Soundbeam which enables children to create sounds through small movements. A range of resources are available including videos and training materials.

Soundabout
Ormerod School
Waynflete Road
Oxford OX3 8DD
Tel and Fax: 01865 744 175
Email: deepizzo@soundabout.freeserve.co.uk

VICTAR (Visual Impairment Centre for Teaching and Research)

VICTAR is a research centre in the School of Education at the University of Birmingham which undertakes research, offers professional development as well as providing advice and resources in the area of visual impairment and education.

VICTAR
University of Birmingham
School of Education
Edgbaston
Birmingham B15 2TT
Tel: 0121 414 6733
Fax: 0121 414 4865
Email: victar-enquiries@bham.ac.uk
www.education.bham.ac.uk/research/victar

David Fulton Publishers
The Chiswick Centre
414 Chiswick High Road
London W4 5TF
Tel: 0208 996 3610
Fax: 0208 996 3622
www.fultonpublishers.co.uk

Project SALUTE (Successful Adaptations for Learning to Use Touch Effectively)

Chen, D., Downing, J. and Rodriguez-Gill, G. (2000) 'Tactile learning strategies for children who are deaf-blind: concerns and considerations from Project SALUTE,' *Deaf-Blind Perspectives* **8**(2), 1–6.

This project, based at California State University, addresses the unique learning needs of children who are deafblind, who have severe visual impairments, and require a primarily tactile mode of learning. The aims of the project are:

- to identify, develop, document and validate tactile learning strategies for children who are deafblind and who do not use symbolic communication;
- to develop guidelines that assist in: a) determining which learning strategy will be most useful; b) identifying how or when each of these strategies should be used, and c) evaluating the effectiveness of these learning strategies for an individual child;
- to produce materials to assist service providers and family members to interact more effectively with children who are deafblind.

The Project SALUTE website provides a wide range of information on the work and findings of the project to date and is recommended for those seeking more information about research in this area.

Project SALUTE, Department of Special Education, California State University, Northridge, 18111 Nordhoff Street, Northridge, CA-91330-8265, USA. www.projectsalute.net

Distributors of tactile books

Bag Books
60 Waltham Grove,
London SW6 1QR
Tel/Fax: 020 7385 4021
Email: bagbooks@appleonline.net

Clear Vision Project
Linden Lodge School,
61 Princes Way,
London SW19 6 JB
Tel: 020 8789 9575
Email: info@clearvisionproject.org

National Library for the Blind
Far Cromwell Road,
Bredbury, Stockport SK6 2SG
Tel: 0161 355 2000
www.nlbuk.org

Tango Books
3D West Point,
36/37 Warple Way,
London W3 ORG
Tel: 020 8996 9970
Fax: 020 8996 9977
Email: sales@tangobooks.co.uk

References

Aitken, S. (1995) 'Educational assessment of deafblind learners,' in Etheridge, D. (ed.) *The Education of Dual Sensory Impaired Children: recognising and developing ability.* London: David Fulton.

Aitken, S. and Buultjens, M. (1992) *Vision for Doing: assessing functional vision in learners who are multiply disabled.* Edinburgh: Moray House Publications.

Appelle, S. (1991) 'Haptic perception of form: activity and stimulus attributes', in Heller, M.A. and Schiff, W. (eds), *The Psychology of Touch.* Hillsdale, NJ: Lawrence Erlbaum Associates.

Ayres, A. J. (1972) *Sensory Integration and Learning Disorders.* Los Angeles: Western Psychological Services.

Baldwin, J. M. (1925) *Mental Development in the Child and in the Race.* London: Macmillan.

Barraga, N. C. (1986) 'Sensory perceptual development', in Scholl, G. T. (ed.) *Foundations of Education for Blind and Visually Handicapped Children and Youth.* New York: American Foundation for the Blind.

Bartley, S. (1980) *Introduction to Perception.* New York: Harper and Row Publishers.

Bates, E. (1976) *Language and Context.* New York: Academic Press.

Bayley, N. (1969) *The Bayley Scales of Infant Development.* New York: The Psychological Corporation.

Best, A. B. (1992) *Teaching Children with Visual Impairments.* Milton Keynes: Open University Press.

Best, A. B. (1994) 'Developing and sustaining appropriate provision', in Summerscale, J. and Boothroyd E. (eds) *Deafblind Education: developing and sustaining appropriate provision.* Proceedings of the UK Conference, Birmingham, 23 March. London: SENSE.

Best, C. and Brown, N. (1994) 'Introduction to multi-sensory impairment', Birmingham Distance Education Unit 2, School of Education, University of Birmingham.

Bloom, L. (1990) *Object Symbols: a communication option*. North Rocks, Australia: The Royal New South Wales Institute for Deaf and Blind Children and North Rocks Press.

Bower, T. G. R. (1977) *A Primer of Infant Development*. San Francisco: W.H. Freeman.

Bozic, N. and Murdoch, H. (1996) 'Introduction', in Bozic, N. and Murdoch, H. (eds) *Learning through Interaction*. London: David Fulton.

Bradley, H. (1991) *Assessing Communication Together*. Penarth, Glamorgan: MHNA (Mental Health Nurses Association).

Bridgett, G. (1999) 'Social relationships and behaviours', in McInnes, J. M. (ed.) *A Guide to Planning and Support for Individuals who are Deafblind*. Toronto: University of Toronto Press.

Brown, N., McLinden, M. T. and Porter, J. (1998) 'Sensory needs', in Lacey, P. and Ouvry, C. (eds) *People with Profound and Multiple Learning Disabilities*. London: David Fulton.

Buekelman, D. R. and Mirenda, P. (1992) *Augmentative and Alternative Communication: management of severe communication*. London: Brookes.

Bushnell, E. W. and Boudreau, J. P. (1991) 'The development of haptic perception during infancy', in Heller, M.A. and Schiff, W. (eds) *The Psychology of Touch*, 139–61. Hillsdale, NJ: Lawrence Erlbaum Associates.

Bushnell, E. W. and Boudreau, J. P. (1993) 'Motor development and the mind: the potential role of motor abilities as a determinant of aspects of perceptual development', *Child Development,* 64, 1005–21.

Bushnell, E. W. and Boudreau, J. P. (1997) 'Exploring and exploiting objects with the hands during infancy', in Connolly, K. (ed.) *The Psychobiology of the Hand*. Cambridge: MacKeith Press.

Buultjens, M. (1997) 'Functional vision assessment and development in children and young people with multiple disabilities and visual impairment', in Mason, H., McCall, S., Arter, A., McLinden, M., and Stone, J. (eds) *Visual Impairment Access to Education for Children and Young People*. London: David Fulton.

Case-Smith, J. (1995) 'Grasp, release, and bimanual skills in the first two years of life', in Henderson, A. and Pehoski, C. (eds) *Hand Function in the Child: foundations for remediation*. St. Louis, MO: Mosby.

Chapman, E. K. and McCall, S. (1989) 'Visually handicapped children: current issues', in Jones, N. (ed.) *Special Educational Needs Review Volume 2*. Lewes, East Sussex: The Falmer Press.

Chen, D., Downing, J. and Rodriguez-Gill, G. (2000) 'Tactile learning strategies for children who are deaf-blind: concerns and considerations from Project SALUTE', *Deaf-Blind Perspectives*, **8**(2), 1–6.

Cholewiak, R. W. and Collins, A. A. (1991) 'Sensory and physiological bases of touch', in Heller, M.A. and Schiff, W. (eds) *The Psychology of Touch*. Hillsdale, NJ: Lawrence Erlbaum Associates.

Clark, C. (1981) 'Learning words using traditional orthography and the symbols of Rebus, Bliss, and Carrier', *Journal of Speech and Hearing Disorders* 46, 191–6.

Clunies-Ross, L. and Franklin, A. (1997) 'Where have all the children gone? An analysis of the new statistical data on visual impairment amongst children in England, Scotland and Wales', *British Journal of Visual Impairment* **15**(2), 48–53.

Conolly, K. (ed.) (1997) *The Psychobiology of the Hand*. Cambridge: MacKeith Press.

Conolly, K. and Elliot, J. (1972) 'The evolution and ontogeny of hand function', in Jones, B. (ed.) *Ethological Studies of Child Behaviour*. Cambridge: Cambridge University Press.

Corbetta, D. and Mounoud, P. (1990) 'Early development of grasping and manipulation', in Bard, C., Fleury, M. and Hay, L. (eds) *Development of Eye-hand Coordination Across the Life Span*. Columbia, SC: University of South Carolina Press.

Coupe, J., Barton, L., Barber, M., Collins, D. and Murphy, D. (1985) 'The object related scheme assessment procedure: a cognitive assessment for development-ally young children who may have additional physical or sensory handicaps', *Mental Handicap* **13**, March, 22–4.

Coupe, J., O'Kane, J. and Goldbart, J. (1998) *Communication Before Speech*. 2nd edition. London: David Fulton.

Daniels, H. (1996) 'Foreword', in Bozic, N. and Murdoch, H. (eds) *Learning Through Interaction*. London: David Fulton.

Davidson, P. W. (1985) 'Functions of haptic perceptual activity in persons with visual and developmental disabilities', *Applied Research in Mental Retardation* **6**, 349–60.

Detheridge, T. and Detheridge, M. (1997) *Literacy Through Symbols*. London: David Fulton.

DfEE (2001) *Supporting the Target Setting Process: Guidance for effective target setting for pupils with special educational needs*. Annesley, Nottingham: DfEE Publications.

Douglas, G. and Dickens, J. (1996) 'The development of early tactile reading skills', in Bozic, N. and Murdoch, H. (eds) *Learning Through Interaction*. London: David Fulton.

Dunst, C. and Lowe, L. (1986) 'From reflex to symbol: describing, explaining and fostering communicative competence', *Augmentative and Alternative Communication* **2**, 11–18.

Eliasoon, A. C. (1995) 'Sensorimotor integration of normal and impaired development of precision movement of the hand', in Henderson, A. and Pehoski, C. (eds) *Hand Function in the Child: foundations for remediation.* St. Louis, MO: Mosby-Year Book.

Erhardt, R. P. (1994) *Erhardt Developmental Prehension Assessment (EDPA).* Tucson, AZ: Therapy Skill Builders.

Exner, C. E. and Henderson, A. (1995) 'Cognition and motor skills', in Henderson, A. and Pehoski, C. (eds) *Hand Function in the Child: foundations for remediation.* St. Louis, MO: Mosby-Year Book.

Ferell, K. A., Trief, E., Dietz, S. J., Bonner, M. A., Crux, D., Ford, E. and Stratton, J. M. (1990) 'Visually impaired infants research consortium (VIIRC): first-year results', *Journal of Visual Impairment and Blindness* **84**, 404–10.

Folio, M. R. and Fewell, R. R. (1983) *Peabody Developmental Motor Scales.* Allen, TX: DLM Teaching Resources.

Foulke, E. (1991) 'Braille', in Heller, M. A. and Schiff, W. (eds), *The Psychology of Touch*, 219–33. Hillsdale, NJ: Lawrence Erlbaum Associates.

Fraiberg, S. (1977) *Insights from the Blind.* London: Souvenir Press.

Geenens, D. L. (1999) 'Neurobiological development and cognition in the deafblind', in McInnes, J. M. (ed.) *A Guide to Planning and Support for Individuals who are Deafblind.* Toronto: University of Toronto Press.

Gibson, E. J. (1988) 'Exploratory behavior in the development of perceiving, acting, and the acquiring of knowledge', *Annual Review of Psychology* **39**, 1–41.

Gibson, J. J. (1962) 'Observations on active touch', *Psychological Review* **69**, 477–91.

Gibson, J. J. (1966) *The Senses Considered as Perceptual Systems.* Boston: Houghton-Mifflin.

Glenn, S., Cunningham, C. and Shorrock, A. (1996) 'Social interaction in multisensory environments', in Bozic, N. and Murdoch, H. (eds) *Learning Through Interaction.* London: David Fulton.

Goldbart, J. (1988) 'Communication for a purpose', in Coupe, J. and Goldbart, J. (eds) *Communication Before Speech.* London: Chapman and Hall.

Goldstein, E. B. (1989) *Sensation and Perception*, 3rd edition. Belmont, CA: Wadsworth Publishing Company.

Goold, L. and Hummell, J. (1993) *Supporting the Receptive Communication of Individuals with Significant Multiple Disabilities: selective use of touch to enhance comprehension.* North Rocks, Australia: North Rocks Press.

Gregory, R. L. (ed.) (1987) *The Oxford Companion to the Mind.* Oxford and New York: Oxford University Press.

Griffen, H. and Gerber, P. (1982) 'Tactual development and its implications for the education of blind children', *Education of the Visually Handicapped,* Winter, **XIII**(4), 116–23.

Hall, N. (1987) *The Emergence of Literacy.* London: Hodder and Stoughton.

Hatwell, Y. (1987) 'Motor and cognitive functions of the hand in infancy and childhood', *International Journal of Behavioral Development* **10**(4), 509–26.

Hatwell, Y. (1990) 'Spatial perception by eyes and hand: comparison and cross-modal integration', in Bard, C., Fleury, M. and Hay, L. (eds) *The Development of Eye-hand Coordination Across the Life Span.* Columbia: University of South Carolina Press.

Heller, M. A. (1986) 'Central and peripheral influences on tactual reading', *Perception and Psychophysics* **39**, 197–204.

Heller, M. A. (1991) 'Haptic perception in blind people', in Heller, M. A. and Schiff, W. (eds), *The Psychology of Touch*, 243–5. Hillsdale, NJ: Lawrence Erlbaum Associates.

Heller, M. A. and Schiff, W. (eds) (1991) *The Psychology of Touch.* Hillsdale, NJ: Lawrence Erlbaum Associates.

Hendrickson, H. (1997) 'Development of early communication', in Mason, H., McCall, S., Arter, A., McLinden, M. and Stone, J. (eds) *Visual Impairment Access to Education for Children and Young People.* London: David Fulton.

Hendrickson, H. and McLinden, M. (1996) 'Using tactile symbols: a review of current issues', *Eye Contact* **14**, Spring, Supplement.

Hogg, J. and Sebba, J. (1986) *Profound Retardation and Multiple Impairment. Vol. 1: Development and Learning.* London: Croom Helm.

Hull, T. (1993) 'The nature and development of spatial processing blind children and young adults: an approach based on the use of tactile maps'. Unpublished PhD. Department of Psychology, University of Birmingham.

Huss, A. J. (1977) 'Touch with care or caring touch', *American Journal of Occupational Therapy* **31**, 295–309.

Kangas, K. A. and Lloyd, L. L. (1988) 'Early cognitive skills as prerequisites to augmentative and alternative communication use: what are we waiting for?', *Augmentative and Alternative Communication*, 211–21.

Karlan, G. and Lloyd, L. (1983) 'Examination of recall comprehension learning by moderately retarded individuals responding to oral and manual cues'. Paper presented at the 107th Annual Meeting of the American Association on Mental Deficiency, Dallas, Texas.

Katz, D. (1925) 'Der Aufbau der Tastwelt'. *Zeitschrift für Psychologie*, 11, Leipzig: Barth. Translated in Kruger, L. E. (1989) *The World of Touch.* Hillsdale, NJ: Lawrence Erlbaum Associates.

Kelley, P. (1998) 'Children with vision impairments and intellectual or physical disabilities', in Kelley, P. and Gale, G. (eds) *Towards Excellence: effective education for students with vision impairments.* Australia: North Rocks Press.

Klatzky, R. L. and Lederman, S. (1993) 'Towards a computational model of constraint-driven exploration and haptic object identification', *Perception* **22**, 597–621.

Klatzky, R. L., Lederman, S. J. and Metzger, V. A. (1985) 'Identifying objects by touch: an "expert system"', *Perception and Psychophysics* **37**, 299–302.

Klatzky, R. L., Lederman, S. and Reed, C. (1987) 'There's more to touch than meets the eye: the salience of object attributes for haptics with and without vision', *Journal of Experimental Psychology*, **116**(4), 356–69.

Langley, M. B. (1986) 'Psychoeducational assessment of visually impaired students with additional handicaps', in Ellis, D. (ed.) *Sensory Impairments in Mentally Handicapped People*. London: Croom Helm.

Lederman, S. J. and Klatzky, R. L. (1987) 'Hand movements: a window into haptic object recognition', *Cognitive Psychology* **19**, 342–68.

Lee, M. and MacWilliam, L. (1995) *Movement Gesture and Sign*. London: RNIB.

Lee, M. and MacWilliam, L. (2002) *Learning Together*. London: RNIB.

Lewis, V. and Collis, G. M. (1997) *Blindness and Psychological Development in Young Children*. Leicester: British Psychological Society.

Lloyd, L. and Blischak, D. (1992) 'AAC terminology policy and issues update', *Augmentative and Alternative Communication* **8**(2), 104–9.

Lochman, J. J. (1986) 'Perceptuomotor coordination in sighted infants: implications for visually impaired children', *Topics in Early Childhood Special Education* **6**(3), 23–6.

Longhorn, F. (1988) *A Sensory Curriculum for Very Special People*. London: Souvenir Press.

Lorimer, J. (1978) 'The limitations of braille as a medium for communication and the possibility of improving reading standards', *The British Psychological Society Occasional Papers* **2**(11), 60–7.

Magee, L. E. and Kennedy, J. M. (1980) 'Exploring pictures tactually', *Nature* **283**, 287–8.

Martin, J. H. and Jessell, T. M. (1991) 'Modality coding in the somatosensory system', in Kandel, E. R., Schwartz, J. H. and Jessell, T. M. (eds), 3rd edition. *Principles of Neural Science*. New York: Elsevier.

Mason, H., McCall, S., Arter, A., McLinden, M. and Stone, J. (eds) (1997) *Visual Impairment Access to Education for Children and Young People*. London: David ⌐ ⌐on.

S. and McLinden, M. (1996) 'Literacy – a foot in the door?', *Eye Contact*, ˥ent, **16**, Autumn.

nd McLinden, M. (2001) 'Accessing the National Literacy Strategy: Moon with children in the United Kingdom with a visual impairment and additional learning difficulties', *The British Journal of Visual Impairment* **19**(1), 7–16.

McCall, S. and McLinden, M. (2001) 'Literacy and children who are blind and who have additional disabilities: the challenges for teachers and researchers', *International Journal of Disability, Development and Education* **48**(4), 354–75.

McCall, S., McLinden, M. and Stone, J. (1994) 'Moon as a route to literacy project: summary of findings', *British Journal of Visual Impairment* **12**(1), 34–5.

McInnes, J. M. (1999) *A Guide to Planning and Support for Individuals who are Deafblind.* Toronto: University of Toronto Press.

McInnes, J. and Treffry, J. (1982) *Deafblind Infants and Children.* Toronto: University of Toronto Press.

McLinden, M. (1997) 'Children with multiple disabilities and a visual impairment', in Mason, H., McCall, S., Arter, A., McLinden, M. and Stone, J. (eds) *Visual Impairment: Access to Education for Children and Young People.* London: David Fulton.

McLinden, M. (1998) 'Assessment of children with multiple disabilities and a visual impairment', *Eye Contact* **21**, Summer, Supplement.

McLinden, M. (1999) 'Hand on: haptic exploratory strategies in children who are blind with multiple disabilities', *British Journal of Visual Impairment* **17**(1), 23–9.

McLinden, M. (2000) 'Haptic exploratory strategies and children who are blind with multiple disabilities'. Unpublished PhD thesis. The University of Birmingham.

McLinden, M. and Douglas, G. (1999) 'Developing haptic perception', *Eye Contact* **22**, Spring.

McLinden, M. and Douglas, G. (2000) 'Haptic exploratory strategies in blind children with multiple disabilities: preliminary case study findings', *Journal of South Pacific Educators in Visual Impairment* **1**, 5–10.

Miles, B. and Riggio, M. (1999) *Remarkable Conversations: a guide to developing meaningful communication with children and young adults who are deafblind.* Watertown, MA: Perkins School for the Blind.

Millar, S. (1994) *Understanding and Representing Space: theory and evidence from studies with blind and sighted children.* Oxford: Oxford Clarendon Press.

Millar, S. (1997) *Reading by Touch.* London and New York: Routledge.

Millar, S. and Aitken, S. (1996) 'Voice output communication aids', in Bozic, N. and Murdoch, H. (eds) *Learning Through Interaction: technology and children with multiple disabilities.* London: David Fulton.

Millar, S. and McEwan, G. (1993) 'Passports to communication', in Wilson, A. and Millar, S. (eds) *Augmentative Communication in Practice.* Edinburgh: CALL Centre.

Murdoch, H. (1997) 'Multi-sensory impairment', in Mason, H. and McCall, S. (eds) *Visual Impairment: access to education for children and young people*. London: David Fulton.

Murray-Branch, J., Udvari-Solner, A. and Bailey, B. (1991) 'Textured communication systems for individuals with severe intellectual and dual sensory impairments', *Language, Speech and Hearing Services in the Schools* **22**, 260–8.

Musselwhite, C. and Ruscello, D. (1984) 'Transparency of three communication symbol systems', *Journal of Speech and Hearing Research* **27**, 436–43.

Musselwhite, C. and St. Louis, K. (1982) *Communication Programming for the Severely Handicapped*. San Diego, CA: College-Hill Press.

Nielsen, L. (1979) *The Comprehending Hand*. Copenhagen: Socialstyrelsen.

Nielsen, L. (1988) *Spatial Relations in Congenitally Blind Infants*. Kalundborg, Denmark: Refsnaesskolen.

Nielsen, L. (1990) *Functional and Instruction Scheme: the visually impaired child's early abilities, behaviours, learning*. Copenhagen: Sikon.

Nielsen, L. (1991) 'Spatial relations in congenitally blind infants: a study', *Journal of Visual Impairment and Blindness* **85**, 11–16.

Nielsen, L. (1992) *Space and Self: Active Learning by Means of the Little Room*. Copenhagen: Sikon.

Nielsen, L. (1993) *Early Learning Step by Step*. Copenhagen: Sikon.

Nielsen, L. (1996) 'How the approach of guiding the hands of the visually impaired child can disturb his opportunity to build up strategies for tactile orientation', *British Journal of Visual Impairment* **14**(1), 29–31.

Norris, M., Spaulding, P. J. and Brodie, F. H. (1957) *Blindness in Children*. Chicago: University of Chicago Press.

Ockelford, A. (1994) *Objects of Reference: promoting communication skills and concept development for visually impaired children who have other disabilities*. London: RNIB.

Ockelford, A. (2002) *Objects of Reference: promoting early symbolic communication*. London: RNIB.

Olson, M.R. (1981) *Guidelines and Games for Teaching Efficient Braille Reading*. New York: American Foundation for the Blind.

Pagliano, P. (1999) *Multisensory Environments*. London: David Fulton.

Pagliano, P. (2001) *Using a Multisensory Environment: a practical guide for teachers*. London: David Fulton.

Park, K. (1995) 'Using objects of reference: a review of the literature', *European Journal of Special Needs Education* **10**(1), 40–6.

Park, K. (1997) 'How do objects become objects of reference? A review of the literature on objects of reference and a proposed model for the use of objects in communication', *British Journal of Visual Impairment* **24**(3), September, 108–14.

Pease, L. (2000) 'Creating a communicating environment', in Aitken, S., Buult-jens, M., Clark, C., Eyre, J. and Pease, L. (eds) *Teaching Children who are Deafblind*. London: David Fulton.

Pehoski, C. (1995) 'Cortical control of skilled movements of the hand', in Henderson, A. and Pehoski, C. (eds) *Hand Function in the Child: Foundations for Remediation*, 3–15. St. Louis, MO: Mosby-Year Book.

Piaget, J. (1926) *The Language and Thought of the Child*. New York: Harcourt Brace Jovanovich.

Piaget, J. (1953) *The Origins of Intelligence in Children*. London: Routledge and Kegan Paul.

Piaget, J. (1954) *The Child's Construction of Reality*. New York: Basic Books.

QCA (2001a) *General Guidelines Planning Teaching and Assessing the Curriculum for Pupils with Learning Difficulties*. Sudbury, Suffolk: QCA Publications.

QCA (2001b) *English: planning, teaching and assessing the curriculum for pupils with learning difficulties*. Sudbury, Suffolk: QCA Publications.

Reed, L. and Addis, C. (1996) 'Developing a concept of control', in Bozic, N. and Murdoch, H. (eds) *Learning through Interaction: technology and children with multiple disabilities*. London: David Fulton.

Revesz, G. (1950) *Psychology and Art of the Blind*. New York: Longmans, Green and Co. Translated from *Die Formenwelt des Tastsinnes*, The Hague: Martinus Nijhoff, 1933.

Rex, E. J., Koenig, A. J., Wormsley, D. P. and Baker, R. L. (1994) *Foundations of Braille Literacy*. New York: American Foundation for the Blind.

Reynell, J. (1981) *The Reynell-Zinkin Scales Developmental Scales for Young Visually Handicapped Children – Part 1 Mental Development*. Windsor: NFER-Nelson.

Roberts, R. and Wing, A. M. (2001) 'Making sense of active touch', *British Journal of Visual Impairment* **19**(2), 48–56.

Rochat, P. (1989) 'Object manipulation and exploration in 2- to 5-month-old infants', *Developmental Psychology* **25**, 871–4.

Rogow, S. M. (1988) *Helping the Visually Impaired Child With Developmental Problems*. New York: Teachers College Press.

Rosen, S. (1997) 'Kinesiology and sensorimotor function', in Blasch, B. B., Wiener, W. R. and Welsh, R. L. (eds) *Foundations of Orientation and Mobility*. New York: American Foundation for the Blind.

Ross, S., Tobin, M. J. and Fielder, A. R. (1997) 'Effective spoon use by blind and partially sighted infants'. Birmingham: University of Birmingham, Research Centre for the Education of the Visually Handicapped (Mimeo).

Rowland, C. and Schweigert, P. (1989) 'Tangible symbols: symbolic communication for individuals with multisensory impairments', *Augmentative and Alternative Communication* **5**, 226–34.

Royeen, C. and Lane, S. (1991) 'Tactile processing and sensory defensiveness', in Fisher, A., Murray, E. and Bundy, A. (eds) *Sensory Integration: theory and practice*. Philadelphia: F.A. Davis.

Ruff, H.A. (1982) 'Role of manipulation in infants' responses to invariant properties of objects', *Developmental Psychology* **18**(5), 682–91.

Ruff, H.A. (1984) 'Infants' manipulative exploration of objects: effects of age and object characteristics', *Developmental Psychology* **20**(1), 9–20.

Ruff, H.A. (1989) 'The infant's use of visual and haptic information in the perception and recognition of objects', *Canadian Journal of Psychology* **43**, 302–19.

Scardina, V. (1986) 'A Jean Ayres Lectureship', *Sensory Integration Newsletter* **14**(3), 2–10.

Schiff, W. and Foulke, E. (eds) (1982) *Tactual Perception: a sourcebook*. Cambridge: Cambridge University Press.

Schwartz, A.S., Perey, A.J. and Azulay, A. (1975) 'Further analysis of active and passive touch in pattern discrimination', *Bulletin of the Psychonomic Society* **6**, 7–9.

Siegel-Causey, E. and Downing, J. (1987) 'Nonsymbolic communication development: theoretical concepts and educational strategies', in Goetz, L., Guess, D. and Stemel-Campbell, K. (eds) *Innovative Program Design for Individuals with Dual Sensory Impairments*. Baltimore: Paul H. Brooks.

Stillman, R.D. and Battle, C.W. (1986) 'Developmental assessment of communicative abilities in the deaf-blind', in Ellis, D. (ed.) *Sensory Impairments in Mentally Handicapped People*. London: Croom Helm.

Stilwel, J.M. and Cermak, S.A. (1995) 'Perceptual functions of the hand', in Henderson, A. and Pehoski, C. (eds) *Hand Function in the Child: foundation for remediation*, 55–80. St Louis, MO: Mosby-Year Book.

Stratton, J.M. and Wright, S. (1991) *'On the Way to Literacy: early experiences for visually impaired children'*. Louisville: American Printing House for the Blind.

Sutherland, P. (1992) *Cognitive Development Today: Piaget and his critics*. London: Paul Chapman Publishing.

TTA (Teacher Training Agency) (1999) *National Special Educational Needs Specialist Standards*. London: Teacher Training Agency.

Tilstone, C. (ed.) (1998) *Observing Teaching and Learning: principles and practice*. London: David Fulton.

Tobin, M.J. (1994) *Assessing Visually Handicapped People: an introduction to test procedures*. London: David Fulton.

Tobin, M.J. (1996) 'Optimising the use of sensory information', in Bozic, N. and Murdoch, H. (eds) *Learning Through Interaction*. London: David Fulton.

Tortora, G. J. and Anagnostakos, N. P. (1987) *Principles of Anatomy and Physiology*, 5th edition. New York: Harper and Row.

Ungar, S., Blades, M. and Spencer, C. (1997) 'The ability of visually impaired children to locate themselves on a tactile map', *British Journal of Visual Impairment* **90**(6), 526–35.

Vygotsky, L.S. (1978) *Mind in Society: the development of higher psychological processes.* Cambridge, MA: Harvard University Press.

Walker, E., Tobin, M. and McKennell, A. (1992) *Blind and Partially Sighted Children in Britain: the RNIB survey. Volume 2.* London: HMSO.

Walker, M. (1985) *Line Drawing Illustrations for the Revised Makaton Vocabulary.* Camberley, Surrey: Makaton Vocabulary Development Project.

Ware, J. (ed.) (1994) *Educating Children with Profound and Multiple Learning Difficulties.* London: David Fulton.

Warren, D.H. (1982) 'The development of haptic perception', in Schiff, W. and Foulke, E. (eds) *Tactual Perception: a sourcebook*, 82–129. Cambridge: Cambridge University Press.

Warren, D.H. (1994) *Blindness and Children: an individual differences approach.* Cambridge: Cambridge University Press.

Wood, D., Bruner, J.S. and Ross, G. (1976) 'The role of tutoring in problem solving', *Journal of Child Psychology and Psychiatry* **17**(2) 89–100.

Index